"It's so easy to get caught up in the stresses of our day-to-day and miss living for what matters most. John Bevere's powerful book *Driven by Eternity* will motivate, inspire, and equip you to live your life today in ways that will impact eternity."

—CRAIG GROESCHEL, Pastor of Life.Church and author
of *#Struggles: Following Jesus in a Selfie-Centered World*

"*Driven by Eternity* is the answer to your exploration for a life of purpose. This vital message will position you to think beyond your day-to-day. This is a must-read!"

—JOHN C. MAXWELL, best-selling author and speaker

"The ten-year anniversary edition of *Driven by Eternity* authored by my friend John Bevere is a great reminder that life is more than the sum of our days. You will find peace and hope as this book reminds you to align your life with a higher calling."

—STEVEN FURTICK, Pastor, Elevation Church and *New York Times*
best-selling author

"In *Driven by Eternity*, John uses scripture to explain how critical it is for us to have a mindset focused on eternity. I believe his teaching will help believers in Christ gain greater wisdom and understanding about how they can live this way today."

—JOYCE MEYER, best-selling author and Bible teacher

"*Driven by Eternity* bravely tackles one of the great 'mysteries' of human existence: eternity. With the clarity and thoroughness that characterizes all his work, John Bevere examines the Bible's wisdom on the subject, inspiring his readers to live eternity-focused lives that extend beyond themselves."

—BRIAN HOUSTON, senior pastor of Hillsong Church

D0009519

"*Driven by Eternity* should be an annual read for every person who wants to build an eternal legacy and advance God's kingdom. With thorough biblical support, John challenges and inspires readers to make the most of their most precious resource—their time on earth—so they can have the greatest impact for eternity. This book is a contemporary classic!"

—CHRIS HODGES, Senior Pastor, Church of the Highlands and author of *Fresh Air* and *Four Cups*

"In *Driven by Eternity*, John Bevere demystifies eternity and creates a compelling case for how our decisions today will reverberate beyond our final breath. You can't afford to miss this."

—MARK BATTERSON, *New York Times* best-selling author of *The Circle Maker* and Lead Pastor of National Community Church

"In *Driven by Eternity*, John Bevere challenges readers to always be motivated by the eternal. John is a dear friend and I'm honored to recommend this book."

—JENTEZEN FRANKLIN, senior pastor of Free Chapel, Gainesville, GA, and *New York Times* best-selling author

"*Driven by Eternity* will transform your perspective of time and how you use it. John brilliantly unpacks biblical truths that will empower you to live each day with a purpose that transcends your temporal reality."

—BISHOP T.D. JAKES, *New York Times* best-selling author and CEO of TDJ Enterprises

"Wow! Powerful, riveting, humbling. I couldn't put it down. I want everyone to read it. Please make time for it."

—BILL MCCARTNEY, Promise Keepers

DRIVEN BY ETERNITY

*Make your life
count today
and forever*

Driven By Eternity

Revised & Expanded
10th Anniversary
Edition

*Make your life
count today
and forever*

John Bevere

Best-selling author of *Good or God?* and *The Bait of Satan*

DRIVEN BY ETERNITY: 10TH ANNIVERSARY EDITION
PUBLISHED BY MESSENGER INTERNATIONAL, INC.
PO Box 888
Palmer Lake, CO 80133
MessengerInternational.org

SPECIAL MARKET SALES
Organizations, churches, pastors, and small group leaders can receive special discounts when purchasing this book and other resources from John Bevere. For information, please call 1-800-648-1477 or write to orders@messengerinternational.org.

I dedicate this book . . .
to all who labor tirelessly to build lives for eternity.
Be encouraged in your quest.
His coming is certain and His reward is with Him.
"And this is eternal life,
that they may know You, the only true God,
and Jesus Christ whom You have sent."
JOHN 17:3

CONTENTS

Section 5

Section 6

About This Book

riven by Eternity may be read cover to cover just like any other book. For those who wish to use this book as an individual or group study, it has been divided into six sections, each of which is followed by a set of discussion questions. This study was designed to be used over the course of six weeks, but feel free to adapt it to your needs.

The sections and their corresponding chapters are as follows:

Section 1	Chapters 1–3
Section 2	Chapters 4–5
Section 3	Chapters 6–7
Section 4	Chapters 8–10
Section 5	Chapters 11–12
Section 6	Chapters 13–14

If you're reading this book as part of the *Driven by Eternity* study, we recommend that you watch or listen to each week's teaching session and answer the discussion questions for the corresponding section as a group. Then have each group member read the relevant book chapters before your next meeting. There is one teaching session for each week of the study.

Enjoy!

PREFACE

The day will come when each of us will stand before God. The question is, will we be ready?

Scripture exhorts us, "Brothers and sisters, make every effort to be *sure* of your calling and election" (2 Peter 1:10 NET). The operative word here is *sure*.

Were you ever sure of something only to later find out you were wrong? It can be vexing. As a typical male, I'm often sure of the route, the instructions, the procedure, the formula, or the method—only to discover that I'm in the wrong neighborhood or that the project, assembly, or formula must be started again, this time following the instructions. It's frustrating. I've wasted gas, time, resources, or money. I was *sure* I knew, but in reality I didn't.

I didn't want to make the same mistake with eternity.

Writing this book personally impacted me more than any other. Since its release a decade ago, countless reports of changed lives have found their way back to me and my team. When we discussed the daunting task of revising and updating this book for rerelease, I knew we had to do it. I had such an overwhelming sense that the message on these pages was both urgent and critical. As stewards of the gospel, we have no greater call than to prepare others for eternity with grace and truth. I want you eternally *sure*.

The sobering fact is that when we stand before our Creator, *it is too late for a do-over*. My hope and prayer is that as you read or re-read this message, the Holy Spirit will use it to move you forward to your greatest eternal potential—forever changed by His grace and mercy.

Sincerely,
John Bevere
May 2016

Introduction

What is it about the word *eternity* that catches our attention—in fact, has the potential to influence an entire nation? Such is the story of Arthur Stace, an Australian born into a life of hopelessness at the turn of the century. His life was that of a bum, filled with petty crime and alcoholism between the First World War and the Great Depression. All this changed when he met Jesus on August 6, 1930, and soon afterward heard his pastor cry, "I wish I could shout *eternity* through all the streets of Sydney!" He felt driven to make this cry a reality.

Arthur would rise early each morning, pray for an hour, and leave his home between 5:00 and 5:30 a.m. to go wherever he felt God lead him. For hours he would write one word, *eternity,* approximately every hundred feet on the sidewalks of Sydney. For more than twenty years his work was a mystery. Who was writing this single word that caused countless thousands to pause and ponder its meaning, both immediate and long range? Had this mystery man captured the impact and portion of this single word's power? It wasn't until 1956 that the puzzle was solved.

Two years after Arthur's death in 1967, Sydney poet Douglas Stewart published these words and immortalized the word of this graffiti preacher:

That shy mysterious poet Arthur Stace
Whose work was just one single mighty word
Walked in the utmost depths of time and space
And there his word was spoken and he heard
ETERNITY, ETERNITY, it banged him like a bell
Dulcet from heaven sounding, sombre from hell.

A one-word sermon touched a nation. Arthur's message was secured for generations by architect Ridley Smith, who put it in copperplate in Sydney Square. It was later viewed by over four billion souls worldwide as they watched the Opening Ceremony of the Sydney Olympics on television, and again when it was emblazoned in fireworks on the Sydney Harbor Bridge on the eve of the new millennium.

Eternity arrests the attention of all mankind. No race, tribe, or gender can resist its draw. We were created with eternity in our hearts and sense the immanent unknown extension of our existence. Therefore, it's wise to delve deeper into what our Creator says concerning eternity. After all, His Word states, "From eternity to eternity I am God. No one can oppose what I do" (Isaiah 43:13 TLB). This is the very reason you've picked up this book. I believe your choice was wise.

Let's pray together before beginning. I've prayed this aloud in my study in anticipation of you praying with me now:

> Dear God of Eternity, Creator of all, and Lord of the Universe, I come to You in the name of Jesus Christ, Your Son. I ask in agreement with Your servant John Bevere that this day You would anoint my eyes to see and my ears to hear, and that You would give me a heart to perceive and understand what You are saying to me through this message. I acknowledge my need for the Holy Spirit's help to know Your will and ways for my life. It is my desire to please You all the days of my life as well as throughout all eternity. Show me not only Your ways but also Your heart that I may know You, for this is eternal life: to know You intimately as my Heavenly Father. Thank You for Your amazing faithfulness, grace, and mercy.

Let's begin, knowing the Holy Spirit will give you insight and understanding you couldn't have obtained on your own. How exciting!

SECTION 1

CHAPTER 1

The Eternal

*Teach us to make the most of our time . . . and make
our efforts successful. Yes, make our efforts successful!*
—Psalm 90:12, 17 NLT

Most people want to live a life that counts. This is a right and godly aspiration. It was Moses's request in the above prayer. He began by asking for wisdom to make the most of time. Many things lost in life can be restored; however, time misused can never be recovered. Once the sun goes down, the day is forever gone.

Moses's prayer concludes with, "Make our efforts successful." The exact phrase is repeated. Why? Moses didn't have a problem with grammar or memory. Rather, this represents a literary style found in Hebrew writing. The repetition is a form of emphasis. In English, when we want to emphasize the importance of a word or phrase, we have several methods available. We can make it bold, italicize it, underscore it, use all capital letters, or add an exclamation point for emphasis. These are all ways of calling the reader's attention to something that is very important. However, the Hebrew writers would write a word or phrase twice to bring emphasis, and they weren't known to overstate—they were always careful with their words. The fact that this phrase was repeated twice in Scripture shows not only that success is God's will for us, but also that He is passionate about it. He is the one who has placed emphasis on it.

We were created to enjoy success. God wants our lives to be significant! This was God's desire first, not ours. He makes this known throughout Scripture. Let me list just two such occurrences. The first:

"The Lord your God will then make you *successful* in everything you do" (Deuteronomy 30:9 NLT). Notice the word *everything*, not *some things*!

Again we read: "This Book of the Law shall not depart from your mouth, but you shall meditate in it day and night, that you may observe to do according to all that is written in it. For then you will make your way *prosperous*, and then you will have *good success*" (Joshua 1:8).

It takes godly wisdom to enjoy success. Scripture states, "He who loves wisdom loves his own best interest and will be a success" (Proverbs 19:8 TLB). Wisdom gives us the knowledge and ability to make right choices at the opportune time. Wisdom is not just for the mentally sharp; it is for all who fear the Lord and are found in Christ. If your aim is to build a life of eternal significance, you must do it through godly wisdom—and that is what this message is all about.

Wisdom breeds success, which brings enduring satisfaction and rewards: "If you are wise, your wisdom will reward you" (Proverbs 9:12 NIV). Not only does the Lord desire your success, but He also longs to reward you for it. Again we read, "Day by day the Lord observes the good deeds done by godly men, and gives them eternal rewards" (Psalm 37:18 TLB).

The fact that God desires us to succeed has been emphasized in a good segment of the church in recent years, as it should be. However, many times success is perceived the way society defines it rather than the way God views it. It's seen through the eyes of the temporal rather than the eternal. This blurs our vision and understanding, which results in misguided pursuits.

We will all one day stand before the Judge of the universe, Jesus Christ. If we've made our lives count through godly wisdom, we will be rewarded eternally. If we've been misguided in our affairs, we will either be punished or suffer eternal loss. So it's wise to spend a few hours searching out what He is looking for.

That is the focus of this book: making your life count not only today but throughout eternity. The Bible is clear about how to do this. If we are to be motivated by the eternal, let's start off by getting an understanding of it.

Eternity

Read carefully these two scriptures:

"No one can begin to understand eternity." (Job 36:26 TLB)

. . . He has put eternity in their hearts. (Ecclesiastes 3:11)

Eternity. What is it? How can it be defined? How can it be understood? One dictionary defines it as *infinite time*[1]; yet another as *the state of existing outside of time*.[2] How can one dictionary define eternity as existing within the state of time while another defines it as being outside time? And why has this gone unquestioned? Wouldn't we question one of two science books if they defined something in our world as existing in different states? Suppose one book defined a fish to be a vertebrate living in water while another reports they live in environments free of water. We would immediately conclude that one was wrong and throw it out. So why do we not question and throw out one of the dictionaries' definitions of eternity?

The truth is that eternity cannot be mentally comprehended. Our minds are finite, prohibited from grasping perpetual or everlasting concepts.

Allow me to illustrate. Take a moment and imagine where the end of the universe is. Think of its outer limits. If you can, then what do you find at the external boundary? A wall? What's it made of? How thick is it? Would the outer side of the wall be the exact point of the end of the universe? If so, what is beyond the outside of the wall? More space? Wouldn't this constitute a continuation of the universe? Where is the end? Can your mind take in the endlessness of the universe? Just stop and think about it.

Or what about a bottomless pit? Can you imagine falling into a hole in which you never stopped falling? You would never hit or even see the floor. You just keep falling and falling forever. Two things, not just one, short-circuit our mental reasoning here: first, that there is no bottom to the hole; second, that we experience an endless time of falling. It's hard to comprehend, and it sounds like a concept from science fiction, yet such a place is referenced seven times in Scripture.

What about God Himself, man's Creator? Pause a moment and think of His beginning—or, I should say, non-beginning. Scripture declares that He is "from everlasting to everlasting." If He wasn't born—if no one created Him—then how did He begin to be who He is? How did He evolve?

The truth is He didn't evolve into God, for the psalmist declares, "Before the mountains were brought forth, or ever You had formed the earth and the world, even from everlasting to everlasting, You are God" (Psalm 90:2). Meditate on this a while. If you do, you'll frustrate your intellectual reasoning since, as the book of Job says, "No one can begin to understand eternity."

Placed in Our Hearts

What is in truth declared unreachable to our natural minds is placed in our hearts by the Creator. Eternity is known in our hearts. It is born in every human being. This is why "the fool has said in his *heart*, 'There is no God'" (Psalm 14:1). Notice Scripture does *not* say, "The fool has said in his *mind*." There are many atheists who emphatically deny the existence of God, but in their hearts they know He exists, for eternity is planted there. They've not yet hardened their hearts to a completely degenerated state.

I had a friend who, years ago, was a staunch atheist—or so he thought. He wouldn't allow anyone to witness to him. In fact, one day he ripped a Bible from the hands of a coworker, threw it on the ground, and stomped on it, cursing the man and his Bible. He accused this Christian man of being weak and brainless.

Later, after years of confessed atheism, the man suffered severe chest pains. Doctors opened him up for exploratory surgery. They immediately closed him up and told him he had less than twenty-four hours to live.

While he lay on the bed that night, he realized he was going to his eternal abode and it was not at all where he wanted to end up. How did he know that, since he would not allow anyone to share the Scriptures with him? Could it be he had eternity planted in his heart? Just as Scripture states of all mankind, "For the truth about God is known to them instinctively; God has put this knowledge in their hearts" (Romans 1:19 TLB).

That night my friend's heart stopped. He left his body and descended into deep darkness. The darkness was so thick he felt he was wearing it; not a glimmer of light could be seen. After falling for what seemed to be quite some time, he heard the horrifying screams of tormented souls. He was pulled by a strong force right up to the gates of hell when suddenly he was able to retreat back to his body. He had been revived.

The next morning he called for the only Christian man he knew. His friend came and proclaimed the good news of salvation through Jesus Christ. Once the man had received Jesus Christ into his life as Lord and Savior, his friend prayed for his healing. Three weeks later he walked out of the hospital. He lived decades more before he passed on to his eternal reward. He was a walking miracle.

As an atheist, this man proclaimed there was no God, yet eternity was planted in his heart. The fool, on the other hand, is the one who has not just denied God mentally but has also resisted in his heart to the point of a seared conscience. He is beyond reach. It's one thing to hold firm to a belief in your intellect. That can be changed. But it is quite another thing to completely harden your heart. *The New Unger's Bible Dictionary* gives this definition: "In Scripture the 'fool' primarily is the person who casts off the fear of God and thinks and acts as if he could safely disregard the eternal principles of God's righteousness."[3]

A fool may actually acknowledge God mentally, but he denies His existence in his heart, which is reflected in how he lives. The fear of God is what keeps our hearts within reach of the Holy Spirit. If it is lost, there is no hope left for us. Paul said, "Men and brethren, sons of the family of Abraham, and those among you who *fear God*, to you the word of this salvation has been sent" (Acts 13:26). Only those who fear God are capable of hearing the words of eternal life.

Eternity Defined

Eternity has been planted in our hearts, even though it's impossible to comprehend it with our minds. So in defining it, I ask you to listen with your heart. In fact, the same is necessary for you to benefit from this entire book. How do you do this? First of all, acknowledge your need for the Holy Spirit to help you, and ask for His assistance. He will commune with your innermost man, not your head. Second, stop to ponder and meditate when your heart is stirred or gripped by a statement of truth. Don't race through this book; if you do, the benefit will be limited.

To receive the full impact of God's eternal word to you, apply these two steps and you will be changed forever. David says, "Your word I have hidden in my heart, that I might not sin against You" (Psalm 119:11). Don't just read for mental understanding, which can be easily forgotten or lost, but let God's Word be hidden in your heart through contemplation and prayer.

Eternity is everlasting; there is no end to it. However, it's not just a matter of ceaseless time, as it is not subject to time. Eternity transcends time. To speak of eternity merely in terms of perpetual duration is to miss the full picture.

To capture the best view of eternity, we must look at God Himself. He is not limited in power, knowledge, wisdom, understanding, or glory—just to name a few. He is self-existent; forever He was and forever He will be God. He is called the "Everlasting Father" (Isaiah 9:6).

Young's literal translation of that phrase reads "Father of Eternity."[4] He is called the "King of eternity" (1 Timothy 1:17 AMP). All that is eternal is found in Him; in fact, eternity itself is found in Him. All that is outside of Him is temporal and will change. No matter how good, noble, powerful, or enduring it may seem, it will eventually cease. Even the earth and universe will change, but He will not:

> Lord, in the beginning you laid the foundation of the earth, and
> the heavens are the work of your hands. Even they will perish, but
> you remain forever. They will wear out like old clothing. You will
> roll them up like an old coat. They will fade away like old clothing.
> But you are always the same; you will never grow old. (Hebrews
> 1:10–12 NLT)

Not only will He never cease, but He remains eternally the same. Scripture declares:

> "All flesh is as grass, and all the glory of man as the flower of the
> grass. The grass withers, and its flower falls away, but the word of the
> Lord endures forever." Now this is the word which by the gospel was
> preached to you. (1 Peter 1:24–25)

God is eternal; therefore, what He speaks is eternal. He cannot lie, nor can what He says be broken. If it weren't so, then all would collapse into utter darkness, for He is light and upholds all things by His Word. There can never be a change to what He says, or else He would no longer be eternal. That is a sure foundation upon which we can build our lives.

Eternal Judgments

Many today are not building their lives on the eternal (God's Word) but rather on cultural thinking, tradition, assumptions, and feelings about who God is. This doesn't just apply to people who are not Christians but to many believers as well. It's a scary thing to believe that something temporal is eternal truth. If a person does this, their foundation is faulty. They are setting themselves up for a sure fall. They believe a lie and are in a deceived state.

I am amazed at how many people I meet who base their lives on what's not eternal. Some will tell me of God and their belief in His Son, but the One they declare just isn't the One revealed in His Word. The deception runs deep. How can they believe what they have simply imagined within their own minds, ideas shaped by a society that has already been declared to operate contrary to God's nature? Jesus said:

> He who . . . does not receive My words, has that which judges him—
> the word that I have spoken will judge him in the last day. For I have
> not spoken on My own authority; but the Father who sent Me gave
> Me a command, what I should say and what I should speak. (John
> 12:48–49)

There is a Judgment Day, which has been appointed from the foundation of the world (see Acts 17:31). That day will not bring new revelations of truth; rather, it will measure all things by what has already been spoken. God's Word, which we currently possess, will judge us in that last day. It is eternal. It is final. There are no exceptions, alterations, or revisions. Wouldn't it benefit us to know and live by what He says—rather than make assumptions about what He said?

The judgments to be made that day are called *eternal* (see Hebrews 6:2). In other words, the decisions made that day—which will be based on how we aligned our lives with God's eternal Word—will determine how we spend the rest of eternity! There will never be any changes to those decisions, for they are *eternal judgments*.

So many, both believers and nonbelievers, are ignorantly allowing the appointed judgment to hasten toward them without investigation.

They've taken false hope in concepts that are not found in the Bible. Some think God will take into account all the good they've done, and if it outweighs the bad, they will find favor. Others who profess a new birth experience have thought they will not stand before Jesus as Judge because He is their Savior. They believe they are exempt from any form of judgment. They will be most surprised. Then there are some who think everything will just pan out. They are trusting in an unscriptural mercy.

None of these concepts are what the New Testament reveals and teaches. These notions and many others that people have devised in their own imaginations are temporal and will not stand in that day. There will be stunned men and women, and I personally think there will be more professing Christians than unbelievers who are shocked on Judgment Day.

Confidence at the Judgment

We don't have to go to the Judgment Day in fear. We can go with confidence:

> And as we live in God, our love grows more perfect. So we will not be afraid on the day of judgment, but we can face him with confidence because we are like Christ here in this world. (1 John 4:17 NLT)

Notice the words "as we live in God, our love grows more perfect." The key that will give us confidence on Judgment Day is the love of God being made perfect (or mature) in us.

Now, here is where many in the church falter. They see the love of God in the light of the temporal, not the eternal. There is an understanding of love and goodness that is admired by society and many in the church, but it is determined by human measures. These concepts are actually contrary to the love of God. Let me illustrate a few such occurrences that are common.

"We love each other so much and are planning to get married." This is often stated when two people are having sex outside of marriage. Not only is this sinful even if they do follow through and get married, but many times I've witnessed that those who make such statements end up not getting married. They've forgotten the clear exhortation, "Marriage should be honored by all, and the marriage bed kept pure, for God will judge the adulterer and all the sexually immoral" (Hebrews 13:4 NIV). Notice the writer of Hebrews does not say, "The adulterer and sexually immoral who don't attend church." No, it is all who practice this lifestyle.

"I know it wasn't quite the truth, but it will help close the deal, and we will make sure they get fair treatment." Businesspeople often say this when they want to secure a sale they really believe is good for the customer but they need to twist the facts a little to get them to move forward. Not only is this the sin of lying, but the deal is almost always better for the one making the statement. Have they forgotten the warning that states, "All liars (those who knowingly convey untruth by word or deed)—[all of these shall have] their part in the lake that blazes with fire and brimstone" (Revelation 21:8 AMP)?

"What I said about him is the truth." This is often said when people are talking in a negative light (gossiping or slandering) about a fellow worker, friend, boss, etc. The fact is, you can be 100 percent right and still be wrong according to eternal standards. If you recall, Noah's youngest son, Ham, reported his father's nakedness and drunken state accurately to his brothers. However, as a result of his dishonoring his father, a curse came on his lineage that lasted generations. Have those who gossip and slander forgotten the exhortation to believers that states, "Don't grumble about each other, my brothers and sisters, or God will judge you. For look! The great Judge is coming. He is standing at the door" (James 5:9 NLT)?

The examples are endless, but the common denominator is that they are contrary to God's eternal will. The scary fact is that many who live in this manner and make such seemingly harmless statements may attend church, be very kind in their mannerisms, and be looked upon as model citizens. But how do they measure up to the eternal?

John gave the answer to perfecting (maturing) the love of God earlier in his letter:

> Whoever says, I know Him [I perceive, recognize, understand, and am acquainted with Him (Jesus Christ)] but fails to keep and obey His commandments (teachings) is a liar, and the Truth [of the Gospel] is not in him. But he who keeps (treasures) His Word [who bears in mind His precepts, who observes His message in its entirety], truly in him has the love of and for God been perfected . . . (1 John 2:4–5 AMP)

Recall that it is the perfected (matured) love of God that gives us confidence to stand before our Judge. John makes it clear that the love of God is perfected in keeping His commandments, not in behaving in a way that is good in society's eyes. Keep in mind that Eve was not drawn to the *evil* side of the tree of the knowledge of good and evil; rather, she was enticed by the *good* side! "The woman saw how *beautiful* the tree was and how *good* its fruit would be to eat" (Genesis 3:6 TEV). Human reasoning can create a form of beauty and goodness that is contrary to the eternal love of God.

Scripture also states that we cannot observe a percentage of God's commands and believe that we will have confidence on Judgment Day. It is when we carefully observe all of His Word in its entirety that the love of God is matured. This is why God gives us grace: it empowers us to obey His Word completely, in a way that is acceptable to Him. "Therefore, since we are receiving a kingdom which cannot be shaken, let us have grace, by which we may serve God acceptably" (Hebrews 12:28).

The key is to know what the King desires and looks for, not what seems good to society or human reasoning. For this reason God tells us, "Do not be conformed to this world, but be transformed by the renewing of your mind, that you may prove what is that good and acceptable and perfect will of God" (Romans 12:2). What may seem good to our culture may be an affront to God's desires—the eternal.

Allow me to illustrate. I'm currently sitting in a hotel in Singapore, where I'll be preaching to close to twenty thousand people this weekend. I've been to this great nation many times. I've also preached the gospel in the Netherlands a few times. In the Netherlands, it is not against the law to have marijuana in your possession. The people there can smoke it legally and not fear penalty. However, in Singapore if you are caught with a certain amount of drugs (and it is a small amount), you will be arrested and severely punished. If caught with certain drugs, the punishment is death by hanging! When you fly into Singapore, this policy is written right on the entry card: "Death to Drug Traffickers under Singapore Law."

Now, can you imagine a young Dutchman who regularly smokes marijuana traveling to Singapore and sharing his pot with Singaporeans? He gladly states to his new friends, "Hey guys, this stuff is great. It calms you, gives you an enjoyable buzz, and takes your frustrations away. Would you like some? I'd love to share it with you."

The young man is immediately arrested. He's in shock. The first question out of his mouth to the police officers is, "Why are you arresting me?"

Judgment day arrives. The Dutchman stands in the court before the judge, believing with all his heart this is some kind of fluke. The judge pronounces his guilt and punishment.

The man, in shock, says, "Your honor, where I come from it's fine to share marijuana with your friends."

The judge then says, "You're not in Holland. You're in Singapore, and in this nation, it is against the law!"

The Dutchman's confidence is gone; he has nothing to stand on. There is no recourse. He is standing before the highest court of the land, doomed with no defense.

While I was in Singapore several years back, a young American was arrested for vandalizing an automobile. He was arrested, judged guilty, and sentenced to several strokes of Rotan. This is a punishment that inflicts permanent physical damage by whipping a person on the hind side with a type of bamboo plant treated with chemicals. The verdict seemed extreme. Even the president of the United States tried to get the young man's sentence lightened. However, he had no success. The young man broke the laws of Singapore and had to serve his sentence.

All of us will stand before the highest court of the universe. This court's decision will be *eternally* final. Many will be shocked by the verdict about their lives, but they don't have to be. You don't have to be.

Are you ready? According to the Word of God, we can go before the Judge of the universe with confidence. This book is designed to help you prepare. If that young Dutchman would have taken time to learn and prepare to enter Singapore, he would have avoided severe penalty. How much more important is it for us to prepare for our own judgment, for the decisions that are made at the Judgment Seat will be forever.

Rewards

There will be more than one judgment in eternity. There will be one for unbelievers, another for believers, and even one for angels. The decisions made will vary. There will be loss and punishment, and there will be rewards. We'll go into this in depth in upcoming chapters, but let me point out again that the decisions made will be eternal. This cannot be overemphasized; try again to mentally grasp never ending! It is God's will that we know this in advance and that we labor for the rewards that come from adhering to His Word. Paul says:

> Do you not know that in a race all the runners compete, but [only] one receives the prize? So run [your race] that you may lay hold [of the prize] and make it yours. Now every athlete who goes into training conducts himself temperately and restricts himself in all things. They do it to win a wreath that will soon wither, but we [do it to

receive a crown of eternal blessedness] that cannot wither. Therefore I do not run uncertainly (without definite aim). I do not box like one beating the air and striking without an adversary. But [like a boxer] I buffet my body [handle it roughly, discipline it by hardships] and subdue it . . . (1 Corinthians 9:24–27 AMP)

Paul clearly says, "I do not run uncertainly (without definite aim)." Another version says it like this: "So I run straight to the goal with purpose in every step" (verse 26 NLT). That is exactly what every human being should do—run with certainty and purpose to win. We are not competing against others, only ourselves.

Driven by Eternity

Just thinking everything will pan out for good at the Judgment Seat is not enough. We have no excuse, for God has made His will available to us. There will be scores of people at the judgment who believe they've done well in comparison to those around them, yet they will not have allowed the eternal to direct and fuel their lives. Hence the title of this book: *Driven by Eternity.*

The word *driven* means "to propel." It also means to "guide, control, or direct." Another definition is "to supply the motive force to." What is guiding and motivating our lives on this earth? Is it the eternal or is it the temporal? Is it based on divine wisdom? Or are we comparing ourselves with others? Have we listened to flattery, tradition, or myths proclaimed in certain pulpits or schools? Will what we've built our lives upon stand before God at the Judgment Seat, or will our efforts be forever lost? Remember, we already know what will be the standard at our judgment: "The word that I have spoken will judge him in the last day" (John 12:48).

Many professing Christians will be shocked when they stand before Jesus Christ at the judgment. They will be those who took security in a part of what the New Testament teaches but neglected to carefully search out the entire picture. My question to you is this: do you want to find out the truth after the *eternal* decision has already been made and it's too late to change, or do you want to know now the standard by which you will be judged?

The next chapter will open with an allegory that will continue into the following chapter. Read it carefully and remember the details, for we will refer back to it often. The story will then conclude in chapter eight, and the truths it contains will be discussed through the rest of the book. This book revolves around this allegory, so please don't skim it. You may also want to refer back to it as the teaching progresses.

God has dealt with me personally about most of what is shared in this book. I will share many of my own faults, which have been scrutinized by the Holy Spirit under the microscope of His truth. My hope is that this will stir you to carefully search the Scriptures, that you may have a firm foundation to stand upon on Judgment Day. I will share some of the greatest misconceptions in our society that cause men and women to grow further from the One they profess as Savior. You will be shocked, shaken, and chastened at times, but it will all be followed by promise, hope, and comfort.

If you are courageous, desire the truth, and have a heart for God, then let's proceed. You'll be glad you did! Take to heart the following exhortation:

> God's gift has restored our relationship with him and given us back
> our lives. And there's more life to come—an eternity of life! You can
> count on this. I want you to put your foot down. Take a firm stand
> on these matters so that those who have put their trust in God will
> concentrate on the essentials that are good for everyone. (Titus 3:7–8
> The Message)

CHAPTER 2

THE KINGDOM OF AFFABEL: LIFE IN ENDEL

*And [Jesus] taught them many things in parables
(illustrations or comparisons put beside
truths to explain them) . . .*
—Mark 4:2 AMP

There was once a world similar to our own yet different in many ways. In this world there were no independent nations, only one great kingdom named Affabel. Though this kingdom spanned the entire known world, it had a single capital city from which all leadership was administered. It was called The Great City of Affabel, which we will refer to from this point on as simply Affabel.

This enchanted city was presided over by a remarkable king named Jalyn. King Jalyn was adored and greatly admired by his subjects. He exuded a depth of love that seemed inexhaustible. He was strong and wise, yet at the same time was kind and possessed a great sense of humor. Though his manner was regal, Jalyn was also personable. To be with him was to find oneself encompassed in an atmosphere of goodness. His presence raised every aspect of life to a higher level. His vision and foresight were astounding, and he had an uncanny ability to see beyond the actions of people into the motives of their hearts.

Jalyn's father, who founded Affabel, was known as the Founding King Father. Once order had been established, he turned all leadership of the kingdom over to his son. The residents of the great city helped administrate the rule of Jalyn in the outlying territories of the kingdom. This was accomplished through a hierarchical system of authority and leadership in the ruling city.

The city was enormous, with a landmass of approximately two hundred square miles. It was so well planned that even though it was densely populated, it never felt overcrowded. It was a composite of suburbs, town residences, and villas.

Located in the flatlands, which lay toward the western end of Affabel, were the modest homes of the laborers. (Their modest homes would be considered extravagant in our world.) Even though their jobs were labor intensive, these residents were thankful just to inhabit the king's city.

The mountainous terrains of the northern and southern borders were home to the artisans. These were the ones skilled in the creative arts of music, writing, artwork, and design. These homes had beautiful vistas and were more expansive than those of the laborers.

The most inviting section of the city was the eastern district, which contained an abundance of beautiful villas. This area was known as the Regal Center. This large neighborhood is where the king resided and spent most of his time. It was also home to those who worked closest to the king; here his administration and co-leaders socialized and worked together.

The Regal Center was poised like a jewel on a cliff overlooking the shores of the Great Sea. A constant gentle breeze blew up from the azure ocean and refreshed the city. These waters were fringed by the most pristine white beaches, which were surpassed in beauty only by the royal gardens. The gardens wove throughout the Regal Center, adding color and vibrancy at every turn. This was without doubt the most desirable place of residency in Affabel. Each home was exceeded in elegance only by the king's royal palace.

In the midst of Affabel stood the tree of life. Only the king's subjects were privileged to partake of its wondrous fruit. The fruit was not merely delicious and lovely to behold; it also had within its fragrant flesh the power of the miraculous.

The Community of Endel

To the west of Affabel's flatlands lay the Outer Wilderness, which stretched for almost sixty miles to the Great River Adonga. Once you crossed the Adonga, you would find yourself in another part of the kingdom, which was called Endel. At birth, the children of the citizens of Affabel were brought immediately to the province of Endel. Before their first week had passed, they were entrusted to the care of the king's nurses. Once these young citizens—or Endelites—were five years of age, they were brought to the School of Endel where they received training for a period of ten years. There they learned the ways of Affabel and of the great King Jalyn.

Only the king's nurses and the teachers had enjoyed the opportunity to meet Jalyn. Every five years or so, he would visit Endel in secret to share his heart for the school and the children. He never made his presence known to all, but even so, his goodness was evident in every aspect of Endel.

The ten years in the School of Endel were to prepare students for the life ahead of them. At the age of fifteen, they would have a short season to apply all they had been taught. In this span of time they would be entrusted with portions of wealth and responsibility. How they stewarded their young lives and resources determined how and where they would spend the rest of their lives, which in their world totaled one hundred and fifty years. Though the season of testing was exactly five years, none of the students were aware of its duration. All they were told was it would not exceed ten years. At the end of this time, each would appear before the king to give account of their life choices.

This span of testing determined the students' allegiances. Those who followed the ordinances of Jalyn with their words and actions acknowledged his leadership. They were admitted as residents of Affabel. Their choices secured rewards for them accordingly.

If, however, the students rebelled and lived only for themselves during the season of testing, they were exiled to the land of Lone. Lone was a desert land of utter darkness where loneliness and hopelessness reigned. There the rebellious ones suffered torment and imprisonment for the duration of their lives.

The first person banished to this desolation was Dagon, who became the founding dark lord of Lone. Though he had rebelled against Jalyn many years before, his influence lingered in the land of Endel. Inhabitants of Endel who acknowledged Jalyn's lordship broke free of the dark power of Dagon. However, those who refused to serve Jalyn remained under this fallen lord's sway.

To isolate any further infiltration of darkness in his kingdom, the great King Jalyn was compelled to establish a decree to protect both the integrity and the social infrastructure of Affabel. All who followed in the way of Dagon and refused to acknowledge Jalyn as king by word and action would be banished for the remainder of their lives to the land of Lone.

So begins our story. We will follow the lives of five students of Endel. Their names are as follows: Independent, Deceived, Faint Heart, Selfish, and Charity. Let me introduce each.

Independent

Independent constantly questions the existence of Affabel. He really can't believe someone called Jalyn, who he has never met or seen, would require not only his allegiance but also such strict adherence to a "list of rules." He suspects this is a scheme to keep him and others under the control of the teachers. In contempt, he refuses to attend classes and learn of this imaginary kingdom.

Independent ridicules others for believing such nonsense. He intends to live as he sees fit and remain free of the laws of Jalyn. The only exception will be if the king's edicts serve his purpose. Then he'll adhere, but only because it's his idea. He has no qualms about letting others know he won't be yielding his life to the will of another.

Deceived

Deceived doesn't question the existence of Affabel. He believes in King Jalyn and even delights in his promises. He mentally and verbally agrees with the school's teachings and policies, yet large portions of his lifestyle conflict with those teachings. He celebrates his allegiance to the king and his teachings and participates in the school's functions when they are delightful, but if he doesn't see any self-benefit, his outlook quickly changes. His lifestyle is contrary to that of a true follower of Jalyn, and due to his strong personality, he subtly draws others into his ways. He never really stops to consider his pending season of testing and judgment.

Deceived gets along well with Independent, even though they disagree about Jalyn's existence. Deceived is fun and they both have similar interests, so Independent likes his company.

Faint Heart

Faint Heart is the most enthusiastic of all the students. She speaks up frequently in class and consistently makes some of the best grades. She is very active and usually initiates extracurricular activities to help promote the students' involvement in the community. Anyone who assessed the students would say she was the most passionate for Jalyn's cause.

Selfish

Selfish also believes in Jalyn and his teachings. He does not doubt the existence of Affabel and is quite vocal as well. He believes Jalyn is such a wonderful ruler and kind judge that he will be gracious to all who profess allegiance to him. He is, however, focused on his limited perception of Jalyn's teachings and character. He has forgotten that Jalyn is a just and holy leader as well as a loving and merciful one. So Selfish has developed a distorted view of who Jalyn really is. He believes that Deceived, Faint Heart, and Charity will no doubt be a part of Jalyn's glorious kingdom, though he has some concerns about the sheer resistance of Independent.

Selfish believes all who acknowledge Jalyn verbally and live a life that doesn't break any major laws will gain entrance to Affabel. However, in keeping with his name, he's largely self-seeking, and often the good he does is motivated by personal benefit. At times, he is motivated by compassion, but when push comes to shove, Selfish looks out for his own best interest.

Charity

Our final young lady, Charity, is one who takes to heart and obeys King Jalyn's laws. Not only has she learned his principles, but she also searches to know the heart behind each edict. She spends a lot of time seeking to know and understand the will of Jalyn. This means long hours of study and freely giving herself for the good of the school and community of Endel. She knows once she reaches the age of fifteen, she will have a short amount of time to carry out the wishes of the great king. Her aim is to live completely for Jalyn's glory, and she will not allow what would benefit her to get in the way of this primary purpose.

Charity loves Jalyn and longs for the day they will meet. She fervently obeys him and frequently speaks with others of his goodness. For this she is often ridiculed and isolated. Though she has suffered for her stance of unwavering loyalty to Jalyn's laws, nothing will deter her from being faithful to the king.

The Graduates

All five of these Endelites turned fifteen. The appointed day arrived, and they graduated along with two thousand other students. Each was entrusted with a specific commission and a corresponding sum of startup funds. This amount was predetermined by Jalyn and was distributed by the headmaster upon graduation.

Among our five students the distribution looked like this: Independent received fifty-five thousand entrustments, Deceived and Faint Heart received forty thousand each, Selfish received the most at seventy-five thousand entrustments, and Charity received twenty-five thousand. With their money in hand, the young citizens were released with some final instructions.

The Salesman

Though Independent rarely attended classes, he still felt as though some of the teachings hung over his head. There were times when he wondered if some of the school's lunacy could actually be true. If so, he hoped his behavior would not affect how much he would be given once his schooling expired.

Independent's hands trembled as he received the envelope filled with his entrustments. Upon opening it, he had to suppress his surprise and relief at the amount he had been given. He was even more excited when he realized that he received fifteen thousand more than Faint Heart and more than twice as much as Charity. He thought, *What a waste! Charity and Faint Heart spent all their time in those useless classes and put in so many extra hours, and now they have little to show for it.*

This experience actually affirmed Independent's belief that Jalyn didn't exist. He reasoned that the students' parents, who disappeared so many years ago, had left the money. This furthered his views that the story of King Jalyn was all a scam created by the school to control their young lives and keep them from being freethinkers.

After a couple weeks of celebrating his graduation, Independent realized he had to set up a business. He was beginning to panic over the rapid pace at which he had started to run through his entrustments.

Independent started a car dealership and realized he was a great salesman. Business went amazingly well. Many of the new graduates used part of their startup funds to buy used or even new cars from Independent's lot. As his finances multiplied, he expanded into other business ventures and found success in those as well. As his assets increased, he expanded and enhanced his personal lifestyle. He realized quickly that money was an amazing source of influence, and it seemed to have the power to purchase happiness. His wealth, assets, and rapidly expanding lifestyle also had the power to attract women, which made life even more invigorating.

Independent didn't attend the community's weekly gatherings, but he was still considered a very good citizen by most because they appreciated his support of community projects. It appeared life couldn't get any better for this hard-working Endelite.

The Builder and Developer

Deceived was more than happy to celebrate with Independent for a couple weeks. Though he hadn't receive as much as others had, he was glad to have more than Charity did. It affirmed his distorted perception of Jalyn as a king of such extreme mercy that certain issues really didn't matter.

Deceived had been sexually loose with a couple girls he had dated in the school, even though this was contrary to the teachings he had received. He saw no conflict in it because he firmly believed in Jalyn and his kingdom. He had formed his own approach to life: *As long as I continue to affirm my allegiance to Jalyn and do not hurt anyone too severely,*

I will remain in good standing with the king. He reasoned that Jalyn understood that everyone has needs and no one is perfect. He was sure all his faults would be covered at the judgment by Jalyn's mercy and grace because he believed in the king with all his heart.

A few weeks after graduation, Deceived started his own business. He became a homebuilder. In the beginning, he struggled to find customers. His model home was excellent in every way, but he couldn't find committed buyers. Some thought his prices were too high; others simply couldn't afford to buy such nice houses. Desperate, Deceived lowered his prices.

Deceived still used his nice model home to draw customers. He continued to make all the promises he had previously made, but he started putting in much lower grade materials than he had previously featured or promised. In fact, some of his materials violated Endel's codes and standards. Deceived rationalized that the lawmakers who set these marks were overly cautious. He was sure the materials he had chosen would hold up under any stress or weather conditions. Because Deceived's homes seemed to be such amazing bargains, interested Endelites started signing contracts faster than he could build the houses. Business had finally taken off.

After a couple years, Deceived decided to turn to land development. He was tired of complaining customers. He felt that once the land was sold, he'd be done with it all. He wouldn't have to deal with fixing warranty items any longer.

Deceived was ecstatic when he came across some land for roughly a thousand entrustments an acre. The deal seemed almost too good to be true. But further investigation revealed the land was a flood plain. This information was only known by a handful of people, all of whom were Deceived's friends. He persuaded a city councilman who was a buddy of Independent's to approve his development without proper geological testing. After all, there hadn't been any floods in his lifetime, so was there really a problem? The deal went through without a hitch. After this, it seemed life couldn't get any better for the young entrepreneur.

The Teacher's Assistant

Immediately following graduation, Faint Heart got together with a few girlfriends for a weekend of shopping. She thought this would be good for two reasons: first, she could spend time celebrating with her closest friends; and second, she could get the clothes and accessories she would need for her new career. Faint Heart's deepest desire was to be a teacher's assistant at the School of Endel. She couldn't remember ever wanting anything more. Her interview was the following Friday.

On the second day of shopping, one of Faint Heart's friends, Gossip, shared with her how a mutual friend, Slander, had told the headmaster that Faint Heart had slept with one of the young male students. Faint Heart burned with anger as she listened to the news. This could severely hinder her chances of being brought on as a teacher's assistant. It was an absurd lie without an ounce of truth in it. She had kept herself pure the entire time of her schooling. She felt certain Slander had done this out of sheer envy and possibly even hatred.

Faint Heart was furious. She was deeply offended, and for the remainder of the weekend her thoughts were consumed with the treachery of this supposed friend. She vowed to make Slander pay for what she had done.

The day of the interview arrived, and to Faint Heart's surprise she was chosen for a position. The headmaster informed her that he had indeed heard the rumor, but after some investigation he was convinced it wasn't true.

Not only did Faint Heart get a position, she was assigned as an assistant to one of her favorite teachers. His name was Double Life, and he was one of the most gifted teachers at the school. He was twenty-five and had been instructing young Endelites for a number of years. (The teachers' judgments did not come at twenty years of age, as with the others, but when they were thirty.) Faint Heart was amazed that she was chosen to work with such a dynamic leader.

The semester began, and things were going extremely well, but Faint Heart still carried a nagging offense against her former friend. No matter how well things went, it seemed she could not really get over Slander's treachery.

Even though things looked great, trouble was brewing below the surface. Double Life's name was indicative of who he was. He lived one way as a teacher but quite another way in his private life. His judgment would be the most severe because as a teacher, he had the privilege of personally seeing Jalyn.

One evening when Faint Heart and Double Life were alone together, he made a pass at her. Shocked and outraged, she left his presence immediately. He didn't give up but persisted in pursuing her over the next several weeks. She began to question her reaction and listened to his persuasion because he was such a great and knowledgeable man. She enjoyed his attention. He was gentle and kind and was considered to be one of the nicest looking men in the community. After a long internal battle, Faint Heart finally gave her virginity to Double Life, and the two entered into a passionate affair.

Faint Heart had never known such exhilarating feelings of passion and love. Each time she saw Double Life, he took her breath away. Thoughts of rendezvousing with him on their set evenings consumed her and temporarily averted her attention from the deep and now hidden offense she still carried against Slander.

However, after four months, Double Life suddenly dumped her. Faint Heart was distraught and devastated; she had to know why. She replayed every encounter in her head and pressed him for an answer. Finally Double Life told her that he had heard about Slander's report of her past affair with a fellow student. This was not the real reason for his change of affection; he had just lost interest in Faint Heart. He was already flirting with another young lady in the community. Young women were hard-pressed to resist the seductive and persuasive powers of this prominent teacher.

Faint Heart was outraged. She couldn't bear the thought of seeing Double Life each day. Unable to go on, she immediately resigned her position at the school.

After several days of sulking, Faint Heart opened a beauty salon with what she had left of her forty thousand entrustments. She stopped going to the weekly gatherings at the school even though Jalyn instructed his subjects not to forsake such meetings. Faint Heart didn't want to associate with hypocrites, and most of the people at the gatherings seemed to be just that.

Faint Heart grew harder by the day. She rarely mentioned the school or Jalyn. Indifference and cynicism replaced the passion she'd previously expressed so freely. When asked, Faint Heart would confess her allegiance to Jalyn, but deep down she blamed him for allowing such a corrupt man to be a teacher in his school.

By the time her days of testing were over, Faint Heart was a very offended and bitter woman, though if asked she would emphatically deny it. She spent the rest of her days trying to get even with those who had hurt her so deeply.

The Mayor of Endel

And now we turn to Selfish. He was simply amazed by the amount of money he'd received. He celebrated, but he knew enough of Jalyn's teachings to steer away from illicit revelry. After a few days' break, he started investing. His trading proved profitable, and he quickly multiplied his startup funds. As his finances grew, he steadily increased in popularity with his peers.

Selfish bought a house in one of Endel's nicest neighborhoods and invited the influential and powerful to his home. Government officials, professional athletes, business executives, and other notables enjoyed the wealth of his hospitality. He was quickly becoming one of the most connected men in the community.

After three years, Selfish decided to run for mayor of Endel and easily won because of his financial clout and social connections. Once in office, he found himself faced with many decisions. One had to do with the school. Due to an increase in population, there was an urgent need for more space. This meant buying land and securing contractors, building expenses, and everything necessary to outfit the school.

The first step was for the community to raise money. In the weekly city gatherings, Selfish heard of their need for more funding. At the end of the fundraising drive, he had given just under a thousand entrustments.

Then came the tough decision. The school finally had enough to buy a particular plot of land. It was an amazing deal, and the price was within their budget. However, there was a large department store that wanted to purchase the same land. The city council was divided. The school was a nonprofit organization, so it would not yield any tax revenue. The store, on the other hand, would bring in huge sums of tax revenue and create additional jobs for the city's residents.

Since the council was split, the deciding vote had to be cast by the mayor. Selfish was conflicted. The owners of the department store had been very supportive of his campaign by contributing large sums of money as well as leveraging their influence on his behalf. They had been guests in his home on frequent occasions.

Selfish voted in favor of the department store. He justified his choice to the public by stating it was for the overall good of the citizens of Endel. He had paved the way for more employment opportunities as well as increased the city revenue. He recommended the school explore their options in expanding their current facility, even though he knew this was not feasible. His choice disappointed the sincere followers of Jalyn, but the community at large applauded his decision.

Selfish's two-year term was coming to a close, and it was time to campaign for reelection. Feeling a bit remorseful, he made a personal contribution of five thousand entrustments to the School of Endel. With it came a promise to find another plot of ground suitable for them to build on.

This helped him regain the confidence of many of the followers of Jalyn. It looked as though the young leader would easily win a second term.

The Restaurant Owner

Upon graduating, Charity gave three of her twenty-five thousand entrustments as a contribution to the School of Endel's land drive. She was thankful for all she had learned from her teachers and wanted to express it. With the remaining twenty-two thousand, Charity was eventually able to start a restaurant.

Charity loved anything to do with the culinary arts. Coupling this with the fact that she was a savvy businesswoman, running a restaurant appeared to be the best way to utilize her gifts and serve her community. She was able to bring in some of the best chefs in the land. By coordinating their knowledge, she assembled an outstanding menu. Her restaurant was an immediate success.

Though Charity won awards for her restaurant, she always credited her success to Jalyn's wisdom. In interviews she repeatedly thanked her former teachers and praised her fine employees. She refused to boast about her efforts or claim her success as her own. She knew it was only because of Jalyn.

Charity used her prosperity to help both the community and the School of Endel. She contributed food to the school's soup kitchen. Often she would set aside an evening to work the outreach food line. She enjoyed serving hot meals to the poor. She made a commitment to give 25 percent of all her restaurant profits to the school. At the end of the five years, she had given over two hundred thousand entrustments.

Charity was always helping others who were working hard but found it difficult to make ends meet. In addition to financial aid, she was quick to share Jalyn's principles of wisdom and success. She constantly told those she aided how she would never have made it had it not been for Jalyn.

Even though Charity's restaurant was successful, she was never included in the social events at Selfish's home. Neither was she asked to participate in leadership roles in the community. She was seen as too radical in her adherence to Jalyn. Being excluded by the influential Endelites didn't deter or discourage Charity. She was focused on reaching the less fortunate. She loved the weekly gatherings at the school and was always offering to help by giving or serving in various roles. Charity was a fulfilled young woman.

The Appointed Judgment Day

The final day of testing arrived. Those who were about to be judged knew it would happen sometime in the next five years because the first five years had already passed. No one imagined it would be so soon.

The day began just like any other, but it ended very differently. Late in the night, the Royal Guards of Affabel swept the two thousand graduates away. Their secret exodus happened while the other Endelites slept.

These two thousand young citizens were ushered through a secret passageway. It was a deep tunnel that brought them beneath the Adonga River. Once through the channel, they traveled an additional two days across a barren wilderness. Throughout the journey, the Chief Guard provided their every need from a store of food, water, and supplies.

The guards were kind yet reserved. All their energy was focused on the task before them. Though they would answer some questions, the Endelites posed others that were not permitted to be answered. The guards' standard reply to these questions was, "All will be made known in due time." This only served to heighten the travelers' curiosity.

The Endelites almost didn't notice the discomfort of the wasteland as they sojourned toward the long-awaited city. As the third day dawned, they crested a hill. There, silhouetted by the morning sun, was the majestic city. Affabel was even more magnificent than any of them had dared to imagine.

As they approached the city, the revelation of its wonder grew and expanded. Even in their approach from the flatlands, it was apparent Affabel was without compare. Endel was puny in comparison to the outskirts of this city.

As the men and women from Endel entered the central portion of the city, they discovered that in Affabel everything was vibrantly alive. It was such a magical place that the birds not only sang but also had the gift of language. Their wondrous and melodic songs interpreted the beauty they beheld and served to further magnify the glory of the city.

This did not come as a total surprise to the Endelites, who had heard the horses of the Royal Guards speak. These noble beasts not only spoke to each other but conversed with their riders as well. It was obvious there was an affectionate relationship between the horses and their riders. It was now apparent all the creatures within Affabel had been gifted with speech and with the capacity for affection and joy.

In every direction the young Endelites turned, they beheld breathtaking vistas. They were enraptured with the awe of Affabel. The air alone was invigorating. It brought both clarity of mind and strength to their travel-weary bodies. The water that flowed throughout the city intrigued them. Somehow it seemed more substantive, as though it glistened with life. Threads of enchanting music permeated the atmosphere and soothed their excited souls with an abiding sense of peace. Everything ranging from the smallest plants to the very air seemed more than alive; it all possessed the ability to give life. Each element was full to overflowing in this miraculous land.

The young citizens could not help but extend their hands and touch everything within their reach as they passed through the concourse of the great city. They longed to run free and explore but somehow knew it wouldn't be permitted at this time.

They were led straight into the large anteroom of a massive auditorium. Here the males and females were separated. This superstructure the young people had been escorted to was so vast it appeared to have unlimited capacity. At least one hundred thousand people could have been contained within its marble walls without issue.

Within the anteroom, the Endelites were allowed to refresh themselves in fragrant baths or showers and were given robes in preparation for their audience with the king. They were all too happy to discard their dusty clothes from Endel. Their old garments seemed awkward and strangely out of place in this radiant city. A deep desire to dwell in Affabel wove itself into the fiber of each Endelite's being. They had the strangest sense of homecoming.

After bathing and dressing, the group gathered again for a meal. This breakfast banquet was set up in a magnificent courtyard where they were allowed to eat and fellowship for a short time. After they ate, the group was separated again, this time by name. Charity, Selfish, and approximately five hundred others were brought to an adjacent hall on the right. Faint Heart, Deceived, and Independent were led with the remaining fifteen hundred to another auditorium on the left. As they entered the halls, they noticed each had a name inscribed over its threshold. The names were strange and in a language unknown to the young Endelites. The name of one auditorium was the Hall of Life; the other, the Hall of Justice.

The Halls of Justice and Life

As he crossed the threshold into the hall on the left, Independent found himself strangely disturbed, almost to the point of being terrified. He reached back into his school memories and tried to comfort himself with what he had briefly heard about Jalyn. It all seemed so confusing now. He found himself regretting that he had missed so many classes.

Obviously, he had been wrong; both the city and the king existed. He tried to block his rising fear and focus on what he remembered of Jalyn's love and merciful nature. At that moment, he did not want to consider Jalyn's justice and holiness, even though they were what now fought for his attention. He attempted to reassure himself by recalling the ways he had been a good citizen and supported the volunteer services in the community.

Taking a deep breath, Independent began to look around and take stock of the company he was in. He could not help but notice he was among some of the worst in Endel. He recognized thieves, swindlers, and drunkards. There were both those who rarely worked and those who worked everything to their advantage. His fear mounted, but just as panic threatened to overwhelm him, he caught sight of Faint Heart. Independent closed his eyes and released a sigh of relief. He immediately remembered her as one of the most outspoken and enthusiastic followers of Jalyn in his class. Hadn't he even heard she had worked at the school? If she was in this hall with him, it would most likely turn out for his good.

As Independent moved in Faint Heart's direction, he bumped into Deceived. Another good sign! Though he had lost touch with Faint Heart, Independent knew Deceived was a strong believer. They even used to argue about Jalyn. As he embraced his old friend, Independent's mood totally changed.

Deceived was both boisterous and positive in his manner. The two men engaged in conversation as all Independent's fear subsided. Jalyn's mercy must have been even vaster than they had known. Look how freely he had forgiven the ones Independent wouldn't have imagined making it. How could this be anything but true? Wasn't the great teacher Double Life just a little way off from them? Independent felt more assured that all would be well. However, he was slightly troubled by the absence of Charity and Selfish. He also found it difficult to ignore that some people wept in the corners of the room. But maybe they were just overwhelmed by Jalyn's goodness.

The other hall was filled with emotion as well. Friends who had lost touch after graduation were thrilled to again be reunited. There was an overwhelming excitement that dominated every conversation: they would soon behold Jalyn! The time had come to enter their true purpose and promised destiny.

All were abuzz with the wonder of the city. They had always known it would be a better place than Endel, but their initial impression exceeded their expectations. It was more than they could take in. Could it possibly be true they'd spend the rest of their lives in such a glorious place? Any one of them would willingly clean floors to have such an honor! All who waited in this hall knew they'd followed Jalyn, but as time passed, a solemn attitude overtook the room. Had they been faithful? Time would soon tell. Excitement intertwined with a measure of fear as these humble servants waited to see their king.

The first to be judged were those waiting in the Hall of Life. However, we will return to them later. For now our story will take us into the Hall of Justice.

The Summons

It was midday. The inhabitants of the Hall of Justice had been restored to a level of comfort and confidence that all would go well for them. They attributed anything that seemed confusing or out of step to Jalyn's mercy or the mystery of his ways. This reasoning comforted them.

The first of the fifteen hundred Endelites in the hall to be called was Independent. Four Royal Guards came to escort him to the Great Hall of Judgment. In an attempt to lighten the solemn mood, he smiled and winked at one of the guards who happened to make eye contact with him as they left the room. He was surprised when this drew no response.

As he heard the hall door shut behind him, Independent found his questions returning. His heart beat against his chest like a drum. It was so loud he imagined the guards heard it, but if they did they gave no sign. He wished Deceived could have come with him. He would soon stand before the Judge and he preferred to not be alone. Independent was rapidly losing confidence.

Before they entered the Great Hall, one of the guards briefed Independent on the appropriate protocol. He nodded, though he feared he would not remember what was said. His pulse was pounding in his ears and threatened to impair his hearing. The guard nodded his acknowledgement of Independent's understanding of procedure, and the doors of the hall were thrown wide open.

As Independent took his first steps into the enormous hall, he noticed his body was trembling. Beads of sweat collected on his usually cool brow. He was completely disoriented because what he saw blew his mind!

CHAPTER 3

THE KINGDOM OF AFFABEL: THE DAY OF JUDGMENT I

Jesus constantly used these illustrations when speaking to the crowds. In fact, because the prophets said that he would use so many, he never spoke to them without at least one illustration. For it had been prophesied, "I will talk in parables; I will explain mysteries hidden since the beginning of time."

—Matthew 13:34–35 TLB

Before continuing our allegory, I'd like to highlight Jesus's statement concerning the coming judgment once again. He announced in John 12:48, "The word that I have spoken will judge him in the last day." We already know the standard by which we will be judged by before His throne: the Holy Scriptures.

Because of this, superscript numbers will appear by many of Jalyn's statements in the Judgment Hall scenes that follow. These numbers refer to scriptures from various translations, whose references can be found at the end of this book. Most of Jalyn's words are composed of scriptures organized in a way that applies to the characters in our story.

With this in mind, let's return to Affabel.

The Judgment of Independent

The Great Hall was more spectacular than anything Independent had imagined. If given the chance to report his experience to the fifteen hundred people still waiting, he would have had no words or frame of reference to describe its grandeur. Its architecture made anything he'd known in Endel obsolete. The auditorium was filled with quite possibly one hundred thousand people in attendance. Independent had never seen so many in one place at one time.

As he stepped closer, Independent caught a glimpse of the citizenry of Affabel. First he noticed that they were regal with radiant faces. Then, almost as an afterthought, he was taken aback by their astounding beauty. It was as though they were from another world. This transformation was because they were all permitted to eat from the tree of life.

Independent wondered, *Is it possible these are former Endelites?* Then he caught sight of one he knew. Her name was Goodness. She was a few years older than Independent, and he remembered how she was constantly ridiculed for her homely appearance. Now she was gorgeous. Her features were the same, making her recognizable, but somehow she was now more beautiful than any person he had ever known in Endel. In fact, everyone he beheld—even the least in beauty—was far more attractive than any he had ever seen in his homeland.

After recovering from his initial shock, Independent noticed that all of those in attendance were focused on an area just ahead of him. It was like nothing he had ever seen.

It was a throne. But this description did not do it justice, for it was indeed a most glorious throne. Independent's eyes took in the one who sat upon it, and in an instant he realized the source of all the majesty of the city. It all proceeded from the man seated on the throne. *This must be Jalyn*, thought Independent. Suddenly he profoundly believed in the one he'd so emphatically denied.

Jalyn's features were handsome yet stern, at least at that moment. Wonderful but frightening would be a more accurate description. His whole appearance was enthralling, yet with every step Independent took toward him, terror grew steadily in his heart. Any confidence he'd once had was now completely gone. What would become of him?

Independent tried to maintain composure by repeating to himself that he was approaching a merciful leader. He was conflicted because he was beginning to doubt he would receive a favorable judgment.

As Independent continued his approach, he was ordered to remain on a narrow platform. Towering above him on the throne was Jalyn. He was the essence of resolute in purpose, and he addressed the assembly: "All . . . shall recognize and understand that I am He who searches minds (the thoughts, feelings, and purposes) and the [inmost] hearts, and I will give to each of you [the reward for what you have done] as your work deserves."[1]

Independent was listening with the others when suddenly Jalyn was looking him straight in the eyes and commanding, "Give an account of your stewardship."[2]

Before Independent could utter a word, a hologram appeared and began to play back his life in Endel from the first day of school until the previous day. Every deed, word, and motive was displayed and revealed to this crowd of witnesses. He was awed by the revelation he now possessed of Jalyn: "Not a creature exists that is concealed from His sight, but all things are open and exposed, naked and defenseless to the eyes of Him with Whom we have to do."[3]

Independent cringed as he watched his foolish, wicked, and selfish ways replayed. Encountering all this before such a large assembly was unanticipated, embarrassing, and shocking. What had seemed insignificant and even harmless in Endel now looked ghastly before this glorious judge and the regal citizens of Affabel. He was horrified by his own behavior. How could he have been so misdirected, so insensitive, so foolish? He strained for a glimmer of hope and found it; he felt there were more good deeds in his number than bad.

When the replay of his life was over, he was relieved, even though he expected a terrible scolding and some form of punishment. He would be happy to be least in the assembly. He felt certain Jalyn would see that his good outweighed his bad.

Jalyn then asked the Chief Scribe, "Is Independent's name found in the Book of Life?"

Without hesitation the Chief Scribe answered, "No, my lord."

Jalyn then spoke. "Independent, you are guilty of choosing an evil nature and are to be taken to the forsaken land of Lone to spend the rest of your life in the torment of utter darkness, hopelessness, and loneliness."

Shocked, Independent cried out, "Lord, why?"

"You did not believe in me," responded Jalyn. "Your teachers taught, 'If you do not believe that I am He, you will die in your sins.'[4] They also taught, 'And there is salvation in and through no one else, for there is no other name under heaven given among men by and in which we must be saved.'"[5]

Independent continued, "But Lord Jalyn, what about my good works? Didn't they outweigh my evil?"

Lord Jalyn replied, "It is not a matter of how little or much you break the law for, 'the person who keeps every law of God but makes one little slip is just as guilty as the person who has broken every law there is.'"[6]

Independent mustered some boldness and countered, "How then can anyone be saved?"

Jalyn didn't immediately respond to this question but rather glanced over to a female citizen of Affabel. She seemed to be an underruler to Jalyn, for she sat on a similar but smaller throne. The woman spoke. "Did not your teachers tell you? 'Jalyn saved you by his special favor when you believed. And you can't take credit for this; it is a gift from Jalyn. Salvation is not a reward for the good things we have done, so none of us can boast about it.'"[7]

Jalyn followed her, saying, "Long ago I paid the price for the laws that had been and would be broken by the citizens. It was impossible for anyone to not sin against me or to redeem themselves from their treasons, but because I loved all, I paid for their wrongs myself. So my salvation is a gift that cannot be earned; you couldn't have done enough good deeds to merit citizenship in Affabel. Your access comes through believing in me. Yet you rejected what I did to save your life."

Stunned, Independent was silent for a few moments, then soberly replied, "I see." He felt as though he was about to drown in a sea of hopelessness. Grasping for something to latch onto, he questioned, "Then all I did was for nothing?"

Jalyn responded, "Again it is written, 'The dead know nothing. They have no further reward, nor are they remembered. Whatever they did in their lifetime—loving, hating, envying—is all long gone. They no longer have a part in anything.'[8]And again, 'For the evil have no future; their light will be snuffed out.'"[9]

Independent was taken aback by Jalyn's words and remained speechless. He regretted all the classes he skipped. Perhaps if he had attended he might have heard the truth and not made this fatal mistake with his life.

In the moments of silence that followed, another thought came to him. It was the one he'd comforted himself with all day. He rallied his courage again and said, "Yes, what you have said is all true, but, Jalyn, you are a merciful king! How can you send me away if this is so?"

Jalyn responded, "I am a merciful king, and that is exactly why I'm sending you away. By choosing to spend your time in Endel the way you did, you permanently chose your nature, that of the dark lord Dagon. How could I be merciful, true, and loving if I allowed your immoral ways to pollute the purity of this great city? I would put the innocent of Affabel in harm's way. Your chosen nature would soon manifest and thus corrupt thousands of pure lives. You have chosen your own way. You will be recompensed for it exactly as the one you followed, Dagon, has been. If I give you less than I gave him, then I would be an unjust leader, and that I am not!"

Jalyn then addressed the entire assembly and quoted the ancient sayings of his father. "He who despises the word will be destroyed, but he who fears the commandment will be rewarded."[10]

What transpired next left the assembly solemn. The king said to the servants, "Bind him hand and foot, take him away, and cast him into outer darkness; there will be weeping and gnashing of teeth. For many are called, but few are chosen."[11]

Screams of horror and the agony of dread seized Independent as he was bound by the Chief Guard and carried toward the side door of the auditorium. Not a sound could be heard among the thousands in attendance. They watched in sorrow as one who had so unwisely wasted his life was carried out to his lifelong punishment.

Once out of the building, Independent was placed in another large waiting room. Here there were thousands of small, barred cells, which held the condemned until the number of all who would be sentenced to exile was completed. Over the entrance to this area these words were written:

> Blessed are those who do His commandments, that they may have the
> right to the tree of life, and may enter through the gates into the city.
> But outside are dogs and sorcerers and sexually immoral and murder-
> ers and idolaters, and whoever loves and practices a lie.[12]

Independent stared at the words. Rage boiled within him. He was now completely under the influence of his nature. Any good that was in his character before was now swallowed up by the very moral fiber he had chosen. His behavior was rapidly deteriorating into that of a mad dog. Without the influence of the king, he was completely given over to a reprobate mind.

Deceived before Jalyn

A few hours passed. Many had already been called out of the Hall of Justice; still waiting amongst the few hundred who remained were Deceived, Faint Heart, and Double Life. Deceived still carried an optimistic attitude, and his demeanor kept the others hopeful as well.

The doors opened and the four Royal Guards once again appeared, this time calling for Deceived. Tension gripped him, and he began to quiver. His time had come. To cover his nervousness, as he was clever at doing, he said to those who yet remained, "Well, guys, my number's up!"

After Deceived was briefed on protocol, the doors to the Judgment Hall swung open and he was escorted down the main aisle. He experienced feelings similar to those Independent had. He likewise saw the size and beauty of the hall and the countenances of the citizens. As he walked down the aisle, he recognized several people he had known from the School of Endel who had graduated a year or two before him. He recognized more citizens than Independent had since Deceived almost never missed a meeting at the school.

One person he recognized who didn't attend classes was a man named Ruthless. He was one of the most notoriously wicked men in the community. Deceived stopped in his tracks, wondering, *What is he doing here?* The Chief Guard motioned to Deceived that it was fine for him to speak to this man.

Deceived walked over to him and asked, "Are you Ruthless?"

The man responded, "I was once known as Ruthless, but at his Judgment Seat, Lord Jalyn changed my name to Reconciled."

Deceived blurted out, "How in the world did you ever get in here? You were considered a wicked man by most in our community. You never went to school and you opposed Jalyn more than anyone I knew."

Reconciled replied, "Yes, this is true. But I hated who I was and what I did. Since I didn't attend school, I had never heard Jalyn's life-changing word. However, a week before my Judgment Day, I went for a meal at Charity's restaurant. She knew my life was a wreck and somehow detected my pain. She paid for my dinner with one condition: that I stay and talk with her. She then spent two hours telling me of Jalyn, his goodness, his salvation, and of this place called Affabel."

Reconciled continued, "She explained it was not too late for me to give my life to this great leader. I could still be forgiven unconditionally and accepted as a citizen in his kingdom. I was overwhelmed by Jalyn's love and pledged the rest of my life to his lordship. Though I was only able to serve him in Endel for a week, I did so with all my heart. I went to those I had oppressed or stolen from and asked their forgiveness. In some cases where it was appropriate I gave back even more than I'd taken."

Deceived was speechless. He looked back at the guard, who nodded his head in affirmation. Reconciled then stepped back into his place, and Deceived proceeded toward the throne.

As Deceived walked, he couldn't help but ponder what he had just heard. He had been told of the great mercy of Jalyn but had now witnessed it in a manner that was staggering. This man had been one of the worst he had ever known, and now he was as regal as the others. Deceived was more convinced than ever that he would find favor with Jalyn because he was such a strong believer in him.

Once Deceived stood before the throne, he was given the same order as Independent: "Give an account of your stewardship."

Just as Independent had, Deceived witnessed his life from the first day of school till the day prior in the three-dimensional hologram. What a relief to see his faithful school attendance and outspoken support of Jalyn before the assembly.

However, Deceived was soon appalled. His lifestyle accused him. He had justified his ways, but as they came to light before this majestic judge and the morally pure witnesses, he was embarrassed and ashamed. When his sexual promiscuity was made known before this regal assembly, he wanted to crawl into a hole and hide.

Not only were his acts brought to the light but his intentions and motives as well. How could Jalyn know these things? How could he judge Deceived for things no one even knew? His deepest secrets were no longer hidden. The entire assembly beheld his lust for gain in his business transactions, in the sales of his homes, and in his land development. They saw the slander and gossip he habitually used to get what he desired. It seemed everything he did was motivated by his desire for more.

He wanted his own way in everything, and he wanted everything for himself. There was no arguing with the facts. However, Deceived comforted himself in the knowledge that none of this really mattered because he believed in Jalyn and professed his allegiance to him.

Once Deceived's life had been fully reviewed, Jalyn turned to the Royal Scribe and asked, "Is Deceived found in the Book of Life?"

The scribe responded, "No, my lord."

Jalyn announced, "Deceived, you are guilty of denying me. You are to be taken to the forsaken land of Lone to spend the rest of your life in the torment of utter darkness, hopelessness, and loneliness."

Deceived was paralyzed with utter shock. His mind raced. *No, this is a mistake. This cannot be happening! I'm a believer in Jalyn. What does he mean, "denying me"?*

He blurted out, "How have I denied you?"

Jalyn said, "Did you not listen when your teachers warned of those who 'claim they know Jalyn, but they deny him by the way they live'?"[13]

Again Deceived countered, "But, great king, I attended your school. I was faithful to not miss classes, and I was involved in many activities. I even called you lord!"

Jalyn immediately said, "Why do you call me, 'Lord, Lord,' and yet don't do what I tell you?[14] Did you not hear my words when I said not all who sound religious are really godly people? They may refer to me as 'Lord' but still won't get to Affabel. For the decisive question is whether they obey my Father. At the Judgment many will tell me, 'Lord, Lord, we told others about you and used your name.' But I will reply, 'You have never been mine. Go away, for your deeds are evil.'"[15]

Deceived was frantic. "But I had faith. I believed in you, so according to your word, I should be saved!"

Jalyn was patient but resolute. He looked to a citizen in the assembly, a former teacher in the school who now sat on a smaller throne. "Read to Deceived what you taught in your classes."

This gentleman read from the sacred writings, "Dear brothers and sisters, what's the use of saying you have faith if you don't prove it by your actions? That kind of faith can't save anyone. It isn't enough just to have faith. Faith that doesn't show itself by good deeds is no faith at all—it is dead and useless. Now someone may argue, 'Some people have faith; others have good deeds.' I say, 'I can't see your faith if you don't have good deeds, but I will show you my faith through my good deeds.' Do you still think it's enough just to believe that there is one Jalyn? Well, even the demons believe this, and they tremble in terror! Fool! When will you ever learn that faith that does not result in good deeds is useless?"[16]

Jalyn reiterated, "You say you had faith, yet faith is not faith unless it is accompanied by corresponding actions of obedience. It is not enough to say you believe, for even the demons believe but are certainly not saved. Those who truly believe will exhibit a changed nature and no longer produce the fruit of an evil one. You continually bore the fruit of the evil lord Dagon, which was only evidence that you never truly believed in me from your heart."

Deceived was having a hard time comprehending all that was said. He countered, "But what about this evil man Ruthless? I was better than him! How could you let him in and keep me out? You are not being fair!"

Jalyn responded, "You say the Lord isn't being fair! Listen to me. Am I the one who is unfair, or is it you? If a wicked person turns away from his wickedness and obeys the law and does right, he shall save his soul, for he has thought it over and decided to turn from his sins and live a good life. He shall surely live—he shall not die."[17]

Frustrated and angry, Deceived ranted on, "But I shared your word and witnessed to people about you. I even volunteered and substitute taught at your school!"

Jalyn, now stern, replied, "Recite my laws no longer and stop claiming my promises, for you have refused my discipline, disregarding my laws. You see a thief and help him, and spend your time with evil and immoral men. You curse and lie, and vile language streams from your mouth. You slander your own brother. I remained silent—you thought

I didn't care—but now your time of punishment has come, and I list all the above charges against you."[18]

Deceived was silent. He mind was reeling, but he had nothing more to say in his defense.

A few moments passed. Then the king said to the servants, "Bind him hand and foot, take him away, and cast him into outer darkness; there will be weeping and gnashing of teeth."[19]

As the Chief Guard approached, Deceived hurled profanities toward Jalyn, the guards, and the citizens of Affabel. Enraged, he thrashed violently. Any good within him was swallowed up by the revelation of his true nature.

Deceived was bound hand and foot and carried out of the auditorium, cursing the entire way. Like Independent, he was held in a cage until the judgment of all was complete.

Once Deceived was out of the auditorium, Jalyn addressed the gathering of witnesses: "There is a generation that is pure in its own eyes, yet is not washed from its filthiness."[20]

Faint Heart before Jalyn

Less than one hundred were left in the Hall of Justice. Faint Heart and Double Life were in their number. Faint Heart stayed as far away from Double Life as she could, as she yet maintained a bitter resentment toward him. He avoided her as well.

The four Royal Guards entered and summoned Faint Heart. She was nervous about where she was going but grateful to leave Double Life behind. Like the others before her, she was led to the entrance of the great hall, briefed on protocol, and ushered in.

As she passed by the citizens of Affabel, she too recognized many who had gone on before her. Most were not as outspoken and passionate about their faith as she had been while in school. Faint Heart was amazed to see a number of people present who she'd thought would surely be absent.

Faint Heart approached the throne and noticed the smaller thrones surrounding it. She recognized a few teachers and others she would have expected to see as leaders in the kingdom. However, there were many more who surprised her sitting on these thrones. They were the lesser-known citizens of Endel. There were some present who had been wealthy as well. *How could the rich be in such places of honor?* she thought to herself.

Before her mind could answer, she heard Jalyn's voice. "Give an account of your stewardship."

The hologram displayed her life. Faint Heart was delighted with the review of her schooling period. All her volunteer work, extra study, and class leadership bode well for her. She was proud of her boldness and diligence. However, her mood changed with the showing of her response to Slander's lie. It was clear she had refused to let go of the offense. Her heart issues were exposed, and they weren't pretty.

Then her affair with Double Life began. She had never repented of her involvement with him. She had always felt the victim and laid all the blame on Slander and Double Life. This caused her to never take responsibility for her choices. As her life unfolded, she watched anger, bitterness, and a desire for revenge multiply. Though she had managed to suppress some of these issues, she had never dealt with their root. This revealed itself not only in her perpetual offense against Double Life and Slander but in the fact that she actually blamed Jalyn for her hardships as well. How could he have allowed a man like Double Life to teach in his school? Her resentment and unforgiveness were being exposed as hard and relentless.

As the review concluded, it was clear Faint Heart was an embittered woman who lacked goodness toward others. However, even with all this revealed before the great assembly, she was confident her previously strong commitment would secure her favor with the king. She dreaded a little scolding but never foresaw what was coming.

Jalyn turned to the Chief Scribe. "Is Faint Heart's name found in the Book of Life?"

The scribe responded, "No, my lord."

Jalyn pronounced his judgment. "Faint Heart, you are guilty of falling away from righteousness and denying me by treason. You are to be taken to the forsaken land of Lone to spend the rest of your life in the torment of utter darkness, hopelessness, and loneliness."

Faint Heart was stunned beyond description. Hers was an even greater shock than that of any of the others before her. This couldn't be happening! She was trapped in a bad dream—no, a nightmare—and somehow she must wake herself! Maybe she had misunderstood.

In disbelief, she questioned, "Jalyn, did you say I am to be taken to the dreaded land of Lone?"

"Yes, Faint Heart, you heard correctly," replied the king.

"How can this be, Lord Jalyn? I believe in you. This was clearly shown in my life review. I had a good life to back my beliefs. I know my heart became hardened and the love within me died, but that wasn't my fault. It was the fault of Slander and Double Life. Their treachery caused me to grow cold."

Jalyn responded, "Did you forget my warnings through your teachers? 'Such will be the spread of evil that many people's love will grow cold. But whoever holds out to the end will be saved.'[21] You did not endure to the end."

Faint Heart continued, "But, Lord Jalyn, I am a righteous person because of my belief in you. I may have lost my witness, but I believed that once a person was saved, they would always be saved and could never lose their salvation. Even some of the teachers proclaimed this. According to them, no one could pluck me out of your hand."

Jalyn responded, "Yes, this is true. No one can pluck you out of my hand, but I never said you couldn't walk away. You alone hold that power. For did you not read the sacred writings? 'If people have escaped from the corrupting forces of the world through their knowledge of our Lord and Savior Jalyn, and then are again caught and conquered by them, such people are in worse condition at the end than they were at the beginning.

It would have been much better for them never to have known the way of righteousness than to know it and then turn away from the sacred command that was given them.'[22] If I stated it would have been better for such people to not have known the way of righteousness because they are now worse off than they were before being saved, how could you believe it was impossible to lose salvation? If it could never be lost, then how could they be worse off than before?

"Why did you listen to teachers who taught contrary to what my word stated? I recorded it carefully so all could know the way of righteousness. Why did you allow yourself to be deceived? If you had believed what I said, you would have confronted the bitterness in your heart. Instead you allowed it to grow unchecked out of your false comfort in unconditional security and now face a judgment that could have been averted."

Faint Heart pleaded, "But what about all the good I did?"

Lord Jalyn replied, "Again, did you not read what I clearly stated through my prophet? 'If righteous people turn to sinful ways and start acting like other sinners, should they be allowed to live? No, of course not! All their previous goodness will be forgotten, and they will die for their sins. Yet you say, "The Lord isn't being just!" Listen to me. . . . Am I the one who is unjust, or is it you? When righteous people turn from being good and start doing sinful things, they will die for it. Yes, they will die because of their sinful deeds.'[23] It is just as it was written; your goodness and righteous acts are forgotten and will not be credited to you."

Still grasping, Faint Heart said, "But lord, you said if I confessed you as my savior, my name would be written in the Book of Life. How is it possible it is no longer there? Why can't your scribe find my name? How could it have been erased?"

Lord Jalyn, patient but resolute, answered, "Did you not hear what was stated earlier? 'He who endures to the end shall be saved.'[24] Those who endure all the way to the judgment are those who overcome, and I clearly said, 'He who overcomes shall thus be clothed in white garments;

and I will not erase his name from the book of life.'[25] If I stated I will not erase someone's name from the Book of Life, it means it can be erased. Otherwise I would have said, 'If you confess me as lord, your name will be forever secured in the Book of Life.'"

Faint Heart pleaded, "How can you send me to Lone, the place where the living dead are sent?"

Jalyn turned to one of the underrulers. "Read the ancient writings that have been made known to the citizens of Endel."

The ruler read, "A man who strays from the path of understanding comes to rest in the company of the dead."[26]

Faint Heart was rendered speechless. Then the king said to the servants, "Bind her hand and foot, take her away, and cast her into outer darkness; there will be weeping and gnashing of teeth. For many are called, but few are chosen."[27]

As the Chief Guard approached, Faint Heart cursed Jalyn. She was overtaken by the violence of her bitterness and twisted by her twice-fallen nature (see Jude 12). She was like a late autumn tree pulled up by its roots with no fruit of righteousness remaining.

Faint Heart was bound hand and foot and carried toward the side door of the auditorium. She also was held in one of the cages. Once she'd left the auditorium, the Chief Scribe enlightened the congregation of witnesses:

> "Dear friends, if we deliberately continue sinning after we have received a full knowledge of the truth, there is no other sacrifice that will cover these sins. There will be nothing to look forward to but the terrible expectation of Jalyn's judgment and the raging fire that will consume his enemies. For we know the one who said, 'I will take vengeance. I will repay those who deserve it.' He also said, 'The Lord will judge his own people.' It is a terrible thing to fall into the hands of the living Jalyn."[28]

The Judgment of Double Life

The last person to be called out of the Hall of Justice was Double Life. He knew the laws of Jalyn and already knew his judgment would not be favorable. He would soon discover just how much his transgressions had cost him.

Double Life felt faint as he was escorted into the judgment hall and had to be assisted by the guards in order to approach the Judgment Seat of Jalyn. His life was reviewed, and he too heard the woeful words that his name was not found in the Book of Life.

Jalyn firmly announced, "Double Life, you are guilty of treason, falling away from righteousness, and being a stumbling block. You are to be taken to the forsaken land of Lone, where you will receive the greatest punishment and torments."

Double Life listened in horror, then pleaded, "But lord, I was a teacher in your school. I gave my life for your cause."

Jalyn answered, "You were a teacher, but did you not read from the books you taught? 'Dear brothers and sisters, not many of you should become teachers in the school, for we who teach will be judged by Jalyn with greater strictness.'"[29]

Double Life countered, "How was I a stumbling block?"

Jalyn's tone became harder. "You caused many of my little ones to stumble and fall permanently. Faint Heart is just one example. She was entrusted to your care. I gave you authority to protect her, not to use her for your own advantage. You used your influence to satiate your lust and violated her and others. A sister already wounded her and you, who should have brought healing, took advantage of her. You shipwrecked her faith. She has been sentenced to Lone. Surely you remember the warning I gave: 'Whoever causes one of these little ones who believe in Me to stumble, it would be better for him if a millstone were hung around his neck, and he were thrown into the sea.'"[30]

Double Life pleaded, "Jalyn, I know I'm to be banned to Lone, but why am I to receive the greatest torment? Why are you so hard on me? I was one of your servants, not an unbeliever. I wasn't like Independent, who would have nothing to do with you. Why?"

Jalyn, still resolute, said, "You knew and taught the ancient writings. Why do you ask these questions of me? I will remind you so you may remember these words. The ancient writings are clear: 'But if the servant thinks, "My master won't be back for a while," and begins oppressing the other servants . . . the master will return unannounced and unexpected. He will tear the servant apart and banish him with the unfaithful. The servant will be severely punished, for though he knew his duty, he refused to do it. But people who are not aware that they are doing wrong will be punished only lightly. Much is required from those to whom much is given, and much more is required from those to whom much more is given.'"[31]

Jalyn continued, "Independent was far less aware of his transgressions. You had both awareness and knowledge. His punishment, though severe, will be lighter than your own. For you, I've 'reserved a place . . . in the deepest darkness.'"[32]

Jalyn then commanded the Chief Guard, "Bind him hand and foot, take him away, and cast him into outer darkness; there will be weeping and gnashing of teeth. For many are called, but few are chosen."[33]

As the Chief Guard approached, Double Life spewed profanities at Jalyn, the guards, and the citizens of Affabel. He was violent and even tried to break free to physically attack Jalyn. His true nature was completely revealed. Any good within was swallowed up by his duplicity. He was bound hand and foot and carried out the side door of the auditorium, cursing the entire way. He joined the other fifteen hundred people who were immediately transported to the land of Lone.

As soon as Double Life exited the auditorium, the Chief Scribe closed his book and shouted: "The judgments you have made are just. They are getting what they deserve!"

A voice from the altar replied, "True and just indeed are your judgments!"[34]

The Forsaken Land of Lone

The fifteen hundred condemned and caged Endelites were escorted by the Royal Guards on a two-week trip to the blighted land of Lone. This journey brought them into the Great Desert of Fire, where the heat that rose from the parched earth was unbearable. Suddenly, in the middle of nowhere, where the heat was the most unbearable, a very large and foreboding structure loomed in the distance. As they approached, the condemned were able to read the sign: "The Forsaken Land of Lone."

Upon closer inspection, they realized the large structure had no windows or openings other than one large door at the base. Passing through the door, they heard what seemed like tens of thousands of screams coming from inside. Within moments they could make out the pleas directed to the Chief Guard, which came from those imprisoned near the entry. "Hasn't it been long enough? Please ask for mercy on our behalf. Our punishment is too much to bear!"

"How long have they been in this place?" Independent asked a guard.

"Their times range from one year to 129."

Deceived was shocked. He had somehow hoped all that had transpired in the past two weeks would turn out to be a nightmare or scare tactic. He inquired of the same guard, "This is truly where I will spend the rest of my life?"

"Yes. It is exactly as you were forewarned in Endel."

Many of those slated for the greater punishment were placed higher in the metal building where the heat was greater. Those who didn't know the truth but still committed things worthy of exile were placed in the lower portions of the enormous structure. Even this placement was unbearable for a day, let alone for more than one hundred years!

The agony of Double Life's abode was unimaginable, worse even than the fate of those at the highest level of the building. He was taken to a dungeon underground, near the hot sulfur rocks. The smell alone was unbearable, and with no venting, the heat was more intense than in any other location in Lone. This place was not in the building but deep within the bowels of the earth. It was without doubt the greatest place of suffering and torment. Here Double Life would suffer all alone. The area was large enough to separate those who shared the same measure of condemnation. They were unable to hear any voice but their own.

Once the condemned were securely imprisoned, the Chief Guard made his way to the entrance. When the massive iron door shut behind him, not a fragment of light could be found within the confines of the structure. The poor souls inside would spend over 125 years in utter darkness and loneliness. The only hope of light they had was when a new round of prisoners was brought in once a year. Yet not all even saw this, only those who were near the great door. Others, like Double Life, would never again see the light of day. For him, the blackness of darkness was reserved as punishment.

Reflections

These four citizens of Endel regretted for the rest of their existence their choice to not listen to the truth. Alone, they continually pondered the foolishness of not carefully heeding the words of Jalyn, which had been accessible in the land of Endel. They would have done anything for the chance to go back and change their destinies. Oh, how they wished they had not listened to the majority or the popular opinion of their day! If they could do it over again, each would spurn their own foolish reasoning and embrace the ancient writings, which never varied and could never be broken.

The condemned were tormented by images of Affabel, that most remarkable kingdom. In their continual anguish, they could still see the beauty of the city even though they'd only experienced it for a few moments. The contrast magnified their torment. The fiery heat, acrid stench, and darkness of Lone only served to punctuate the truth. Beauty had been theirs for the choosing, and they had forsaken it all through their folly.

DISCUSSION QUESTIONS

SECTION 1: CHAPTERS 1–3

1. Before you started reading this book, how would you have defined *success*? How have your goals, priorities, and habits reflected that definition? In what way is your perspective challenged or affirmed by what you read in this section?

2. When we consider the gravity of a concept like eternity, it almost seems absurd to think anyone could be confident at a judgment that determines their eternal fate. Yet that's exactly what 1 John 4:17 promises. We'll be unpacking this idea throughout the remaining sections—but can you explain, based on what you know now, where you believe that confidence comes from?

3. In this section, you were introduced to the kingdom of Affabel, which acts as a picture of the relationship between life on earth and our eternal destinies. What most stood out to you about this kingdom and its governance? Did anything excite or surprise you? How does Scripture shine light on those elements of the story?

4. Let's talk about the inhabitants of Endel. What was your reaction to the first four judgments? Would you have expected them to go differently? If so, why?

5. What are your most pressing questions or concerns as we move forward in our study?

SECTION 2

CHAPTER 4

ETERNAL HOME OF THE DEAD

And when His disciples asked Him the meaning of this parable,
He said to them, To you it has been given to [come progressively
to] know (to recognize and understand more strongly and
clearly) the mysteries and secrets of the kingdom of God . . .
—Luke 8:9–10 AMP

In the next four chapters, we'll break from our allegory and focus on the specific truths revealed by the judgments of Independent, Deceived, Faint Heart, and Double Life. We'll then finish the allegory by discussing Selfish and Charity and for the remainder of the book focus on the truths revealed by their lives. The better part of this book will focus on the eternal rewards of those who follow Jesus Christ.

Foundational Truth

In our allegory, Jalyn represents Jesus Christ, and the King Father is Almighty God the Father. Dagon is Satan, life in Endel represents a human being's life on this earth, and Affabel reflects the heavenly city of God. The forsaken land of Lone represents the Lake of Fire, where every individual without the saving grace of Jesus Christ will spend eternity. The individuals discussed in the previous chapter represent various scenarios of those who will be forever condemned; God's Word makes this very clear.

Yes, you read that correctly, forever condemned. In preparing to write this message, I struggled with how to bring you the reader to a place of being able to relate to what Scripture refers to as "eternal judgments." Read carefully the following:

> Therefore let us go on and get past the elementary stage in the teachings and doctrine of Christ (the Messiah), advancing steadily toward the completeness and perfection that belong to spiritual maturity. Let us not again be laying the foundation of . . . eternal judgment and punishment. [These are all matters of which you should have been fully aware long, long ago.] (Hebrews 6:1–2 AMP)

As you can see, I left out the other five foundational doctrines, some of which are repentance from dead works and faith toward God, in order to emphasize that eternal judgment and punishment are *elementary* teachings of Christ.

One dictionary defines *elementary* as "constituting the basic, essential, or fundamental part."[1] It's the essential part we must have right from the start to build upon; it's a foundation. To understand, consider our education system. In elementary school, we get the basic tools used to further build our education, such as reading, writing, and arithmetic. Lacking these as a foundation, we will never have the ability to develop a proper education. The same is true for believers. If we do not have eternal judgments firmly established in our understanding, then we will not be capable of building a proper life in Christ. It could be compared to trying to advance your education without being able to read, write, add, or subtract.

Yet I've discovered after almost twenty years of traveling ministry that many—and I'm including devoted followers of Jesus Christ—are unaware of these issues. Notice the writer states, "These are all matters of which you should have been fully aware long, long ago." He didn't say we are to be acquainted with these issues but to be *fully,* or *completely,* aware. His words, "long, long ago" only emphasize that these are foundational to our basic faith, as the ability to read and write are to our education.

We'll see shortly why "eternal judgment" is an elementary doctrine we must understand in order to build a healthy Christian life. Keep this in mind as you continue to read. Without this understanding, it may be too difficult to take in what we're about to discuss, and you may succumb to the thought, *What's the point?*

Hell—Figurative or Real

Before I began to write this book, I wrestled with this thought: *How do I communicate to a generation who "lives for the day" the reality of the eternal decisions that will shortly be made about our lives by the Judge of the universe?* After several days of struggle, in prayer another thought arose. I realized that Jesus, to communicate spiritual truths to the minds of human beings, told stories. Thus the idea for the allegory of Affabel.

As I was writing of the judgment of the individuals in Affabel and their lifelong punishment in the land of Lone, I trembled within myself. In fact, I wrote the final part of the previous chapter while flying home one Sunday evening. I preached three times that day. My assistants were sound asleep, but I couldn't stop typing. Upon arriving home well after midnight, I couldn't sleep, fearing for all those who will eventually find themselves in an unspeakably worse situation called the Lake of Fire— and, according to Jesus, it will be the majority of people who do:

> "Go in through the narrow gate, because the gate to hell is wide and
> the road that leads to it is easy, and there are many who travel it. But
> the gate to life is narrow and the way that leads to it is hard, and there
> are few people who find it." (Matthew 7:13–14 TEV)

While lying in bed that night, I reflected back a couple years when I was asked to preach the gospel to a top-security male prison in South Africa. I remember walking into that dreadful place, witnessing horrors like terrible smells, revolting living conditions, and cells that held twenty to thirty men with bunks inches from each other. There were even condoms hanging on the walls. I had ministered in several prisons in America, but never had I seen such despairing conditions. Our prisons looked like country clubs in comparison.

I couldn't imagine living a week in that vile place, let alone forty to fifty years. Most of the prisoners were there for life. You could see utter despair on the faces of those who were not believers in Jesus. I could almost hear their thoughts: *At least one day I'll get out of here through death.* Yet on the other hand, they were terrified by the unknown reality of dying. It was a very terrible quandary indeed. They were in a complete state of hopelessness. If you'd lived in the free world—as all of them had—and you were facing this place for the rest of your life, it would be sheer torment.

While there, I thought that as horrific as this was, it was beautiful compared to hell. At least these inmates had companions and sunlight streaming through a few barred windows in this prison. In hell, there are neither companions nor light, except for the fire that is never quenched. In the Lake of Fire, there is no relief, forever and ever; souls will be in perpetual anguish! In hell, the people cannot think, *One day I'll get out of this place.* They've received *eternal* punishment!

Because it is one of His elementary teachings, Jesus discussed hell frequently, much more often than the subject is mentioned from pulpits today. He didn't see bringing up its description—the torment involved, as well as the fact that it was never-ending—as a lack of compassion. Rather He saw it as essential to reaching us as the Good Shepherd. His addressing and teaching on it, therefore, was motivated by love, since all He did and taught was out of a heart of compassion. So my question is, are we doing the best service to people by not mentioning hell from our pulpits today? Is that true love?

There are several names given to hell in Scripture. *Sheol* (in the Old Testament only), *Hades*, and *the grave* are a few of the names given to the intermediate chambers of death. *Gehenna* and the *Lake of Fire* are the names given to the eternal hell. We will discuss the difference between the intermediate and eternal shortly.

Scripture tells us hell is a real place, not figurative as our society has endeavored to promote. In Numbers 16 the earth opened up and three families were physically swallowed into Sheol before a multitude of witnesses. In the New Testament, we are told concerning the Antichrist and his False Prophet, "Both of them were hurled alive into the fiery lake that burns and blazes with brimstone" (Revelation 19:20 AMP). They didn't die with just their souls taken to this place; rather, their physical bodies and souls were cast into the Lake of Fire.

Lazarus and the Rich Man

In the Gospel of Luke, Jesus tells of an actual incident involving a rich man who lived entirely for himself, neglecting a beggar daily laid before his house. We know this is not a parable because Jesus opens the story with, "There was a certain rich man." Second, He uses Abraham's name and gives a specific name to the beggar, Lazarus. It was not customary for Jesus to give names or mention actual people in His parables.

Lazarus died and was carried by angels to Abraham's bosom, which was the holding area of comfort for the Old Testament saints until Jesus made the way for them to come into the presence of God in heaven. The rich man died and found himself in Hades. We read:

". . . And in Hades, where he was in great pain, he looked up and saw Abraham, far away, with Lazarus at his side. So he called out, 'Father Abraham! Take pity on me, and send Lazarus to dip his finger in some water and cool off my tongue, because I am in great pain in this fire!'" (Luke 16:23–24 TEV)

Notice that the rich man was in great pain. Other translations use the words *agony, anguish,* and *torment.* In other words, the suffering was very great. Hell is a place of conscious torment. Also notice that the man recognized Abraham as well as Lazarus and that they could also recognize him. People are very much human beings in hell; they still have their reasoning faculties, emotions, wills, physical features, and senses. This man could see, hear, and feel pain. They also have some form of flesh; you can see the rich man's intense desire just to have his tongue cooled. Jesus says that both body and soul are eternally destroyed in hell (see Matthew 10:28). In other words, people's flesh will be continuously afflicted and marred by its fires and worms.

Also notice that the rich man was pleading for mercy, just like those who were begging for mercy in the dungeon of Lone in our story. Hell is a place of no escape, forever! There is nobody who will ever come from the outside to comfort its inhabitants, even though such relief is greatly longed for. It also seems this reality never completely sinks in. Abraham had to remind this rich man, "There is a great chasm separating us. Anyone who wanted to cross over to you from here [*to bring comfort*] is stopped at its edge, and no one there can cross over to us" (Luke 16:26 NLT). I know an individual who experienced hell; he later reported that everyone he saw cried out that it was too much to bear. This is exactly what you hear this rich man cry out in the above verse.

Continuing to read:

"But Abraham said, 'Remember, my son, that in your lifetime
you were given all the good things, while Lazarus got all the
bad things. But now he is enjoying himself here, while you are
in pain . . .'
      "The rich man said, 'Then I beg you, father Abraham, send
Lazarus to my father's house, where I have five brothers. Let him go
and warn them so that they, at least, will not come to this place of
pain.'" (Luke 16:25, 27–28 TEV)

You've heard of the old saying, "Misery loves company." Why doesn't it apply here? Why didn't this rich man want others there with him? The answer is that in hell there is no companionship or fellowship. Some think there will be parties in hell; others think they will enjoy their friends. If that were so, the rich man would have wanted all his closest comrades to join him, but he was desperate to see that they would not come to this place of torment. Hell is a place of utter loneliness and hopelessness. It is also a place of eternal remembrance, which I personally believe is one of its great torments.

Hear how Abraham responds to the man's plea for his brothers:

"Abraham said, 'Your brothers have Moses and the prophets to warn them; your brothers should listen to what they say.'

"The rich man answered, 'That is not enough, father Abraham! But if someone were to rise from death and go to them, then they would turn from their sins.'

"But Abraham said, 'If they will not listen to Moses and the prophets, they will not be convinced even if someone were to rise from death.'" (Luke 16:29–31 TEV)

There is such a powerful truth conveyed here. Many would like extraordinary experiences to prove to themselves or others the validity of the gospel. Yet Jesus shows us nothing is greater than the Word of God to produce the belief it takes to follow God completely to the end. Don't misunderstand me. Most who witnessed the supernatural would be startled and changed for a short while, but they would not be permanently convinced in their hearts by these experiences.

When I was a teenager—a profane young man and party animal— my dad took me to see the movie *The Ten Commandments* starring Charlton Heston. I vividly remember fixing my eyes on that huge screen when the earth opened up to swallow the people into hell; it shook me tremendously. I walked out of that theater, and my life was changed. I straightened up and walked differently for about a week, only to return to all my old ways. Why? Because I hadn't heard the Word of God, repented of my ways, and committed my life completely to Jesus in order for His grace to change me.

My friends and I had other extraordinary experiences that shook me as well, but I wasn't changed by any supernatural experiences. It wasn't until one of my college fraternity brothers came to my room and presented the Word of God through the gospel of Jesus Christ that my life was changed. We are specifically told, "Faith comes by hearing, and hearing by the word of God" (Romans 10:17), and, "You have been born again, not of perishable seed, but of imperishable, through the living and enduring word of God" (1 Peter 1:23 NIV). For this reason, it is so important that we teach and preach the Word of God, not just our experiences.

On the other hand, having clarified this, let me now stress this fact: *if experiences complement or help amplify the Word of God, they are tremendous and even needful.* Testimonies play a huge part in communicating the gospel, but it is the Word of God received and believed that will cause us to abide forever.

"Why Am I Going This Way?"

So now allow me to share a testimony that will complement what we've discussed from Scripture. My wife and I sat in the living room of a friend one evening, and he shared with us what happened to him as a young man. He was raised in the Caribbean and during the rainy season fell into a pit used to gather rainwater for construction. His brother jumped in and tried to save him but couldn't, so he got out and ran for help, for our friend couldn't swim. By the time help arrived, he had been dead for approximately thirty minutes.

He told us that once he left his body, all of his senses were intact. He found himself being pulled rapidly downward into a very deep darkness. He said the darkness was so deep he couldn't see his hand in front of his face; it was so dark he felt as if he were wearing it. He said, "The fear was so great I thought, *It cannot get any worse.* Yet the more I fell, the more intense it became. I have never experienced fear like that on the earth. There is no way to describe it in words."

He continued, "Then I saw the flickering lights, and I knew I was headed for hell. I started screaming, 'Why am I going this way? I'm a Christian!'" Our friend's mother and father were strong believers, but he was simply going to church because his parents told him he had no choice.

He then reported hearing screams of fear and torment. I vividly remember him saying, "John and Lisa, there are some screams that are ordinary. Then there are other screams that make your blood freeze in its veins. These are the screams I heard.

"Then I came face to face with a creature that had scales who kept saying to me, 'Come to me. You are mine.'

"I was fighting with the creature. At first I couldn't say anything because of the fear, but then I yelled, 'Let me go, let me go!'"

"Then suddenly I found myself screaming in my body and bit the doctor who had his finger down my throat—so I was told by my mother after I explained to her my experience. At the same time, my mother was sitting outside the operating room (now at the hospital) and crying out to God, 'Father if you give my son back to me, I will give him to You forever!'" Our friend later in life pioneered a ministry in the Caribbean.

You may question this man's experience; however, there have been quite a number of men, women, and children who have undergone similar occurrences. These near death experiences (NDEs) occur frequently enough in the presence of doctors that a few have researched them.

One such researcher is a man named Melvin Morse, a doctor who conducted extensive study on children who have had NDEs. Dr. Morse studied two groups of children. The first group of 121 patients consisted of those who were critically ill but not near death. They were on artificial lung machines, in intensive care or on heavy medication, and ranged in age from three to sixteen years of age. Not one of them reported leaving their bodies.

The second group, which consisted of twelve children of a similar age group, had experienced heart failures from drowning, car accidents, cardiac arrest, and the like. In this smaller group, every one of the twelve patients had out of body experiences. Some had briefly seen their bodies and described to doctors the procedures they were using while working on them.

Some may think our friend's experience was hallucinated; however, the studies done on these other children would strongly show otherwise. Besides, how could he have hallucinated when he was clinically dead for almost thirty minutes?

Hades Versus the Lake of Fire

Our friend, as well as the others I know who have experienced hell, saw the intermediate place of torment called Hades. This is not the eternal abode of those outside of salvation. Rather, it's a waiting place of torment where they are held until the Great White Throne Judgment. The permanent place where human beings, demons, and fallen angels will spend eternity after their judgment is called the *Lake of Fire*. This is clearly seen in the following Scripture:

> Then I saw a great white throne and the One Who was seated upon it . . . And the sea delivered up the dead who were in it, death and Hades surrendered the dead in them, and all were tried and their cases determined by what they had done [according to their motives, aims, and works]. Then death and Hades were thrown into the lake of fire. This is the second death, the lake of fire. And if anyone's

[name] was not found recorded in the Book of Life, he was hurled into the lake of fire. (Revelation 20:11, 13–15 AMP; two parenthetical statements omitted for clarity)

I first want to point out that all those who were in the intermediate place of torment, Hades, were brought before the judgment. Once this judgment is complete, everything that offends and all those who practiced lawlessness will be hurled into the Lake of Fire—everything including demons, fallen angels, and yes, even Hades itself.

A Vision of the Lake of Fire

My wife and I have friends who are Greek. The wife, whose name is Joy, is a third-generation minister. Her grandmother was born and raised in Greece and from a young age started seeking God. Her questions to those around her were met with apathy and downright mockery. She wanted to go to a church but she was told that "there is no God" and to stop with that nonsense.

One day, as Joy's grandmother was dancing a folk dance with her friends in the village square during a Greek festival, a voice spoke to her and said, "Efrosyni, seek the eternal dance."

She was startled! *Who said that?* she wondered. Immediately, she quit the dance and ran home, hoping to find some clarity. As she ran, a tremendous burden began to come on her like a heavy weight on her back.

Once inside her home, Efrosyni went straight to her bedroom, fell on her knees, and started to cry. She wanted to talk to that voice. Who was talking to her? What were the words that were spoken to her? What was He trying to communicate? These were the questions that tormented her mind—but not for long. No sooner had Efrosyni touched the floor than she felt something like fire come into the room, engulfing her. She fell backward and came into a vision.

In the vision she saw an angelic being come to her dressed in white.

He lifted her and transported her to a place where light was dim. He left her there. When she focused, she realized in total amazement that she was standing in front of the scene at Golgotha. The Lord was hanging on the cross, blood dripping from His wounds. She saw the agony on His face as He was being tormented.

At the same time, Efrosyni heard screams coming from a distance. She turned to see where they were coming from and saw a great chasm between the cross and the place across the chasm, where huge waves of fire belched from the earth. It was an ocean of fire. She could hear the screams of what seemed like multitudes of people. They were cursing God. At that moment she felt a force pushing her head down through a gaping chasm in the earth, and the voice she had heard before spoke to her and said, "This is where you too belong."

She was terrified! She started to cry and plead for mercy. She fell at the foot of the cross, carrying on her back the great burden she felt before. She stayed there crying for quite some time. When the voice, full of love and compassion, spoke to her again, it said, "He did it for you! He died for you! If you ask for forgiveness and accept His sacrifice for you, you won't have to go there [to the lake of fire]!"

At that, Efrosyni cried even more, responding immediately to what the voice said. She asked for forgiveness, and immediately the burden she had been carrying was lifted and rolled over to the foot of the cross.

She looked up and saw the Lord Jesus standing in front of her, dressed in His glorified form. He picked her up and carried her toward the most beautiful green hill. She was now able to communicate with Him through her mind. She would ask a question, and He would answer. It was amazing! She asked Him where they were going and He said, "To meet your heavenly Father!"

As they approached the top of the mountain, she could see a light coming out of a gate. Beautiful, angelic music and singing were emanating from flowers and trees everywhere. They reached the peak and entered the gate. It was incredible. The beauty was indescribable!

They went straight to the throne. Efrosyni did not see God's face, for it was shrouded, but she saw a great big book and a hand coming out of the clouds. It started to write. She leaned forward to see what was being written, and to her amazement she saw her name written down in the Book of Life! (Although she did not know at that time this was the Book of Life.)

When the heavenly Father wrote her name in the Book of Life, He said, "Welcome to the family!" and gave Efrosyni a kiss on the forehead. At that moment, she saw the angels forming circles as they began dancing and singing and making great joy! She could recognize her name being sung by the angels as they were dancing. She joined them. It was much later that she found out that what the angels were doing was a great celebration in her honor because she had been saved.

After a while, the Lord spoke to her and said it was time for her to return to earth because He had a great work planned for her. She would have to go through fiery trials for His name's sake, but He would be with her, and when all this was done she would return to be with Him forever.

At that, Efrosyni found herself back in her room. She was greatly disappointed to be back on earth after the heavenly trip she had just experienced, but she had no choice in the matter.

When news spread in the village about Efrosyni's experience, the persecution began. It started with her father, who threatened to kill her with an ax if she didn't renounce what she believed. She told him that she could never renounce what she had experienced.

The persecution greatly intensified until one evening, Efrosyni's sister came to her and warned that certain people were planning to come the next morning and bring her to the village square, where the Greek Orthodox church was. They would bring out the icon of Mary, and if she didn't bow down to worship it and kiss it, they would pour gasoline all over her and set her on fire.

Efrosyni didn't believe the people would go that far, but it seemed they had determined to do so, for the same night an angel of the Lord came to young Efrosyni and woke her up by tapping her on the shoulder. Once she was awake, the angel told her to get dressed and go to the front door. She obeyed, and when she reached the porch, she felt someone lifting her off the ground. She was physically transported from her home to safety in a different village miles away.

Unimaginable Torment

Joy's grandmother didn't see Hades. She saw the Lake of Fire, which is also called "the second death." Her destiny changed because she chose to follow Jesus Christ with all her heart. Scripture tells us:

> "But cowards who turn back from following me [Jesus], and those who are unfaithful to me, and the corrupt, and murderers, and the immoral, and those conversing with demons, and idol worshipers and all liars—their doom is in the Lake that burns with fire and sulphur. This is the Second Death." (Revelation 21:8 TLB)

Notice this is a lake that "burns with fire and sulphur." Sulfur is a nonmetallic substance that burns with great heat and produces a very unpleasant smell. Many who have described hell have told of its dreadful aroma. They describe it as "unbearable." In fact, those I know who have experienced this place of the dead tell me there is no possible way to describe in our vernacular the torment and horror to the senses.

Also notice the term *second death*. Jesus says, "He who has an ear, let him hear what the Spirit says to the churches. [Meaning what He is about to say is not to unbelievers.] He who overcomes shall not be hurt by the *second death*" (Revelation 2:11).

You may find it strange that Jesus would say this to the churches. However, notice in the above verse that we see three main categories of people who will burn in the lake of fire. The first are those who turned back from following Him. The second are those who were unfaithful to Him. The third are the sinners who never walked with Him at all. The first two groups would describe those who were once in the church.

Recall the first three individuals we discussed in our allegory: Faint Heart, Deceived, and Independent. Two of them were active in the School of Endel, which is a type of the church. We will go into this in depth shortly.

The *second death* is anguish in the Lake of Fire for the rest of eternity. Again, think of the first chapter when we discussed eternity: forever and ever, no end, no relief, no escape! Some think that this agony will eventually end, yet this is clearly contrary to what the Word of God teaches. It states, "They will be tormented day and night forever and ever" (Revelation 20:10).

To further show that this suffering is never-ending, Jesus says this about all who don't obey His word: "And these will go away into *everlasting punishment*, but the righteous into eternal life" (Matthew 25:46).

Notice the words "everlasting punishment." In other words, the punishment never ends. It's eternal! Jesus tells us:

"And if your eye causes you to stumble and sin, pluck it out! It is more profitable and wholesome for you to enter the kingdom of God with one eye than with two eyes to be thrown into hell (Gehenna)." (Mark 9:47 AMP)

As you can see here, Jesus is talking about Gehenna, the Lake of Fire. Now see what He says in a different translation:

"And if your eye makes you lose your faith, take it out! It is better for you to enter the Kingdom of God with only one eye than to keep both eyes and be thrown into hell. There 'the worms that eat them never die, and the fire that burns them is never put out.'" (Mark 9:47–48 TEV)

Notice the worms that eat them never die, which means they continually have something to eat. Let's compare this to the natural. Once a person physically dies, the worms eat the flesh until it is consumed and only bones are left, and then the worms die. These worms in Gehenna never die because what they consume never ceases to exist. One of the individuals who saw hell reported that she saw huge worms eating the flesh of the people tormented in the flames, yet no matter how long they had been in hell, they still had flesh that was being consumed.

Yes, you are getting it right—this place is unimaginable! What we must keep in mind is that God didn't originally create the Lake of Fire for human beings. Hear what Jesus says to those who are hurled into this dreadful place:

> "Then He will also say to those on the left hand, 'Depart from Me, you cursed, into the everlasting fire prepared for the devil and his angels . . .'" (Matthew 25:41)

The Lake of Fire was created for the devil and his fallen angels, not mankind. However, the devil is deceiving and bringing many with him to eternal punishment. It is similar to what we saw in our allegory: the influence of Dagon resulted in many being deceived, and the wrath of Jalyn, which was originally intended for Dagon, had to be administered to those who succumbed to his influence. Otherwise, Jalyn would not have been just.

Going Well Forever

We saw how vivid the wrath of Jalyn was in the previous chapter. Scripture declares that the man or woman who drinks of "the wine of the wrath of God . . . shall be tormented with fire and brimstone in the presence of the holy angels and in the presence of the Lamb. And the smoke of their torment ascends forever and ever" (Revelation 14:10–11).

Once again, think of "forever and ever." Remember our discussion of eternity in the first chapter? Of trying to comprehend never ending? You can't do it mentally, but you can understand it in your heart. For this reason, God lamented over an entire generation who wouldn't listen to Him, saying:

> "Oh, that they had such a heart in them that they would fear Me and always keep all My commandments, that it might be well with them and with their children forever!" (Deuteronomy 5:29)

Notice the word *forever*. If only these people were motivated by that which endures—were driven by eternity!

Notice also that God said "always keep all My commandments." He didn't say "*for a season of time* keep all My commandments." Nor did He say "always keep *some* of My commandments." No, it is *always* keep *all!* We are commanded to obey His will entirely as well as continuously.

You may think, *I haven't kept all His commandments. I will be found guilty at the judgment!* Yes, that is absolutely correct. The law of God identifies and proves that every human being falls short of God's righteous standard and will be found guilty at the judgment. No one can ever stand before God and say, "I have lived a life worthy of Your kingdom and do not deserve to be punished eternally."

The reason for this shortcoming is that in the beginning, in the garden, man willfully disobeyed God. In doing so, he took on the nature of sin. By his act of treason, he made himself a slave to Satan, bound to his domain. In no way could he redeem or save himself. This fallen nature would be passed down to every descendant of Adam and Eve, which is all mankind, for we are born with our parents' nature.

Out of pure love, God made a promise that even though man was fully responsible for his fallen state, the Lord would send a Savior to rescue us. That Savior is Jesus Christ. It was foretold hundreds of years before His birth that He would be born of a virgin (see Isaiah 7:14). His

Father is God and his mother was a virgin named Mary, a descendant of King David. This would have to be so, for if both parents were human, Jesus would have been bound to the nature of Adam. He would have been a slave to sin. He could not have lived a perfect life and therefore could not redeem us. However, He had to be born of woman because it was a man who fell, and it would have to be a man who would pay the price for our treason. So Jesus was one hundred percent God and one hundred percent man.

When Jesus went to the cross, He took all our sins upon Himself and shed His blood to death, paying the price for our sin. However, because He lived a perfect life of righteousness, the Father raised Him from the dead and seated Him at His right hand. King David, who was also a prophet and an ancestor of Jesus, foresaw what would happen after Jesus's crucifixion over a thousand years before it occurred. Peter refers to his words on the day of Pentecost by declaring:

> "Therefore, [King David] being a prophet, and knowing that God had sworn with an oath to him that of the fruit of his body, according to the flesh, He would raise up the Christ to sit on his throne, he, foreseeing this, spoke concerning the resurrection of the Christ, that His soul was not left in Hades, nor did His flesh see corruption. This Jesus God has raised up, of which we are all witnesses." (Acts 2:30–32)

Jesus was raised from the dead to free us. Notice Peter says He was not left in Hades, which automatically tells us He was there. When was He there? Sometime between the cross and the resurrection. Jesus tasted death, or hell, for everyone so that we would not have to receive our just eternal punishment. Now when we renounce our self-focused lives and give ourselves completely to His lordship, what He did for us—shedding His blood and tasting death—becomes both the ransom to buy us back and our justification before God. We are made in right standing with His righteousness and can stand confidently before His throne of judgment. Praise God forevermore!

For this reason we are explicitly told, "God saved you by his special favor when you believed. And you can't take credit for this; it is a gift from God. Salvation is not a reward for the good things we have done, so none of us can boast about it" (Ephesians 2:8–9 NLT).

If you have never before repented of living independent of God, renounced your sinful ways, and given yourself completely to the lordship of Jesus, then at this point immediately turn to the appendix in the back of the book. In this section I will explain God's plan for your salvation and pray with you to receive Jesus Christ as your personal Lord and Savior.

Most believers are well versed in what I've written in these last few pages. However, I've found many believers do not fully understand what I'm about to discuss in the next couple chapters. In fact, many professing Christians will be shocked at the simple truths revealed in the scriptures we will see in the coming pages. We shall also discover in the upcoming chapters why the truth about eternal punishment is foundational knowledge every believer must have for healthy growth.

CHAPTER 5

The Judgment of Deceived

We know that the judgment of God is according to truth . . .

—Romans 2:2

Jesus came to save us from paying the eternal penalty of sin, which was originally intended for Satan and his cohorts. His life being given for us reveals the amazing love of God.

Think of it. The Lord created mankind, along with the animals, birds, insects, sea creatures, and the rest of the earth—including its atmosphere— perfect in the beginning. We read, "Then God saw everything that He had made, and indeed it was very good" (Genesis 1:31). He then placed a perfect creation in the hands of man to guard and keep. As the psalmist declares, "Heaven belongs to the Lord alone, but he gave the earth to man" (Psalm 115:16 TEV). It would be Adam's responsibility to protect not only himself but all creation from Lucifer, the archenemy of God.

God didn't desire robots that couldn't freely choose to love, obey, and be in relationship with Him. So out of a myriad of trees in the garden, one was accompanied by the following command: "You may eat the fruit of any tree in the garden, except the tree that gives knowledge of what is good and what is bad. You must not eat the fruit of that tree; if you do, you will die the same day" (Genesis 2:16–17 TEV).

The death God spoke of wasn't physical death, for Adam didn't experience physical death until years afterward (though this was also a result of his disobedience). Instead, the Lord showed man he would be cut off from God's life and take on the nature of Lucifer, which is death.

After a period of time, Lucifer deceived Eve by perverting the character of God in her eyes. He was able to get her focus off all the available trees and onto the one prohibited. Once she judged the tree to be good, beneficial, and pleasant, she ate. This was because she now perceived the Lord to be a taker instead of the Giver He is. Yet at this point, mankind still hadn't fallen. It wasn't until Eve's husband partook of the fruit of the tree that God's creation took on the nature of death. For this reason, his sin was greater. She was deceived; he wasn't (see 1 Timothy 2:14).

Consequently, not only Adam but all the creation he was placed over immediately took on the nature of death. Prior to Adam's treason, animals didn't devour and eat flesh, nor did they die. Tornadoes, earthquakes, hurricanes, famines, disease, and pestilence didn't exist. These all resulted from man not guarding what God entrusted to his care. We read:

> Against its will, everything on earth was subjected to God's curse. All creation anticipates the day when it will join God's children in glorious freedom from death and decay. (Romans 8:20–21 NLT)

Nature wasn't cursed with death by its own choice but rather by man's insubordination to God. Adam didn't protect what was entrusted to his care. He subjected not only nature but also himself, his wife, and all their future offspring to what was originally Lucifer's curse: separation from God. What treachery! What treason!

At this point, God could have said, "Mankind, whom I loved, blessed, and created perfect, chose Lucifer over Me. Let them all go to the Lake of Fire and We (Father, Son, and Holy Spirit) will begin all over. We will create another universe with beings who will stay loyal and love Us as We love them."

If the Lord had done this, He would have been perfectly just in His decision. Yet out of His amazing love, He made a promise to mankind that He would send a Redeemer to deliver us from the bondage we placed ourselves under. That Redeemer would be His Son, with whom He created the heavens and earth. In other words, He would pay the terrible price for our sin and the nature of death when He hadn't done anything but love us from the start. This is amazing love.

Thus the reason for Calvary. I find it amazing when Christians are stumped by a nonbeliever saying, "How can a loving God send people who have not heard the gospel to hell?" My simple answer is, "It's not His fault but our own." Jesus paid the terrible price to free mankind. Afterward, He told those of us who already understood this good news to go into the entire world, telling those who hadn't heard that we have been redeemed from the curse we brought upon ourselves and upon all creation. We will have to give an account for our generation. God has done His part!

We Take on God's Nature

Not only is the penalty for our sins paid for by Jesus, but in Him we've also been provided a new nature in the likeness of God's. No longer are we slaves to sin. When a person gives his life entirely to Jesus, he becomes a brand new creation.

> When someone becomes a Christian, he becomes a brand new person inside. He is not the same anymore. A new life has begun! (2 Corinthians 5:17 TLB)

We literally die when we receive Jesus Christ as Lord. Our old nature is put to death, crucified with Christ in God's eyes. A brand new person with the nature of God is born. Thus we are born again. Now we are free from the nature that once dictated our lives. As Scripture clearly shows, "And just as Christ was raised from the dead by the glorious power of the Father, now we also may live new lives . . . Our old sinful selves were crucified with Christ so that sin might lose its power in our lives. We are no longer slaves to sin. For when we died with Christ we were set free from the power of sin" (Romans 6:4, 6–8 NLT). We now can live according to

Christ's nature, not the nature we were bound to due to Adam's treason.

It is complete ignorance for a Christian to disdain an individual who has not received Jesus as their Master because of their lifestyle. This person's spiritual DNA is to sin, and that is just what they do. What is freaky and completely unnatural is a "believer" who habitually or willfully sins. The reason I put *believer* in quotation marks is that a person who practices sin may declare Jesus as their Savior and Lord, but in reality, He is not. If He truly were, that person would manifest a godly nature in their life. Jesus made this clear by saying:

> "Different kinds of fruit trees can quickly be identified by examining their fruit. A variety that produces delicious fruit never produces an inedible kind. And a tree producing an inedible kind can't produce what is good. So the trees having the inedible fruit are chopped down and thrown on the fire. Yes, the way to identify a tree or a person is by the kind of fruit produced." (Matthew 7:17–20 TLB)

What Jesus states here is not complex, and it is definitely unalterable. The cause of what is produced is not the fruit. It is the nature of tree. However, the tree's nature shows up at the fruit level.

If you approach a bush that bears healthy blueberries, you know it is a bush that is good for food. On the other hand, if you find poisonous berries, the bush is not good. The proof, or evidence, that a tree is good or poisonous is in the kind of fruit it produces. Even so, Jesus says the way to identify whether people are genuine Christians is not by what they say, how religious they may seem, or how often they attend Christian gatherings. Rather it is by what they do! Is their fruit selfless and kingdom-focused? Or is it selfish and worldly-focused, like the apostle John describes in his letter:

> Don't love the world's ways. Don't love the world's goods. Love of
> the world squeezes out love for the Father. Practically everything that

goes on in the world—wanting your own way, wanting everything for yourself, wanting to appear important—has nothing to do with the Father. It just isolates you from him. The world and all its wanting, wanting, wanting is on the way out—but whoever does what God wants is set for eternity. (1 John 2:15–17 The Message)

It took Lisa and me a long time to convince our children of this truth. They would attend Christian schools and observe numerous classmates who regularly attended church with their parents and professed to be Christians but were habitually producing self-gratifying fruit, as seen in the above scriptures, rather than Christlike fruit. These classmates lived for themselves rather than desiring, seeking, and delighting in doing the will of God.

Our children's situation at school is only one of countless examples I could give. This problem is found in homes, the business world, and even churches and ministries. There are many who confess to being Christians yet produce fruit that clearly indicates otherwise.

The Typical "Conversion"

The gospel we've preached has been lopsided, with emphasis placed on accepting Jesus by praying a sinner's prayer. We confess Him as "Lord," and once done, we are saved eternally. Yet this is not what Jesus teaches. He says, "Not everyone who says to me, 'Lord, Lord,' will enter the kingdom of heaven" (Matthew 7:21 NIV).

If we would just listen to Jesus's statement—without filtering it through years of unbalanced preaching, teaching, writing, and singing—we would see our modern gospel contradicts it. Jesus's words couldn't be clearer: not everyone who has prayed the sinner's prayer confessing Him as their Lord is going to heaven. And if they are not going to heaven, there is only one alternative, as we saw in the last chapter.

Let's review a typical evangelistic service. The communicator gives a "come to Jesus and get blessings" message. He tells how Jesus will give us joy, peace, prosperity, happiness, health, heaven, and so forth. Don't get me wrong. It's God's desire to bless us. But Jesus never used the blessings to entice people to follow Him.

After the thirty-five-minute-or-so sales pitch, the minister asks the audience to bow their heads. He asks them, if they were to die tonight, would they go to heaven? In some settings he may encourage those in attendance to look to the people to their left and right and ask the same question in order to help recruit them. Would they go to heaven if they died tonight? "If they can't say yes," the leader says, "take them by the hand and bring them forward."

As the candidates come forward, mood-appropriate songs like nineties favorite "Just As I Am" are sung. In other cases, the audience simply claps and smiles as the musicians play a triumphant tune for the march forward.

Once all are up front, the minister asks them to bow their heads and repeat a common prayer such as, "Father, I confess I am a sinner. Forgive me of my sin. This day I ask Jesus into my life as my Lord and Savior. Thank You for making me Your child. In Jesus's name, amen."

The audience cheers, the music plays, and the new "converts" leave the meeting "just as they were." Except now they are deceived. Nothing has been said concerning repentance from disobedient lifestyles, denying their own desires in order to embrace the will of God, and losing their lives for the cause of Christ. They've confessed Jesus as their Lord, but there's been no heart change. Jesus is now just a part of their lives.

Well, let me inform you, the King of Kings and Lord of Lords doesn't come into anyone's life as second—or even first—among rival lovers. He only comes in as our complete and total King, with no person, thing, or activity vying for His place in our hearts. He must be Lord, which means supreme master and owner—meaning we don't own our lives any longer.

Think of it. Would you marry someone who informed you that they would be loyal to you along with their other lovers, but that you would be first? How much more absurd is it to say that to the King of the universe? Will He accept a bride who says, "You are first of all my other lovers"? There is no covenant relationship in that arrangement, no joining together as one. What deception!

These new "converts" have not allowed the cross to slay their selfish, worldly lives and make room for the new nature of Jesus to be formed within. They've just been sold on a better life here and the promise of heaven. It's interesting. In many countries where Christians are persecuted, they come to Jesus knowing they are losing their lives. Today in Western societies, we come to Jesus for a better life and entrance into heaven. But we must lose our lives for His sake as well.

Today, many typical Evangelicals in our society live in deception as a result of the type of gospel we've preached. New converts may be energized by their newfound "faith," participate in Christian activities, attend church, and even get involved in outreach because it is all fresh and exciting. It's like being in a new club, trying a new sport, attending a new school, or working a new job. There's a freshness about it. But these Christians have not done what Jesus commanded all true followers to do: count the cost of following Him and then make the permanent decision to give their lives to His service (see Luke 14:27–33).

Loss for Gain

This is an exchange. We must give our entire lives, and in their place, we get His life (nature). Jesus repeatedly communicates this. He says:

> "If anyone intends to come after Me, let him deny himself [forget, ignore, disown, and lose sight of himself and his own interests] and take up his cross, and [joining Me as a disciple and siding with My party] follow with Me [continually, cleaving steadfastly to Me]." (Mark 8:34 AMP)

We are to continually cleave steadfastly to Him. Salvation is not just a one-time prayer and then life as usual, except that you are now in the "Christian" club and are heaven-bound. Jesus continues, "If you try to keep your life for yourself, you will lose it. But if you give up your life for my sake and for the sake of the Good News, you will find true life" (Mark 8:35 NLT). The Amplified Bible states it this way: "Whoever gives up his life [which is lived only on earth] for My sake and the Gospel's will save it [his higher, spiritual life in the eternal kingdom of God]."

It's a definitive exchange. We give up our rights as owners of our lives. By doing this we are enabled to follow His desires. In return we receive His eternal life. In the gospel that is preached today, we've not emphasized this extremely important aspect of following Jesus. We've only told the benefits. In essence, we've preached the *resurrection promises* without preaching the *impact and call of the cross*.

This could be compared to a young man who sees a military recruiting ad on television. He observes a classy naval man about his age dressed in a sharp uniform and standing on the deck of a remarkable ship, sailing the open seas under a beautiful crystal sky and smiling with his mates. The commercial then shows this sailor in ports all over the world—and all this is free.

The young man immediately goes to the recruiter and signs up. He doesn't read the conditions of joining because he's so focused on the benefits. He is so happy. Now he'll have a blast seeing the world, becoming a part of a great military, and making lots of new friends.

However, the man quickly finds out in basic training that he can't sleep in till nine in the morning as was his custom. He is ordered to cut his cherished long hair. He can't go to many social gatherings because he can't leave base more than a couple days per month. Worst of all, he is on a regimented schedule that doesn't allow time to hang out with other people. All the while, he's cleaning bathrooms and mess halls and doing push-ups and other difficult training exercises. He's lost the abundant leisure time he once had and is collapsing in bed each night from exhaustion.

The young man is still hopeful, as he knows he'll soon be on the ship. Once basic training is over, he's assigned to a vessel—but it's just as labor-intensive, only now the work is on the open seas. War breaks out, and the man finds himself fighting a battle he didn't sign up for.

The man enlisted because military service offered a life he never could have provided for himself, and it was free. He didn't make note of the details at the recruiter's office: this life was free, but it would cost him all his freedoms. In many ways, the young man is now offended. He feels cheated. In his eyes, he was sold a package that showed him only the benefits but didn't make known the personal cost.

We've preached a gospel that speaks of free salvation, which is absolutely accurate, but we've neglected to tell candidates it will cost them their freedom. When I speak of freedom, this isn't a matter of real but of perceived liberty, for all those outside Christ are bound to sin. They are slaves even though they may fully believe they're free.

This could be compared to the movie *The Matrix*. Years ago my oldest son rented the edited version of this movie one evening and showed it to our family, and I saw an amazing parallel.

The Matrix poses an interesting question: "How would you know the difference between the dream world and the real world if you didn't wake from the dream?"[1]

In this film, twentieth-century life flows on as normal, or so it seems. In reality, the story begins late in the twenty-first century. Man develops artificial intelligence, referred to simply as the Machines. These Machines take control of the earth, and man fights back. In the resulting power struggle, the world is decimated and the Machines are victorious.

The Machines discover they can manage to survive using electricity generated by the human body, so they create a grand illusion to fool humans into serving them. The world seems to still be normal (and in the twentieth century), but in fact the bodies of humans are contained in chambers on large "farms." Their minds are linked into a worldwide virtual reality program called the Matrix, which simulates normal life.

Mankind's perceived freedom isn't real. In essence, they are slaves.

It's at this point that the film opens with a select group of men and women who have hacked their way out of the Matrix, discovering their true identity. They form a colony called Zion in the real world, which is otherwise lifeless. A few of them re-enter the Matrix to battle the Machines and set humanity free. The battle is intense and life is not easy, but the crusaders are more interested in genuine freedom than in living a lie of false liberty. They would rather have liberty with difficulty than slavery with deceptive comfort.

Here we see the parallel. Many nonbelievers see Christians as slaves, in bondage and losing freedoms while they themselves are free. However, the truth is that those outside of Christ are the ones bound, not unlike those living a lie on the farms while enslaved by the Machines. They are slaves to sin.

Difficult to Be a Christian

It's not only those who've never heard or refuse to believe the gospel who are in bondage. Many typical "converts" of this generation are enslaved to sin as well. We've created this dilemma by neglecting to proclaim the full message of what it truly means to follow Jesus. Many assume they are free when in reality they aren't, and the evidence is in their lifestyles. Jesus says:

> "I assure you, most solemnly I tell you, whoever commits and
> practices sin is the slave of sin. Now a slave does not remain in a
> household permanently (forever); the son [of the house] does re-
> main forever. So if the Son liberates you [makes you free men],
> then you are really and unquestionably free." (John 8:34–36 AMP)

These words reiterate the truth found in the example of the fruit tree. If someone habitually sins, that is evidence he is still a slave to sin.

He is not a son, for his true nature hasn't changed. He may think he is free because he confessed a sinner's prayer, yet he has not freely given up his personal "rights" in order to follow Jesus. He still wants his freedoms (which are counterfeit) along with the benefits of salvation. You cannot have both!

As stated earlier, these individuals may start their "born again" experience with joy, excitement, and passion because it's fresh and new. However, eventually their unchanged nature will manifest—but it will manifest in Christian circles and be cloaked in an evangelical language and lifestyle. This is why it is most deceptive. Yet the New Testament warns specifically of this deception.

Paul writes, "In the last days it is going to be very difficult to be a Christian" (2 Timothy 3:1 TLB). We are living in the last days. There is no question about it; all prophetic scriptures reveal Jesus is soon to return. Paul foresaw our day as being the most difficult period to be a Christian.

Other translations use the words *perilous* and *terrible* in describing our time. Why is this? In examining Paul's days, we see he encountered great opposition. He received thirty-nine stripes on his back from whippings on five different occasions. Three separate times, he was beaten with rods. Once, he was stoned, and he spent years in prison. He met up with intense persecution everywhere he turned. Yet he says our days will be more difficult to be a Christian! Why? He gives the reason:

> People will be lovers of themselves, lovers of money, boastful, proud,
> abusive, disobedient to their parents, ungrateful, unholy, without
> love, unforgiving, slanderous, without self-control, brutal, not lovers
> of the good, treacherous, rash, conceited, lovers of pleasure rather
> than lovers of God . . . (2 Timothy 3:2–4 NIV)

In examining this statement, you may still wonder what point Paul is trying to make. How does this list differ any from his day? People in his society had all these traits. They loved themselves and loved money. They were unholy, unforgiving, and the like. Peter even said on the day of Pentecost, "Be saved from this crooked (perverse, wicked, unjust) generation" (Acts 2:40 AMP). So why is Paul singling out our generation as having these traits, causing ours to be the most difficult time to be a Christian?

He goes on to give the reason: "For [although] they hold a form of piety (true religion), they deny and reject and are strangers to the power of it [their conduct belies the genuineness of their profession]" (2 Timothy 3:5 AMP). The NKJV states they are "having a form of godliness but denying its power."

So you can see what makes it difficult to be a Christian in our generation. There will be many (according to other references in the New Testament) who profess to be *Christian, born again*, or *saved* who will not have allowed the cross to slay their self-life. They'll not have made the decision to forsake all their own rights and lusts to follow Jesus. They'll sincerely believe He is their Savior, but they'll affiliate with Him for the mere fact of what He can do for them rather than for who He is. It's no different than a woman marrying a man for his money. She may marry him for love, but it's love for the wrong reasons. Out of such a motive, many will seek Jesus for the sake of salvation, community, success in this life, and entrance into heaven in the afterlife. They'll believe sincerely that Christ is their Savior, but they will never have relinquished control of their own lives.

Paul continues to say of these "believers" that they will be "always learning and never able to come to the knowledge of the truth" (verse 7). They will attend services, home groups, and other gatherings, hear the Word of God, yet lack transformation.

Blurred Lines

The difficulty is found in the lines being blurred. Let's look at a person who is self-seeking but who confesses the born-again experience, speaks the language of a true believer, makes friends with the godly, and is even excited about believers' gatherings—yet there is no change in their nature. In essence, this person is unknowingly an impostor, and the difficulty arises in the fact that their self-deception spreads like a disease. Others base their lives off the "norm" in Christian culture, and this norm is out of sync with heaven's way of life, thus making it hard to be a true believer. In Paul's day, if you were a believer, your life was in jeopardy every hour. There was no question about it—if you gave your allegiance to Jesus, you put your life on the line.

In 2 Timothy 3, Paul continues:

> But you know what I teach, Timothy, and how I live, and what my purpose in life is. You know my faith and how long I have suffered. You know my love and my patient endurance. You know how much persecution and suffering I have endured. You know all about how I was persecuted in Antioch, Iconium, and Lystra—but the Lord delivered me from all of it. Yes, and everyone who wants to live a godly life in Christ Jesus will suffer persecution. But evil people and impostors will flourish. They will go on deceiving others, and they themselves will be deceived. (2 Timothy 3:10–13 NLT)

Paul made it clear. It wasn't only what he taught that proved Timothy could trust him. His reliability was also found in what he lived and his purpose in life (one driven by eternity, which we will get to later in this book). Paul's witness wasn't his answered prayers, the miraculous signs that followed him, the popularity of his ministry, or even his excellent ability to teach the Word of God. No, it was not these traits he pointed to. It was his lifestyle. This was, and still is to be, the determining factor.

Paul continued by saying "*evil people* and *impostors*" will flourish. Now, we all know to stay clear from an evil person. However, it's impostors—those who assume an outward identity that does not match their true nature—who are the most dangerous. They are the ones who profess and have a form of Christianity, but their behavior shows no evidence of the life-changing power of grace. Notice Paul says that not only will they deceive others, but they themselves will also be deceived.

This perfectly describes Deceived in our allegory. This young man was active at the School of Endel, professed to be a devout follower, and sincerely believed he was in good standing with the king. He put more emphasis on his professed allegiance than on a life that revealed his loyalty. Not only was he deceived, but he deceived others. Due to the standards Deceived set, many were compromised, from the girls he slept with to the many he influenced by his *message* within the student body.

You may ask, "Message? He wasn't a teacher." Oh yes, I mean *message*, for how we live communicates much louder than what we speak does. For those students in Endel who were true to Jalyn, it was a battle to not be influenced by Deceived's strong personality and lifestyle. Those who didn't stand strong succumbed to his influence.

This is a battle warned about not only by Paul but also by many other writers of the New Testament. Jude tells us:

> My dear friends, I was doing my best to write to you about the salvation we share in common, when I felt the need of writing at once to encourage you to fight on for the faith which once and for all God has given to his people. (Jude 3 TEV)

Notice the urgency in his voice. Jude wanted to discuss the wonderful things we share in salvation, but he had to write about something different. He had to encourage God's people to fight for the faith. What is this fight? He explains by saying:

> For some godless people have slipped in unnoticed among us, persons who distort the message about the grace of our God in order to excuse their immoral ways, and who reject Jesus Christ, our only Master and Lord. Long ago the Scriptures predicted the condemnation they have received. (Jude 4 TEV)

The war is against the influences created by people who have perverted the grace of God in order to excuse their ungodly lifestyles. These assaults are more deadly than all-out persecution against the church. They're more dangerous than laws that oppose biblical principles, laws such as those that legalize abortion, marijuana use, and same-sex marriage or require schools to teach evolution. They're a stronger influence than any cult or false religion. They're eternally fatal!

You might ask how this applies to people in church. The people Jude references reject or deny Jesus Christ. No one could do that in our churches today and still be accepted as a Christian.

But what would make you think believers were more vulnerable in Jude's days? Look again carefully. These people slip into our circles *unnoticed*. No one could stand up in our assemblies today (or in Jude's day), confess with their mouths their denial of Jesus Christ, and go unnoticed. So how do these people renounce Him? The answer is found in another New Testament book: "Such people *claim they know God*, but they *deny him* by the way they live" (Titus 1:16 NLT). They deny Him by their lifestyles, not their words. In fact, they claim to know God. They confess Jesus as their Lord. But they communicate otherwise by their actions. Remember, they not only deceive others. They also deceive themselves. In other words, with all sincerity, they believe they're Christians.

The True Grace of God

Jude states that these people distort the message of God's grace. This is so prevalent in these final days because our teachings have opened the door to it. We've taught grace as God's blanket of protection for worldly and even ungodly lifestyles. You hear this mindset often from many in the church, who make common statements such as, "I know I'm not living the way I should, but thank God for His grace." This is serious deception. Scripture doesn't teach grace as the big Band-Aid but rather as *God's empowering presence within us to do what truth demands of us*.

Grace has been taught as simply God's unmerited favor. It is indeed His favor and cannot be bought or earned. However, it also empowers us to obey Him, and the evidence that we've truly received grace is our godly lifestyle. Our obedience to God's Word confirms grace's reality in our lives. For this reason, James says:

> . . . Faith, if it does not have works (deeds and actions of obedi-ence to back it up), by itself is destitute of power (inoperative, dead). But someone will say [to you then], you [say you] have faith, and I have [good] works. Now you show me your [alleged] faith apart from any [good] works [if you can], and I by [good] works [of obedience] will show you my faith. You believe that God is one; you do well. So do the demons believe and shudder . . . (James 2:17–19 AMP)

James identifies a huge gap in our teaching today. We pull out scrip-tures such as, "Believe on the Lord Jesus Christ, and you will be saved" (Acts 16:31). If just believing that Jesus exists and that He is the Son of God are all that's required to be saved, then as James shows, the demons will be saved because they believe. That is ludicrous! To drive his point home even further, James points out that the demons shudder before God. In other words, the demons fear Him more than do some who say they have faith but lack corresponding actions of obedience.

The evidence of our truly being saved by the grace of Jesus Christ is that we have the lifestyle to prove it. This is why the apostle John states:

> Now by this we know that we know Him, if we keep His com-mandments. He who says, "I know Him," and does not keep His commandments, is a liar, and the truth is not in him. But whoever keeps His word, truly the love of God is perfected in him. By this we know that we are in Him. He who says he abides in Him ought him-self also to walk just as He walked. (1 John 2:3–6)

John clearly states the proof that we do indeed know Jesus Christ is that we keep His commandments. The one who says he knows Jesus but doesn't keep His Word is deceived, a liar estranged from the truth, even though he confesses with his mouth his knowledge of the Word of God. For this reason, John says, "My little children, these things I write to you, so that you *may not sin*. And *if* anyone sins, we have an Advocate with the Father, Jesus Christ the righteous" (1 John 2:1–2).

Notice John does not say, "These things I write to you so that *when* you do sin, you have an Advocate." No, the goal is to not sin. We have the power of God's grace so we can set our sights on a life like Christ's (as 1 John 2:6 says, we are "also to walk just as He walked"), for we are free from the control of the disobedient nature. But if we do succumb to sin, we have an Advocate.

The celebration of the believer is that we now have the ability to serve our God acceptably:

> Therefore, since we are receiving a kingdom which cannot be shaken, let us have *grace*, by which we may *serve God acceptably*. (Hebrews 12:28)

There you have it. Grace empowers us to serve God acceptably.

Why have we not proclaimed the entire gospel, just half the story? Yes, salvation is a gift—it cannot be purchased, and it cannot be earned. This is all true. However, we forgot to tell people that the only way to receive salvation is to lay down our lives and confess Jesus's lordship. In doing so, we will be empowered by grace to live in accordance with His nature. Just as Peter wrote:

> Grace and peace be yours in abundance through the knowledge of God and of Jesus our Lord. His divine power has given us everything we need for life and godliness through our knowledge of him who called us by his own glory and goodness. Through these he has given

us his very great and precious promises, so that through them you may participate in the divine nature and escape the corruption in the world caused by evil desires. (2 Peter 1:2–4 NIV)

Notice a few things: that we've been given *grace* through the knowledge of Jesus Christ, that grace is His *divine power* giving us everything we need to live in a godly manner, and that this godly lifestyle is according to His *divine nature*. Thus we have been redeemed from the corruption that entered the world through Adam, which has been multiplied by the desires of men contrary to God. Don't let anyone, whether by word or action, discourage you from living in the divine nature imparted into your being. Paul clearly states:

For the grace of God that brings salvation has appeared to all men. It teaches us to say "No" to ungodliness and worldly passions, and to live self-controlled, upright and godly lives in this present age, while we wait for the blessed hope—the glorious appearing of our great God and Savior, Jesus Christ, who gave himself for us to redeem us from all wickedness and to purify for himself a people that are his very own, eager to do what is good. These, then, are the things you should teach. (Titus 2:11–15 NIV)

The grace of God teaches us to deny all ungodliness and worldly passions and to live a self-controlled, upright, and godly life. Teachers instruct and empower us, and that is exactly what God's grace does in our lives.

Notice we are to teach these things. In fact, Paul goes on to say, "This is a faithful saying, and these things I want you to affirm *constantly*, that those who have believed in God should be careful to maintain good works" (Titus 3:8).

We are to maintain good works by the power of God's grace in our lives. We didn't have grace before we were saved. Nor did the Old Testament saints. This is God's gift to us through Jesus Christ.

This is why Jesus tells us that in Old Testament times, you were considered a murderer in danger of hell if you took someone's physical life. However, under grace, all you have to do is call your brother a fool, be prejudiced, refuse to forgive, or harbor any other form of hatred, and you will be in danger of hellfire (see Matthew 5:21–22). Why? We now have the ability to live according to God's nature, inwardly and outwardly, through the power of grace.

Affirm Constantly

Notice that in Titus 3:8, we are told to affirm or teach these things *constantly*. Did you hear that? I find these things are *rarely* spoken of from pulpits or amongst believers today, let alone continually. For this reason, we've drifted from understanding the importance of maintaining good works through the grace of God. We are in essence allowing the power that is in us to remain dormant through lack of belief and acknowledgment. Our faith, which accesses grace, must remain active through the verbalization of our beliefs. Paul says, "That the communication of thy faith may become effectual by the acknowledging of every good thing which is in you in Christ Jesus" (Philemon 6 KJV).

If we don't affirm these things constantly, then we will drift away from the truth. This is clearly seen in the words of Hebrews:

Therefore we must give the more earnest heed to the things we have heard, lest we drift away. For if the word spoken through angels proved steadfast, and every transgression and disobedience received a just reward, how shall we escape if we neglect so great a salvation . . . (Hebrews 2:1–3)

By affirming these things constantly, we keep before us the urgent matters of eternity that keep us from drifting away.

I remember when I used to fish as a boy. While my companions and

I were focused on fishing, the boat, if not anchored, would drift unnoticed to us. We'd look up forty-five minutes later and not even recognize our location. The drifting occurred because we had our minds on other matters, namely fishing.

This dynamic has been quite costly for some, as there have been many who have been fishing in certain rivers that led to deadly waterfalls. Countless people have gone over falls to their death because they drifted away from where they were first positioned.

The same is true with the important matters of eternity. If God says we are to affirm these things constantly, then they should be our emphasis. Why are we not highlighting the power of grace, which gives us the ability to maintain godly lifestyles of obedience?

I find that the early church did this. I examined some of the writings of the early church fathers and found they taught things that would almost seem foreign to our teachings today—but they didn't teach things contrary to Scripture. The Christian fathers of the first few centuries believed that works played an essential role in providing evidence of our salvation. Let's look at a few examples.

The first man I'll quote is Polycarp (AD 69–156), bishop of the church at Smyrna and companion of the apostle John who in his old age was arrested and burned at the stake. He wrote: "Many desire to enter into this joy (of salvation), knowing that by grace you are saved, not of works."[2] This would be an accepted statement in today's Evangelical circles. We have stressed the fact that we are not saved by our own good works. However, Polycarp also wrote to believers, "He who raised Him up from the dead will also raise us up—if we do His will and walk in His commandments and love what He loves, keeping ourselves from all unrighteousness."[3] You won't hear this spoken often from our pulpits today.

Notice the word *if.* We are told we have to do God's will and walk in His commandments in order to be raised up in the believer's resurrection. You'll see shortly that this is exactly what Jesus said as well.

The next man I'll quote is Clement of Rome (AD 30–100), a companion of the apostles Paul and Peter and an overseer in the church of Rome. He wrote, "We are not justified by ourselves, nor by our own godliness, or works. But by that faith through which Almighty God has justified all men."[4] This too would be a widely accepted statement in today's Christian circles. However, Clement also wrote to believers, "It is necessary that we be prompt in the practice of good works. For He forewarns us, 'Behold, the Lord comes and His reward is before His face, to render to every man according to his work.' (Romans 2:6–10)"[5]

Could this be why Paul stated, "I was not disobedient to the heavenly vision, but declared first to those in Damascus and in Jerusalem, and throughout all the region of Judea, and then to the Gentiles, that they should repent, turn to God, and *do works befitting repentance*"? (Acts 26:19–21) The NLT version records his words as ". . . and prove they have changed by the good things they do." Since Paul stressed this, it seems to follow suit that his companion, Clement of Rome, would do the same.

The next leader I'd like to point out is Clement of Alexandria (AD 150–200). He was a leader in the church of Alexandria, Egypt, and was in charge of the school of instruction for new believers. He wrote about unbelievers: "Even if they do good works now, it is of no advantage to them after death, if they do not have faith."[6]

This, too, would be heartily cheered among Evangelicals today. We know, as I've already pointed out in the last few chapters, that no matter how many good works an unbeliever accomplishes, they still cannot gain entrance into the eternal kingdom of God. It is by God's grace we are saved. However, look at what Clement wrote to believers:

Whoever obtains the truth and distinguishes himself in good works shall gain the prize of everlasting life . . . Some people correctly and adequately understand how God provides necessary power (to be saved), but attaching slight importance to the works that lead to salvation, they fail to make the necessary preparation for attaining the object of their hope.[7]

Some of you may be thinking, *It sounds like these guys didn't read the New Testament.* But they did. In his book *Evidence that Demands a Verdict*, Josh McDowell points out that Clement of Alexandria took 2,400 of his quotes from all but three books in the New Testament.[8] The same is true of the others quoted here. By contrast, I have to say that many books in our Christian bookstores today have very little Scripture in them. Could it be that we have drifted because we have not affirmed constantly what is important?

Our Incomplete Gospel

Unfortunately, we mostly quote such scriptures as, "If you confess with your mouth the Lord Jesus and believe in your heart that God has raised Him from the dead, you will be saved" (Romans 10:9). We tell people all they have to do is recite the magical prayer and they're in.

But why don't we heed and teach Jesus's own words? He said, "But why do you call Me 'Lord, Lord,' and not do the things which I say?" (Luke 6:46) As we've seen, *Lord* means supreme master. It carries the meaning of ownership. So Jesus is warning, "Don't call me Master and yet still own your own life. Better to call me 'Great Prophet' or 'Teacher' so that you do not deceive yourself."

Now let's reexamine the statement of Jesus with which we opened this entire discussion: "Not everyone who says to me, 'Lord, Lord,' will enter the kingdom of heaven" (Matthew 7:21a NIV).

As we've already stated, not everyone who calls Jesus Christ *Lord* will be in heaven. That emphatically tells us that just saying the "sinner's prayer" doesn't secure us a place in heaven. In that case, my question is this: who will enter into the kingdom of heaven?

Jesus answers by saying, "Only he who does the will of my Father who is in heaven" (Matthew 7:21b NIV).

Interesting. These were almost the exact words of Polycarp. So it is not only confessing Jesus, but both confessing Jesus and doing the will of

God, that will get us into heaven. And the only way we can do God's will is through the grace He gives us when we humble ourselves by denying our own lives and receiving Him as Lord. It is as simple as confessing, but the difficult part comes in yielding ourselves entirely to the reality of His lordship.

Hear now why I've stressed this point so passionately:

> "When the Judgment Day comes, many will say to me, 'Lord, Lord!
> In your name we spoke God's message, by your name we drove out
> many demons and performed many miracles!' Then I will say to
> them, 'I never knew you. Get away from me, you wicked people!'"
> (Matthew 7:22–23 TEV)

In the late 1980s, God gave me a vision. I saw a multitude so large you couldn't see the end of it. It was a sea of humanity. I knew there were no atheists in this group, no self-acknowledged sinners, no followers of other religions. Rather, all professed to be Christians. This multitude had come to the Judgment Seat and were fully expecting to hear Jesus say, "Enter into the joy of your Lord, the kingdom of God." Instead they heard the words, "Depart from Me, you who practice lawlessness" (Matthew 7:23).

I beheld the utter shock and terror upon their faces. Can you imagine feeling secure in a salvation you don't possess? Can you imagine being exiled into the flames of hell forever when you fully believed you were heaven-bound? Forever and ever having to deal with the knowledge that you, and possibly those who preached to you, took your eternal destination so lightly?

Is there room for a seeker-friendly message that shuns the admonitions of Jesus?

Can you understand why we are to proclaim the whole counsel of God, not just the positives or benefits? Yes, we love the benefits, and we should tell of them and enjoy them. But not at the expense of neglecting the commands and warnings of the Scriptures!

I recall once stating at a conference that my reason for preaching these truths is that "I don't want anyone screaming at me at the Judgment, 'Why didn't you tell me the truth?' while their blood is dripping off my hands!"

After my session, a pastor immediately approached me quite upset. In fact, he was irate. He said, "How dare you put that Old Testament theology on us ministers. I won't have blood dripping off my hands for not proclaiming the entire gospel." He obviously liked the positive aspects of God's Word but stayed clear of the confrontational portions.

I said, "Sir, look at what Paul stated to the leaders of Ephesus." Having my Bible in hand, I turned to Acts and asked him to read: "Therefore I testify to you this day that I am innocent of the blood of all men. For I have not shunned to declare to you the *whole* counsel of God" (Acts 20:26–27).

He looked up at me in shock, his eyes and mouth wide open. He said, "All the times I've read the New Testament, I've never noticed this." We then had a friendly conversation. As we talked, I mentioned that in order to present every human being mature in Christ, we must not only teach but also warn them (see Colossians 1:28). What is our warning? To not drift away from truth. To not be swayed by the message propagated by impostors who seduce not only themselves but also countless others from godliness.

In the account of Acts 20, Paul had been with the people of Ephesus for quite some time. He loved them dearly and knew by the Spirit of God he would not see them again until heaven. Think how carefully you would choose your words, knowing they would be your last to those who were like your children. Paul's parting instructions were:

> Keep watch over yourselves and all the flock of which the Holy Spirit
> has made you overseers. Be shepherds of the church of God, which he
> bought with his own blood. I know that after I leave, savage wolves
> will come in among you and will not spare the flock. Even from your
> own number men will arise and distort the truth in order to draw

away disciples after them. So be on your guard! Remember that for three years I never stopped warning each of you night and day with tears. (Acts 20:28–31 NIV)

How would these people distort the truth? Possibly by words, but most likely by actions. Notice that Paul felt so strongly about this that he didn't stop warning the Ephesians day and night for three years. Again, we see the emphasis. We are to affirm these things constantly.

God of Love and Justice

In our allegory, you could feel the shock and agony of Deceived. You gasped at the foreboding dungeon of Lone. You cringed thinking of 130 years in the darkness and unbearable heat, a sweatbox of contaminated air. Yet that is nothing compared to what countless men and women will face if we don't proclaim the whole counsel of God.

If you remember, Jalyn was both loving and just. In his judgment, love was revealed in the fact that he couldn't permit someone who possessed the nature and character of Dagon into the city of Affabel. If he did, that person would pervert and contaminate the entire city, including all its inhabitants. Jalyn's love protected the innocent.

At the same time, Jalyn was just in that he couldn't permit someone who had the nature of Dagon to receive a lesser penalty for disobedience than Dagon himself. For this reason, all who did not choose to follow Jalyn had to be exiled to the same dungeon of Lone.

Even so, God's love cannot permit someone who has the nature of Satan into the eternal city forever. He would be unjust to sentence Satan and his cohorts to the eternal Lake of Fire while making exceptions for those who were under Satan's rule and chose to maintain his nature. All who have his nature will be sentenced with him to the Lake of Fire for eternity. God is, and will continue to be, both merciful and just, and His glory will be known throughout the earth.

DISCUSSION QUESTIONS

SECTION 2: CHAPTERS 4–5

1. Before reading this section, would you have defined eternal judgment as a foundational doctrine for a Christian to understand? What happens when we disciple people without really diving into this subject?

2. Many Christians fail to tell others about the realities of hell because they're afraid of seeming negative or judgmental. But talking about these matters is actually an act of compassion. What might it look like for believers (as individuals and in church settings) to address this subject from a place of love?

3. How would you explain the relationship between faith and fruit (or works)? If salvation is a gift, why is what we do relevant to what we believe?

4. In chapter five, we discussed the idea that we tend to share the gospel's promises without talking about the impact a decision to follow Jesus will have on someone's life. Why is a life of submission to Christ's lordship actually richer than one in which we simply receive spiritual perks without having to change the way we live?

5. Think about everything you've learned so far regarding salvation, judgment, and the impact our lives now have on eternity. How does chapter five's insight on the nature of grace impact your outlook on these topics moving forward?

SECTION 3

CHAPTER 6

The Great Falling Away

"But whoever holds out to the end will be saved."
—Matthew 24:13 TEV

Now we come to the truths reflected by Double Life and Faint Heart. At one time they truly followed Jalyn. However, one didn't follow with right motives, and the other eventually turned permanently from his ways. The end for both was fatal.

"Read What We Believe" or "Believe What We Read"

I've discovered that some of the truths we'll discuss in this chapter are controversial among some in Evangelical circles. However, if we desire the truth and are honest with ourselves, a thorough investigation of Scripture should eliminate controversy. So before we begin to examine what the Bible reveals concerning those like Double Life and Faint Heart, let me first ask that you be willing to read with an open heart and mind.

One of the greatest hindrances to our coming to know the will of God is that when we read Scripture, we *read what we believe* rather than *believe what we read*. Reading what we believe occurs when we choose to see truth through tainted lenses. This tainting results from incorrect knowledge gained from others or taught by our denomination, or from our preconceived notions about God and His ways. This is very danger-ous because it can lead us to deception. An example of this is seen in the book of Job.

Recently I picked up my Bible, and before I could open it, I heard the Spirit of God say, "Go to the book of Job and begin reading from the thirty-second chapter." I turned immediately to this chapter and realized it was the beginning of Elihu's message.

A little backstory. After he experienced great tragedy, Job's perception of God's ways rapidly deteriorated due to his pain and misfortune. He now viewed God through his experience rather than seeking God for His wisdom (see James 1:2–8). Over time, this reasoning moved toward self-justification. Job's three friends, who spoke in chapters prior to the one I was reading that day, became errant self-made theologians attempting to interpret Job's tragedies. This made matters even worse. They found no way to refute Job's wayward reasoning and instead condemned him.

Elihu, as the youngest of the group, waited for a long while to hear God's wisdom from Job or his three friends. But when he perceived the three friends had nothing more to say, he finally spoke up: "I listened patiently while you were speaking and waited while you searched for wise phrases. I paid close attention and heard you fail; you have not disproved what Job has said. How can you claim you have discovered wisdom? God must answer Job, for you have failed" (Job 32:11–13 TEV).

Elihu proceeded to rebuke all the men. He said, "Must God tailor his justice to your demands?" (Job 34:33 NLT) Oh, how accurately he spoke to the error that is so prevalent today. This is one of the main roots of misguided theology in the church: *we allow our experiences to interpret the Word of God rather than allowing the Word of God to establish truth!*

Elihu didn't speak human reasoning or theology formed by events, occurrences, or preconceived notions of who God is. Rather, without tampering with truth, he spoke the pure Word of God. Once he concluded his sayings, we read:

> Then out of the storm the Lord spoke to Job. "Who are you to question my wisdom with your ignorant, empty words? Stand up now like a man and answer the questions I ask you." (Job 38:1–3 TEV)

The Amplified Bible records God's question as, "Who is this that darkens counsel by words without knowledge?" This is exactly what happens when we filter God's words through our experiences, others' opinions, errant theology, or preconceived ideas about who God is. We darken His counsel, thus making it unavailable to all we influence. We actually hide the truth from those who would seek to know it. This is why God was so angry with Job and his friends—and is so angry today when we incorrectly represent His ways. We keep people from knowing the truth!

The Lord then spends four chapters revealing His word to Job. Once He is through, Job contritely says:

"I know, Lord, that you are all-powerful; that you can do everything you want. You ask how I dare question your wisdom when I am so very ignorant. I talked about things I did not understand, about marvels too great for me to know. You told me to listen while you spoke and to try to answer your questions. In the past I knew only what others had told me, but now I have seen you with my own eyes. So I am ashamed of all I have said and repent in dust and ashes." (Job 42:2–6 TEV)

Notice Job says, "In the past I knew only what others had told me, but now I have seen you with my own eyes." There is a powerful truth in this. Scripture states we are changed from glory to glory as we *behold* the Lord (see 2 Corinthians 3:18), not as we *hear about* Him. Jesus is the living Word of God. To see Him is to know Him, to know His ways.

This is what revealed truth does to a person. We hear the Word of God, but there is not a change until we are *enlightened*. When the understanding of God's Word enters our hearts, we cry out, "I see, I see!" At that moment we are enlightened and are transformed further into His likeness.

It is this spiritual truth that motivates Paul to pray, "I . . . do not cease to give thanks for you, making mention of you in my prayers: that the God of our Lord Jesus Christ, the Father of glory, may give to you the spirit of wisdom and revelation in the knowledge of Him, *the eyes of your understanding being enlightened*" (Ephesians 1:15–18). Job was now enlightened like never before, even though he lived a very godly life prior to his tragedies. Now he knew God on a higher level.

Once God is through speaking to Job, He addresses Eliphaz, one of Job's friends, and says, "I am angry with you and your two friends, because you did not speak the truth about me" (Job 42:7 TEV).

The Lord does not take it lightly when we represent Him or His ways incorrectly. This darkens counsel and perverts His justice. For this reason, I find it strange that men will so quickly declare a theology that is not backed by the overall counsel of Scripture. Oh, how frightening! How can we know the truth if we are not willing to be instructed or corrected by it?

After I finished reading the book of Job, the Lord spoke something to me that answered many questions. He said, "Son, did you notice that I did not come on the scene while Job or his friends spoke of Me incorrectly? My presence didn't manifest until someone stood up and spoke the truth!"

I was in awe of what God had spoken to my heart, and I began to ponder His statement. Then I heard Him again say, "This is why so many individuals, churches, or denominations are not experiencing My presence and life-changing power. They are not proclaiming My pure Word but rather their own filtered interpretations or reasonings, no different than Job or his friends. They are darkening My counsel with their words without knowledge."

If we want to know the reality of God's presence and power, we must seek to know truth without tampering with it. Therefore, as we continue to examine what Scripture reveals about God's judgments, don't allow preconceived notions of God, errant theology, or circumstances to alter your understanding of what He has already made clear. Instead, seek Him in the revealed Word of God that you may be enlightened to His ways.

Following for Gain

Let's first discuss the fate of Double Life. We'll start by returning to the words of Jesus that we discussed last chapter:

> "When the Judgment Day comes, many will say to me, 'Lord, Lord!
> In your name we spoke God's message, by your name we drove out
> many demons and performed many miracles!' Then I will say to
> them, 'I never knew you. Get away from me, you wicked people!'"
> (Matthew 7:22–23 TEV)

The NKJV translates Jesus's response as, "I never knew you; depart from Me, you who *practice lawlessness!*" This version is a rendition closer to the original. The Greek word for lawlessness (*anomia*) means acting contrary to the law or will of God. Simply put, it means not being submitted to the authority of God.

Jesus also prefaces the idea of lawlessness with the word *practice*, indicating this is not a person who periodically stumbles or even a babe in Christ who is struggling to be free. Rather, He is describing one who lives contrary to what pleases God and overlooks it, justifies it, or just plays it off. Therefore Jesus's words apply both to one who is deluded, such as Deceived, or to the unfaithful, such as Double Life.

This multitude Jesus addresses will hear proclamations of judgment that will reverberate in their souls throughout eternity in the regions of the damned. It is critically important that we don't overlook or take lightly this warning of the Master.

Let's look a little closer at the second group to whom Jesus is referring in the above scriptures. A portion of those who are turned away from the kingdom of God will be people who cast out demons *in the name of Jesus*.

Who are these people? Could they be men and women who use the name of Jesus just to cast out demons without any other association with the Lord Jesus? To find our answer, we must look at Acts.

A team of Jews who were traveling from town to town casting out evil spirits tried to use the name of the Lord Jesus. The incantation they used was this: "I command you by Jesus, whom Paul preaches, to come out!" Seven sons of Sceva, a leading priest, were doing this. But when they tried it on a man possessed by an evil spirit, the spirit replied, "I know Jesus, and I know Paul. But who are you?" And he leaped on them and attacked them with such violence that they fled from the house, naked and badly injured. (Acts 19:13–16 NLT)

It was impossible for these exorcists to cast out a demon in the name of Jesus! There is a truth established in this account: To cast out a devil, it's not enough to have the name of Jesus alone. You must have some form of relationship with the One who bears it. You have to be one who is actually a follower of Christ, unlike those we discussed in the last chapter.

You may now be thinking, *But Jesus said He had never known them. How could they have cast out devils and done miracles in His name? How can this be?*

There are those who genuinely joined themselves with Jesus for the benefits of salvation but did so purely out of the motive of personal gain. They never came to know the heart of God; they only wanted His power and blessings. Paul warns these are men who possess "corrupt minds and [are] destitute of the truth, who suppose that godliness is a means of gain. From such withdraw yourself" (1 Timothy 6:5).

These people sought Jesus for personal benefit, so their service to Him was gain-motivated, not love-motivated. Jesus will not know them, for we read, "But if anyone *loves God*, this one is *known by Him*" (1 Corinthians 8:3).

He is known by God. This word *known* doesn't mean to merely know of someone, for God knows everything about everyone. He is all-knowing! Rather, it carries the meaning of intimacy. The Amplified Bible brings this out: "But if one loves God truly [with affectionate reverence, prompt obedience, and grateful recognition of His blessing], he is known by God [recognized as worthy of *His intimacy* and love, and he is owned by Him]."

Jesus says to the multitude on Judgment Day, "I never *knew* you." So the ones who don't love God (which is evident because they do not give Him their prompt obedience, affectionate reverence, and gratefulness) are not *known* intimately by the Father or Jesus—even if they have looked to Him for salvation. Loving Jesus means you lay your life down for Him. You no longer live for yourself but for Him.

Judas is an example. He joined himself with Jesus. By the great sacrifice he made to follow Him, it appeared he loved God. Judas left all to join Jesus's ministry team and go on the road with the Master. He stayed under the heat of persecution and even when other staff members left (see John 6:66). He didn't quit. He cast out devils, healed the sick, and preached the gospel (see Luke 9:1).

However, Judas's intentions were not right from the start. He never repented of his self-seeking motives. His character was revealed by statements such as: "What are you willing *to give me* if I . . ." (Matthew 26:15). He lied and flattered to gain advantage (see Matthew 26:25), took money from the treasury of Jesus's ministry for personal use (see John 12:4–6), and the list goes on. He never intimately knew the Lord even though he spent three and a half years in His presence as a disciple. For this reason, Jesus said of him, "'Did I not choose you, the twelve, and one of you is a devil?' He spoke of Judas Iscariot, the son of Simon" (John 6:70–71).

There are those not unlike Judas who make great sacrifices for the ministry—even getting people free from demonic oppression, healing the sick, preaching the gospel, and trusting Jesus for salvation—but who have never intimately known Jesus. Their work is all done out of the motive for self-gain, not out of love of God. This perfectly describes Double Life in our allegory. He followed Jalyn because he loved the influence and power it gave him. Right from the start, his motives were not rooted in love for Jalyn.

For these the greatest condemnation is reserved. Jesus says of Judas, "It would have been good for that man if he had not been born" (Matthew 26:24). To the religious leaders who serve God out of motive for gain and take advantage of people in the name of the Lord, He says, "Therefore you will receive greater condemnation" (Matthew 23:14). These men and women, like Double Life, will find themselves in the darkest and most tormenting places of hell.

Giving Up Salvation

What we have just discussed perfectly describes Double Life in our allegory. However, what about Faint Heart? She truly had a relationship with Jalyn—even loved him—yet she didn't endure to the end. Does Scripture reveal this as well? Let's begin our examination of this question with the words of the prophet Ezekiel:

> "But when a righteous man turns away from his righteousness and
> commits iniquity, and does according to all the abominations that
> the wicked man does, shall he live? All the righteousness which he has
> done shall not be remembered; because of the unfaithfulness of which
> he is guilty and the sin which he has committed, because of them he
> shall die." (Ezekiel 18:24)

First and foremost, God is addressing a *righteous* man, not one who *thought* he was righteous but never was. There is no doubt that this person is not the same as the deceived or impostor we discussed in the previous chapter.

God says He will *not remember* any of this man's righteousness. When God forgets something, it is as if it never happened. We speak about

God forgetting our sin, putting it as far as the east is from the west and burying it in the sea of forgetfulness, which He certainly does. He states, "Their sins and their lawless deeds I will remember no more" (Hebrews 8:12). God forgets our sins once we receive Jesus as Lord. The devil tries to accuse us, but God said He will remember our sins no more. So in His mind, it is as though we have never sinned.

Well, the converse is also true. When God says a man's righteousness will not be remembered, He means He will forget He once knew him. The relationship is terminated.

Let's now closely examine what Scripture states concerning a believer permanently walking away from their salvation. The apostle James writes:

> Brethren, if anyone among you wanders from the truth, and someone turns him back, let him know that he who turns a sinner from the error of his way will save a soul from death and cover a multitude of sins. (James 5:19–20)

The first point to notice is found in the words, "*Brethren,* if anyone among *you* . . ." James is not talking to people who only think they are Christians. He is speaking of a *believer* who wanders from the way of truth. In this passage, a brother who wanders from the truth is called a *sinner.* This doesn't mean he is no longer born again; rather, he is in habitual sin and needs to return to obedience. However, if he persists in his wandering ways, James makes it clear the end result will be death to the soul—a lost soul—if there is no turning back to God (repentance). Proverbs confirms this by saying: "A man who *wanders* out of the way of understanding shall abide in the congregation of the spirits (of the dead)" (Proverbs 21:16 AMP).

Proverbs affirms James's words by showing that the final abode of a person who *wanders* from the ways of God without turning back to righteousness is the assembly of the dead, which is Hades—and eventually, the Lake of Fire.

The Book of Life

The Book of Life is mentioned eight times in the New Testament. Paul and John write that all who will spend eternity with Jesus are recorded in this book. Our names are written in it the moment we are born again.

Recall Efrosyni's testimony from chapter four. Once this young Greek girl gave her life to Jesus, God the Father wrote her name in the Book of Life and said to her, "Welcome to the family!" Likewise Paul writes to a fellow believer, "And I ask you, my true teammate, to help these women, for they worked hard with me in telling others the Good News. And they worked with Clement and the rest of my co-workers, whose names are written in the Book of Life" (Philippians 4:3 NLT).

The converse is also true. All those who are not recorded in the Book of Life are lost. Hear what the book of Revelation states: "Anyone not found written in the Book of Life was cast into the lake of fire" (Revelation 20:15).

John emphatically tells us the only people who will be admitted into the eternal city of God are "those who are written in the Lamb's Book of Life" (Revelation 21:27). The rest will find themselves in the assembly of the dead.

In Revelation 3, Jesus speaks to a church—not a city, not a group of lost people, not worshippers of false gods, and not a "supposed" church. He speaks to those who are truly His and warns: "He who overcomes shall be clothed in white garments, and I will not *blot out* his name from the Book of Life" (Revelation 3:5). The Amplified Bible records His words as "I will not *erase* or *blot out* his name from the Book of Life."

Did you notice the word *erase*? The only way to have your name *erased* from the Book of Life is for it to originally be there. Only those who have been truly born again through faith in Jesus Christ are recorded in the Book of Life. The unbelievers and even the deceived who never truly walked with Jesus were never written in this book, so their names cannot be blotted out. He is speaking to those "in the family."

A Sobering Vision

There is a man of God who served faithfully in ministry for close to seventy years in the twentieth century. His influence in the body of Christ was monumental, with his books numbering over sixty-five million in print and his Bible school graduating over 20,000 people.

He wrote on this subject in one of his books. He records that in 1952, Jesus appeared to him in a vision and showed him a pastor's wife with whom he was familiar. She had come to believe the lie that her abilities and beauty were being wasted in ministry. Over time she entertained thoughts of the fame, popularity, and wealth she could have in the world. She eventually gave in, left her husband, and went out searching for the success she desired.

The Lord specifically said to this minister, *"This woman was a child of Mine,"* and then instructed him *not* to pray for her. The following is taken directly from his book:

"Lord, what will happen to her?" I asked.

"She will spend eternity in the regions of the damned, where there is weeping and gnashing of teeth," He answered. And in the vision I saw her go down into the pit of hell. I heard her awful screams.

"This woman was Your child, Lord. She was filled with Your Spirit and had part in the ministry. Yet You said not to pray for her. I cannot understand this!"

The Lord reminded me of the following Scripture: "If any man see his brother sin a sin which is not unto death, he shall ask, and he shall give him life for them that sin not unto death. There is a sin unto death; I do not say that he shall pray for it" (1 John 5:16).

I said, "But Lord I always believed that the sin referred to in this Scripture is physical death, and that the person is saved although he has sinned."

"But that Scripture doesn't say physical death," the Lord pointed out. "You are adding something to it. If you will read the entire fifth chapter of First John, you will see that it is talking about life and death—spiritual life and spiritual death—and this is spiritual death. This refers to a believer who can sin a sin unto death, and therefore I say that you shall not pray for it. I told you not to pray for this woman because she sinned a sin unto death."

"This really disrupts my theology, Lord. Would you explain some more?" I asked. (Sometimes we need our theology disrupted if it is not in line with the Word.)

Jesus reminded me of the following Scripture:

Hebrews 6:4–6 (KJV)

4 For it is impossible for those who were once enlightened, and have tasted of the heavenly gift, and were made partakers of the Holy Ghost,

5 And have tasted the good word of God, and the powers of the world to come,

6 If they shall fall away, to renew them again unto repentance; seeing they crucify to themselves the Son of God afresh, and put him to an open shame.[1]

There are certain qualifications to note in the above Scripture. First, to fall away from faith, a person must be enlightened and have tasted the heavenly gift. This would apply to those who have received Jesus, as He is that heavenly gift. Second, the person must be filled with the Holy Spirit. Third, he must have tasted the good Word of God and the powers of the world to come. From this list we can see this would not include baby Christians, only mature believers.

In the past, I've had a few people come up to me in tears saying that at one time they told the Lord they didn't want to serve Him any longer. Later they felt deep remorse and repented. They experienced great fear when encountering this passage and a few others like it in their Bibles. However, infants sometimes do stupid things in ignorance, and the Lord knows that. The writer of Hebrews is not talking about a babe in Christ but about one who is mature.

To continue ministering comfort to these troubled souls, I tell them that if they did commit the sin unto death (as seen in the above passage), they wouldn't have a desire to come back into fellowship with Jesus. The very fact that they hungered for Him and did indeed repent, which was accompanied by godly fruit, meant the Holy Spirit drew them back into fellowship. There would be no desire for intimacy with Jesus or to live a holy life if these people permanently walked away, as did the woman in the minister's vision.

Jesus said this woman was truly a child of God. The minister who wrote this testimony was raised in a denomination in which many do not believe a person can walk away from their salvation; they believe in unconditional eternal security. This is why he said, "This really disrupts my theology." As a child of God, the woman had her name written in the Book of Life. She did not endure but permanently returned to the world; therefore, her name was erased, just as Jesus warned the church in Revelation 3. She chose to walk away for good. She was not an "overcomer." For this reason, the writer of Hebrews tells us that it is impossible for a person like this to be restored. She was now *twice dead*. She was once dead in sins, then inherited eternal life, but died in sin again by permanently walking away (see Jude 12).

Once a person comes to this state, they can never again be reborn. This is why the writer of Hebrews says it is "impossible . . . to renew them again unto repentance." So it's quite erroneous to think we can have situations in which people are born again, again.

Again, let me reiterate: if a person commits this sin, they wouldn't have a desire to repent and live all-out for Jesus ever again. No one can draw us to Jesus except the Holy Spirit. Once He departs a true believer as a result of their apostasy—such as in the case of the woman this minister described—He will not return. For this reason, the Holy Spirit is longsuffering. He will not give up easily.

The Blackness of Darkness

The apostle Peter gives us further insight. He says,

> When people escape from the wickedness of the world by knowing our Lord and Savior Jesus Christ . . . (2 Peter 2:20 NLT)

First, let's stop and examine whom Peter addresses. If someone has escaped the pollutions (wickedness) of the world through the knowledge of the Lord and Savior Jesus Christ, this would undoubtedly make them Christians. They would not fall under the category of impostors discussed in the previous chapter—those who profess to know God but in reality don't. Rather, these people have truly escaped the corruption of this world through the saving grace of the Lord Jesus. There is no doubt Peter is addressing people who have truly been born again.

Continuing, we read:

> . . . and then get tangled up and enslaved by sin again, they are worse off than before. It would be better if they had never known the way to righteousness than to know it and then reject the command they were given to live a holy life. (2 Peter 2:20–21 NLT)

Peter is addressing Christians who have given themselves back over to sin's enslavement. It would have been better for them had they never known the reality of salvation through Jesus Christ. They permanently chose the pleasures, lusts, and pride of this life over obedience to live a holy life.

Why would it have been better to have never known the way of righteousness? Jude answers this. As Peter did, Jude addresses those who walk away from their salvation. He states, "Woe to them! For they have gone in the way of Cain, have run greedily in the error of Balaam for profit, and perished in the rebellion of Korah" (Jude 11).

Cain, Balaam, and Korah all had a relationship with the Lord at one time. Two of them were ministers. Cain's error was blatant disobedience to God, Balaam's was the love of money, and Korah's was rebellion against delegated authority.

Jude continues:

These are spots in your love feasts, while they feast with you without fear, serving only themselves. They are clouds without water, carried about by the winds; late autumn trees without fruit, twice dead, pulled up by the roots; raging waves of the sea, foaming up their own shame; wandering stars for whom is reserved the blackness of darkness forever. (Jude 12–13)

In the early church, love feasts were evening meals where members came together as an expression of their close relationship with God and with one another. The love feast usually ended with the sacrament of holy communion.[2] We here learn a most sobering fact: not all who walk away from salvation will leave the organized church, as the woman in the minister's vision did. This makes such people most dangerous because their influence on the babes, the weak in conscience, and the wounded can be fatal.

Korah is an example of this type of person. He was an associate minister to Aaron, but he said to both Moses and Aaron, "You have gone too far! Everyone in Israel has been set apart by the Lord, and *he is with all of us*. What right do you have to act as though you are greater than anyone else among all these people of the Lord?" (Numbers 16:3 NLT) Korah's influence caused a judgment of death to come upon 250 leaders and 14,700 congregation members!

Jude tells us these apostates, referred to as *spots*, remain in our congregations. They possess a false sense of security in a grace they once walked in, but they have perverted it by living to serve themselves and have lost the fear of God. Notice that Korah said God was "with all of us." He too walked in a false sense of security, for the next day the earth opened up and swallowed him alive into hell.

Consequently, these apostates will still know the language of the Christian. They will hang out with other believers, but you will not find them among the overcomers Jesus is returning for. He is coming for a church without *spot* (see Ephesians 5:27).

Jude points out that these people are *twice dead*. How can you die twice? It could be that you were once dead in sin, then received eternal life through new birth, but tragically died again through persistent, unrepentant sin. Remember, James stated that if a Christian wanders from the truth and remains in that state, his soul shall *die*. And John says there is a sin unto death for believers. Both refer to one who is *twice dead*.

Notice Jude states, "For whom is reserved *the blackness of darkness forever*." The *blackness of darkness* means the worst eternal punishment. This is clearly seen in Jesus's words about His coming and the judgment. He says:

> "Blessed are those servants whom the master, when he comes, will find watching. . . . But if that servant says in his heart, 'My master is delaying his coming,' and begins to beat the male and female servants, and to eat and drink and be drunk, the master of that servant will come on a day when he is not looking for him, and at an hour when he is not aware, and will cut him in two and appoint him his portion with the unbelievers. And that servant who knew his master's will, and did not prepare himself or do according to his will, shall be beaten with many stripes. But he who did not know, yet committed things deserving of stripes, shall be beaten with few." (Luke 12:37, 45–48)

There is so much in these verses. Let me point out a few highlights. First of all, notice this is a *servant*, not an outsider, heathen, or sinner. He *knew his master's will* yet did something contrary to it. This would not relate to the behavior of Independent; he would fall under the category of those who did not know and were beaten with *few stripes*. It couldn't apply to Deceived either. Deceived thought he was a servant, but according to Jalyn, he was never a true servant. The person Jesus refers to here is called a *servant*, and he fully understood his master's will. He is one who walked away from his salvation.

Notice that the man beat his fellow servants. This speaks of a lifestyle of taking advantage of others for personal benefit or pleasure. And we see that the man now lives for the day. He is eating, drinking, and getting drunk. He lives to serve himself. Recall that Jude states that the apostate feast with other believers without the fear of God. They serve only themselves. All their decisions, even if they appear noble, are for their own advantage.

Finally, note that concerning this servant's judgment, we're told he was appointed or sent to where the unbelievers (those never saved) were. The unbelievers only received *few stripes*, but the servant who knew his master's will and departed from it was beaten with *many stripes*—thus showing he shall receive the greatest condemnation of the Lake of Fire, or the blackness of darkness, forever!

Bitter Unforgiveness

This would certainly apply to Faint Heart (along with Double Life). Faint Heart knew it was the will of Jalyn to forgive, yet she refused. She chose to hold fast to the offense of Slander. Her bitterness opened the door to her defilement. For this reason, we read of God's people "looking carefully lest anyone fall short of the grace of God; lest any root of bitterness springing up cause trouble, and by this many become defiled" (Hebrews 12:15).

Both in searching the scriptures of the New Testament and through years of experience in the ministry, I've learned that the greatest trap for pulling people away from their walk with God is unforgiveness. As it did with Faint Heart, unforgiveness opens the door to all kinds of other errant beliefs and behavior.

In Matthew 18, Jesus tells the parable of a great king in the process of settling his accounts. A servant who owed him ten thousand talents was brought before him. Now, a talent was not a measure of money but a measure of weight. It was used to measure gold (see 2 Samuel 12:30), silver (see 1 Kings 20:39), and other metals and commodities. In this parable, a talent represents a measure of debt, so we can safely assume Jesus was referring to a unit of exchange such as gold or silver. Let's assume it was gold.

The common talent was equivalent to roughly seventy-five pounds. It was the full weight a man could carry (see 2 Kings 5:23). Ten thousand talents would be approximately 750,000 pounds, or 375 tons. So this servant owed the king 375 tons of gold. When I wrote this book, the price of gold was roughly $1,200 an ounce. So put the math to it. Ten thousand talents of gold would be worth roughly fourteen billion dollars. That is how much this servant owed the king! The point Jesus emphasizes here is that this servant owed an overwhelming debt he could never pay.

The king commanded that the man and his family be sold to make payment toward the debt. The man fell at the king's feet and pleaded for mercy, which the king granted. He forgave the entire debt.

We can see that in this parable, the king represents God the Father. The man forgiven of the debt represents someone who has received His forgiveness through Jesus Christ. When harm is done, a debt is owed. You have heard it said, "He'll pay for this." Forgiveness is the cancellation of that debt. This man, like us, was forgiven of an unpayable debt.

However, we read, "But that servant went out and found one of his fellow servants who owed him a hundred denarii; and he laid hands on him and took him by the throat, saying, 'Pay me what you owe!'" (Matthew 18:28)

A denarius was a common day's wage. Let's assume it equates to $100 in today's money. The total debt owed would be approximately $10,000. So this is not a small offense.

We continue to read, "So his fellow servant fell down at his feet and begged him, saying, 'Have patience with me, and I will pay you all.' And he would not, but went and threw him into prison till he should pay the debt" (Matthew 18:29–30). This man has been forgiven a debt of fourteen billion dollars. A fellow servant owes him $10,000, but this man will not release the debt. He is determined to make the other man pay.

It is important to note that the offenses we hold against each other, when compared with our initial offense against God, are comparable to a $10,000-debt stacked up against one of fourteen billion dollars! No matter how badly someone has treated you, their wrongdoing does not compare with our transgressions against God. You may feel no one has it as bad as you do. You don't realize how badly Jesus was treated. He was innocent, a blameless lamb who was slain and took our fourteen-billion-dollar debt.

A person who cannot forgive has forgotten how great a debt they were forgiven of! When you understand the death and eternal torment Jesus delivered you from, you will freely release others. There is nothing worse than eternity in a lake of fire. There is no relief. The worm does not die, and the fire is not quenched. This was our destination until God forgave us through the death of His Son, Jesus Christ! If a person cannot forgive, they are unaware of the reality of hell. They have not comprehended the love and forgiveness of God.

Let's continue with the parable:

"So when his fellow servants saw what had been done, they were very grieved, and came and told their master all that had been done. Then his master, after he had called him, said to him, 'You wicked servant!

I forgave you all that debt because you begged me. Should you not also have had compassion on your fellow servant, just as I had pity on you?'" (Matthew 18:31–33)

I want to emphasize that Jesus is not referring to unbelievers in this parable. He is talking about servants of the king, born-again believers. This man had already received forgiveness of his great debt (salvation) and was called the master's servant. The one he could not forgive was a fellow servant. So we can conclude this is the final outcome of a "believer" who permanently refuses to forgive.

I find an amazing fact here. When they heard all the other parables in the gospels, people would have to inquire in order to be told the meaning. However, Jesus gives the interpretation of this parable without being asked. I believe it is because what He communicated was so far outside the norm that He had to make sure the people got it. Here is His interpretation:

"And his master was angry, and delivered him to the torturers until he should pay all that was due to him.

"So My heavenly Father also will do to you if each of you, from his heart, does not forgive his brother his trespasses." (Matthew 18:34–35)

There are three major points I want to highlight in these two verses. First, the unforgiving servant is turned over to the torturers. Second, he now has to pay off the original debt of 375 tons of gold. And third, this is what God the Father will do to anyone who does not forgive his brother's offense.

Let's briefly discuss each point. First, the word *torture* means the act of inflicting extreme pain and agony of mind or body and to twist from a normal position. A torturer is one who inflicts torture.

A believer who refuses to forgive will be tormented by demon spirits.

These *torturers* are given permission to inflict pain and agony of mind and body at will. I have often prayed for people in services who could not receive healing, comfort, or deliverance all because they would not release others and forgive from their hearts. This bitterness almost always leads to anger and offense toward God. The person's faith becomes defiled, and if there is no repentance and forgiveness, their end will be fatal.

The second point is that this unforgiving servant now has to pay the original, unpayable debt. He is required to do that which is impossible! This is the debt Jesus paid at Calvary. You may cringe at this, but hear the words of Jesus in another account: "And whenever you stand *praying*, if you have anything against anyone, forgive him, that *your Father in heaven* may also forgive you your trespasses" (Mark 11:25).

Notice whom Jesus is speaking to here. See His words "your Father in heaven." God is not Father to the sinner. He is *God* to the sinner and *Father* to the believer. Also, it isn't normal for sinners to pray. So it is clear that Jesus is addressing children of God.

Let's continue. "But if you do not forgive," Jesus says, "neither will your Father in heaven forgive your trespasses" (Mark 11:26). This is as clear as it can get. Which brings us to the third point: if a person refuses to forgive, they will suffer torment until they pay the unpayable debt. This is impossible, for no one can pay the ransom for his or her own soul (see Psalm 49:7 NLT). Jesus says that if you do not forgive, your Father will not forgive your trespasses. Is that worth it?

We are not talking about someone who is working through an offense and praying to forgive. We're discussing someone like Faint Heart who insistently refuses to forgive. Notice in the allegory that her unforgiveness opened the door to other manners of evil, and she gradually slipped away from her devotion to Jalyn. Was the offense worth her fatal end? Again, this is why the writer of Hebrews emphatically tells us to carefully examine ourselves and let go of any form of bitterness, for by it *many* are defiled.

Now we can understand Jesus's words concerning the latter days of the church. He says, "Many will be *offended*, will betray one another, and will hate one another . . . And because *lawlessness will abound*, the *love* of many will grow cold. But he who endures to the end shall be saved" (Matthew 24:10, 12–13).

Notice it is not a few or even some but *many* who will be offended in the days in which we are living. The word *many* means a vast, very large, or great number. Offense, or unforgiveness, will lead to lawlessness, and the love of a vast number will grow cold.

The Greek word translated *love* here is *agape*, which describes the love of God shed abroad in a Christian's heart the moment they are saved. Jesus is not speaking of impostors, for they have never truly received the love of God. No, He is speaking to believers, for notice He says, "But he who endures to the end shall be saved." You don't say to a sinner or an impostor, "If you endure to the end, you'll be saved." They haven't started the race yet!

Departure from the Faith

Scripture warns us of the *falling away* that will occur among believers in our day. Paul says, "Let no one deceive you by any means; for that Day [of the coming of the Lord] will not come unless the *falling away comes first*" (2 Thessalonians 2:3). And again he foretells, "Now the Spirit *expressly says* that in latter times some will *depart from the faith*" (1 Timothy 4:1).

Why? "For the time will come when they will not endure sound doctrine, but according to their own desires, because they have itching ears, they will heap up for themselves teachers; and they will *turn their ears away from the truth*" (2 Timothy 4:3–4).

Notice that in the above scripture, Paul says people "will depart from the faith." The faith he speaks of isn't an imaginary faith. It is true faith in Jesus Christ. For these people to depart from the faith, they need to have been actually in it at one time.

I've shared truths from almost every New Testament writer concerning the departure of believers from the true faith. Let me now share some of the writings of the noted early church fathers, some of whom were companions of the apostles who wrote the New Testament. I find their writings directly correlate with the words we've seen in Scripture:

Let us then practice righteousness so that we may be saved unto the end.
—Clement of Rome[3]

Even in the case of one who has done the greatest good deeds in his life, but at the end has run headlong into wickedness, all his former pains are profitless to him. For at the climax of the drama, he has given up his part.
—Clement of Alexandria[4]

Some think that God is under a necessity of bestowing even on the unworthy what He has promised [to give]. So they turn His liberality into His slavery . . . For do not many afterwards fall out of [grace]? Is not this gift taken away from many?
—Tertullian[5]

A man may possess an acquired righteousness, from which it is possible for him to fall away.
—Origen[6]

Those who do not obey Him, being disinherited by Him, have ceased to be His sons.
—Irenaeus[7]

Upon hearing my stance on these truths from Scripture, some have incorrectly said to me, "John, you are an Arminian." This is a term the dictionary describes as follows: "of or relating to the theology of Jacobus Arminius and his followers, who rejected the Calvinist doctrines of predestination and election and who believed that human free will is compatible with God's sovereignty."[8]

To these people I simply say, "No, I'm neither a Calvinist nor an Arminian. I'm a Christian who believes the Bible is the infallible Word of God."

Jacobus Arminius lived long after the writers of the Scriptures and even long after the early leaders quoted above. So could you call these writers Arminian? Obviously not, as they lived and wrote before Arminius was born. What I'm writing is not a personal thought, concept, or belief but clearly communicated New Testament truth. And God made His message of warning very clear to those of us who believe. We must be careful to not get hung up on schools of thought but to be open to the context of Scripture as inspired by the Holy Spirit, for:

> All Scripture is inspired by God and is useful to teach us what is true
> and to make us realize what is wrong in our lives. It straightens us out
> and teaches us to do what is right. It is God's way of preparing us in
> every way . . . (2 Timothy 3:16–17 NLT)

It is interesting to note that the false leaders, whom Jesus warned and rebuked sternly, were those who congregated around schools of thought and taught in like manner. However, if you look at what was said of John the Baptist, Jesus, or others who spoke the truth, it was repeatedly reported that they "taught . . . as one having authority, and not as the scribes" (Matthew 7:29). For this reason, Paul instructs Titus, "Speak these things, exhort, and rebuke with all authority" (Titus 2:15). And to Timothy he writes, "Remain in Ephesus that you may charge some that they teach no other doctrine" (1 Timothy 1:3). Paul also instructed Timothy to:

Herald and preach the Word! Keep your sense of urgency [stand by, be at hand and ready], whether the opportunity seems to be favorable or unfavorable. [Whether it is convenient or inconvenient, whether it is welcome or unwelcome, you as preacher of the Word are to show people in what way their lives are wrong.] And convince them, rebuking and correcting, warning and urging and encouraging them, being unflagging and inexhaustible in patience and teaching. (2 Timothy 4:2 AMP)

In Ephesians 6, Paul requests prayer that "I may speak boldly, as I ought to speak" (verse 20). You can see this is a trait among all God's true spokespeople. Their authority is in the Word of God. They will not gather around personal feelings, schools of thought, or the consensus of the majority. The majority can sometimes be wrong. We must know that God means what He says and says what He means!

Keep You from Stumbling

Some have been shaken by this message about falling from grace, which is so clear in Scripture. They've come to me in a panicked state, saying, "I thought we had eternal security."

To this I reply, "Absolutely yes! We do have eternal security! Jesus said He would not lose any the Father gives Him (see John 18:9) because He would never leave or forsake us. But He didn't say that we couldn't leave Him." This usually is met with concerned looks. So then I say, "If you truly love Jesus Christ, why would you ever want out? You will not deny Him if you truly love Him!"

If you love God, you will have no trouble keeping His commandments! If serving God is an obligation, you have entered into a legalistic relationship, and it will be hard to keep His commandments. We should not serve God to earn His approval; we should serve God because we are in love with Him!

Jude goes on to tell us how to keep our love fresh even if there are bad influences in the church. He says, "Keep yourselves in the love of God, *looking* for the mercy of our Lord Jesus Christ unto eternal life" (Jude 21). We are to look for the Lord every moment of the day. We are to long for Him and seek Him continually, that He might reveal Himself in a greater way, for "everyone who has this hope in Him *purifies* himself, just as He is pure" (1 John 3:3). John specifically spoke of the revelation of Jesus Christ.

When you look for Him and fellowship with His Spirit, you will never want out. So there is nothing by which to be shaken. One of my favorite promises in the Bible is at the conclusion of the book of Jude. To those who keep themselves in love with God by looking for the revelation of Jesus, Jude says:

> Now to Him who is able to keep you from stumbling, and to present you faultless before the presence of His glory with exceeding joy, to God our Savior, Who alone is wise, be glory and majesty, dominion and power, both now and forever. Amen. (Jude 24–25)

This is my earnest prayer and desire for you!

CHAPTER 7

The Foundation

. . . The [uncompromisingly] righteous
have an everlasting foundation.
—Proverbs 10:25 AMP

Before returning to the allegory of Affabel to discuss the judgments and rewards of Selfish and Charity, we'll put a cap on what we've discussed in the past three chapters. Recall this passage from chapter four:

> Therefore let us go on and get past the elementary stage in the teachings and doctrine of Christ (the Messiah), advancing steadily toward the completeness and perfection that belong to spiritual maturity. Let us not again be laying the foundation of . . . eternal judgment and punishment. (Hebrews 6:1–2 AMP)

Being without a firm foundation in the truths of eternal judgment and punishment prevents us from building a proper and healthy life in Christ. It could be compared to attempting to advance your education without the basic tools acquired in elementary school, such as the ability to read and write.

Why is this so? In careful study of the gospels, you'll notice that Jesus spoke of and described hell more than He did heaven. He did this to plant a foundation within us—the fear of God. Here's one example:

> "Whatever you have said in the dark will be heard in the light, and what you have whispered behind closed doors will be shouted from

the housetops for all to hear! Dear friends, don't be afraid of those who want to kill you. They can only kill the body; they cannot do any more to you. But I'll tell you whom to fear. Fear God, who has the power to kill people and then throw them into hell." (Luke 12:3–5 NLT)

These words are strong and precise: attaining and maintaining a good understanding of eternal judgment and punishment firmly plants and keeps the fear of the Lord in our hearts.

Allow me to explain. Only God can give the eternal sentence to hell. What we have spoken in secret will be revealed by the light of His glory at the judgment. Not only our words but also our motives, attitudes, actions, and works will be made known. The fear of God keeps us continually aware that nothing can be hidden from Him, even the most secret things. We know nothing will escape His judgment—and His judgment is just. If we lack this understanding, we can become deceived into believing God overlooks or even doesn't see lawlessness, and we will take comfort in an unscriptural mercy that doesn't exist (as Deceived, Faint Heart, and Double Life did). We can easily become among the many in these last days who will drift away from steadfast devotion and into lawlessness.

Those who lack this foundation will surely slip into the fear of man, and we ultimately serve who we fear. If we fear God, we will obey Him even under pressure. If we fear man, we will yield to man—especially under pressure—and drift toward what benefits our own pleasures, fleshly desires, or pride. To consistently yield to the flesh will ultimately lead to serious consequences. So if we lack a conscious understanding of eternal judgment and punishment, we will lack a certain measure of the fear of the Lord, for a holy awe of the judgments of Christ is indeed one aspect of the fear of the Lord. Paul says it like this:

For we must all appear before the judgment seat of Christ, so that each one may be recompensed for his deeds in the body, according to what he has done, whether good or bad. Therefore, knowing the fear of the Lord, we persuade men . . . (2 Corinthians 5:10–11 NASB)

Paul wasn't referring to the Great White Throne Judgment (the one Jesus referred to in Luke 12), at which people will be sentenced to hell. He was referring to the believer's judgment. We will begin to discuss this judgment in the next chapter, but notice that Paul equates Christ's judgment seat with the fear of the Lord. In fact, in the verse above, he actually calls the Judgment Seat "the fear of the Lord." The point is, you cannot separate the fear of the Lord from an understanding of judgment, and the fear of the Lord is the key to a healthy life.

Hear the words of the prophet Isaiah: "He will be the sure foundation for your times, a rich store of salvation and wisdom and knowledge; the fear of the Lord is the key to this treasure" (Isaiah 33:6 NIV).

Holy fear is the key to God's sure foundation. Recall in the previous chapters Jesus foretelling of the multitude who would do miraculous things in His name but would be turned away to eternal punishment. It's not surprising that, in Matthew 7, Jesus immediately continued by explaining the cause of their downfall. It was their foundation. They built their lives on mindsets and beliefs that couldn't weather life's storms. In Jesus's words:

"So then, anyone who hears these words of mine and obeys them is like a wise man who built his house on rock. The rain poured down, the rivers flooded over, and the wind blew hard against that house. But it did not fall, because it was built on rock [God's sure foundation, the fear of the Lord].

"But anyone who hears these words of mine and does not obey them is like a foolish man who built his house on sand. The rain poured down, the rivers flooded over, the wind blew hard against that house, and it fell. And what a terrible fall that was!" (Matthew 7:24–27 TEV)

Those who have endured to the end withstood the storms because of their firm foundation. The fear of the Lord is that foundation; it provides stability for us. It is a storehouse of the riches of God. His salvation, wisdom, and knowledge are all hidden in it.

The Fear of the Lord

What is the fear of the Lord? Is it to be scared of God? Absolutely not. How can we have intimacy with the Lord (which is His earnest desire) if we are afraid of Him? When God came to reveal Himself to Israel, He came to have fellowship with them like He had with Moses—but they all ran back and refused to draw near. Moses told the people, "*Do not fear,* for God has come to test you, and *that His fear may be before you,* so that you may not sin" (Exodus 20:20).

Moses's words sound like they contradict themselves, but they don't. He differentiates between being afraid of God and the fear of the Lord, and there is a distinction. The one who is afraid of God has something to hide. Recall what Adam did when he disobeyed in the Garden of Eden: he hid from the presence of the Lord. On the other hand, the one who fears God is afraid to be away from Him. He runs from disobedience. So the first definition of holy fear is to be terrified to be away from God.

Let's continue to unpack what it means. To fear the Lord is to honor, esteem, value, respect, and reverence Him above anything or anyone else. It is to love what He loves and hate what He hates. What is important to Him is important to us; what is not important to Him is not important to us. When we fear Him, we will *tremble at His word,* which means we obey Him instantly—when it doesn't make sense, when it hurts, when we don't see the benefits. And we obey to completion. So yes, the manifestation of the fear of the Lord is *obedience* to His Word, ways, or commands.

Scripture tells us the fear of the Lord is the beginning of wisdom. Or we can say it like this: it's the *foundation* of wisdom. Wisdom, which we will discuss in great depth in future chapters, is the knowledge and ability to make the right choices at the opportune time. Those who make wrong choices under pressure lack wisdom, and wisdom's source is the fear of the Lord.

Scripture tells us that our lives can be compared to building houses. First comes the foundation; next we build the structure. We read, "Through wisdom a house is built" (Proverbs 24:3). If we are building our lives with the ability to make right choices, then we will build a healthy life with which we'll be able to stand with confidence before the Judgment Seat. The very beginning or foundation of this wisdom is the fear of the Lord.

Kept from Departing

Christians wouldn't backslide if they had the fear of the Lord firmly planted in their hearts. We wouldn't slip or drift away from our steadfast devotion to Jesus. We wouldn't take His Word for granted or treat it casually. We wouldn't flirt with sin, which causes believers' hearts to harden so that they eventually fall away (see Hebrews 3:12–13). We would always know that what is done and spoken in secret will be proclaimed publicly at the Judgment Seat.

Hear what God said to Jeremiah about New Testament people:

"They shall be My people, and I will be their God; then I will give them one heart and one way, that they may fear Me forever, for the good of them and their children after them. And I will make an everlasting covenant with them, that I will not turn away from doing them good; but I will put My fear in their hearts so that they will not depart from Me." (Jeremiah 32:38–40)

Notice God says His people will *"fear Me forever . . . that they will not depart from Me."* I recall a meeting in Malaysia where the Spirit of the fear of the Lord manifested strongly. People were there from all over the Eastern Hemisphere. Bible school students, pastors, and many others packed the auditorium where I was speaking. Toward the close of the service, many were weeping uncontrollably and lying all over the floor near the platform.

The terror of the Lord was so awesome in that atmosphere, I thought, *John Bevere, you make one wrong move, say one wrong thing, and you are dead!* Would that have happened? I don't know, but I can say a man and a woman made a wrong move in a similar atmosphere in the New Testament and died. The immediate result of their judgment was that "great fear came upon all the church and upon all who heard these things" (Acts 5:11).

After this meeting in Malaysia, a couple from India approached me and said, "John, we feel so clean inside."

I responded, "Yes, I do too."

The next morning I was in my hotel room and I found this scripture: "The fear of the Lord is clean, *enduring forever*" (Psalm 19:9).

The Holy Spirit immediately spoke to my heart and said, "Lucifer was the lead worship angel in heaven. He was anointed, beautiful, and blessed. But he didn't fear Me; *he didn't endure forever*."

I contemplated this. I then heard, "A third of the angels who surrounded My throne and saw My glory didn't fear Me. *They didn't endure forever*."

I was struck by what God had revealed. Again I heard, "Adam and Eve walked in the presence of My glory. They fellowshipped with Me, but they did not fear Me. *They didn't endure in My presence forever*."

The fear of the Lord gives us staying power. It keeps us consistently obedient to God's Word. Believers are warned, "Therefore, since a promise remains of entering His rest, let us *fear* lest any of you seem to have come short of it" (Hebrews 4:1). It's interesting that the writer of this verse says *fear* instead of *love*. It is the fear of God that keeps us from drifting back into sin.

A Famous Evangelist

I will never forget the time I visited a famous evangelist who was serving his last year of a five-year prison sentence. His case had been made known to the world and brought much reproach on the kingdom. However, during his first year in prison, he had a genuine encounter with the Lord. When I walked into that facility four years later, one of the first things he said to me was, "John, this prison wasn't God's judgment on my life; it was His mercy. If I would have kept going the way I was living, I would have ended up in hell for eternity."

Now he had my attention. I knew I was speaking to a broken man of God, a true servant of Christ. I knew he started out in ministry very much in love with Jesus. His passion had been evident. I wondered how he ended up so far from the Lord while still at the height of his ministry. So I asked him, "When did you fall out of love with Jesus?"

He looked at me and answered without hesitation, "I didn't!"

Very puzzled, I replied, "But what about the mail fraud and adultery you committed in the past seven years—everything that you're in prison for?"

He said, "John, I loved Jesus all the way through it, but I didn't fear God. He wasn't the supreme authority of my life." Then he said something that riveted me: "John, there are millions of American Christians just like me. They call Jesus their Savior and love Him, but they don't fear Him as their supreme Lord."

A light went on inside me at that point. I realized we can love Jesus, but that alone will not keep us from falling away. We must fear God as well. Recall Moses's words: "God has come to test you, and *that His fear may be before you, so that you may not sin*" (Exodus 20:20). It is the fear of the Lord that gives us the staying power to not drift away from our obedience to God—as did Lucifer, a third of the angels, and Adam, and as will those in the church who fall away in these last days.

Complete Your Salvation

For this reason, Paul tells us to "work out (cultivate, *carry out to the goal*, and *fully complete*) your own salvation with *reverence* and *awe* and *trembling* (self-distrust, with serious caution, tenderness of conscience, watchfulness against temptation, timidly shrinking from whatever might offend God and discredit the name of Christ)" (Philippians 2:12 AMP). We carry out and complete our salvation with reverential *fear and trembling*. This keeps us under the awareness that every thought, word, and deed will be made manifest at the judgment. Having this consciousness keeps us humble, cautious, sober-minded, tender, and aware of temptations to disobey. It compels us to always keep away from what may displease God.

Notice that Paul doesn't say we fully complete or finish our salvation with love and kindness. The fear of the Lord gives us strength to not fall away from His grace into a life of lawlessness. The love of God, on the other hand, keeps us from legalism, which also destroys intimacy with God. Our love for God also fuels our motives and intentions, keeping them passionate and accurate. We must have the great forces of both love and fear in our lives to maintain a healthy relationship with Him. For this reason Paul calls God our heavenly Father and Abba (meaning Daddy) but also says our God is a consuming fire (see Hebrews 12:29). He is love, but He is also just and a holy judge. To not fear Him is to lack enduring stability, and Jesus repeatedly says, "He who endures to the end will be saved" (Matthew 10:22).

Our Influence

The other reason it is critical that we have a firm understanding of eternal judgment and punishment is our influence on others. If we lack the fear of the Lord, we will communicate—either by words or by actions—an unbalanced gospel. This will make those we influence susceptible to slide back or even permanently fall.

As gospel teachers or pastors, if we lack in these foundational doctrines, we will convey extensively the principles found in Scripture about living a blessed, prosperous, happy life. These principles will work, as they were intended to. They will produce health, financial success, peace, better relationships, and so forth. However, without the foundational understanding of eternal judgments, we will shy back from preaching the cross and the price of following Jesus. We will preach more self-gratifying messages rather than the calling to lay our lives down at all costs.

If we are not driven by eternity, we will live and communicate more to benefit this life instead of seeing life from an eternal perspective. We will teach people to live for the day rather than to live like the patriarchs, who "waited for the city which has foundations, whose builder and maker is God" (Hebrews 11:10).

Yes, there are rewards in this life for obeying the principles of God. We've taught them well. But let's not forget we are temporary residents on this earth. We are to succeed in this life, but we're to do so by the standards of heaven, not of our culture. Our real home is not here.

Read carefully the motive of the saints who gave up this world to follow God:

> These all died in faith, not having received the promises, but having seen them afar off were assured of them, embraced them and confessed that they were *strangers* and *pilgrims* on the earth. For those who say such things declare plainly that they seek a homeland. And truly if they had called to mind that country from which they had come out, they would have had opportunity to return. But now they desire a better, that is, a heavenly country. Therefore God is not ashamed to be called their God, for He has prepared a city for them. (Hebrews 11:13–16)

The homeland these saints looked for is the City of God, the New Jerusalem, to which we will turn our attention for the remainder of this book. Those who will live in this city are called *overcomers*. Their reward shall be infinitely better than the very best this life on earth can offer.

DISCUSSION QUESTIONS

SECTION 3: CHAPTERS 6–7

1. What benefits of following Christ do you think you could be most tempted to pursue above intimacy with Jesus Himself? What might help you keep your heart aligned with the right focus?

2. It's a sobering thought that a believer can choose to walk away from their faith. Does this conflict with what you've believed? Discuss your response in light of this truth: as believers, we seek to respond not with mere fear but with the fear of the Lord.

3. Reflect on the parable of the unmerciful servant, found in Matthew 18:23–35. Why do you think God takes the issue of forgiveness so seriously?

4. In your own words, describe how a skewed focus on the mercy of God—without the influence of holy fear—can lead a believer into deception.

5. Our eternal perspective affects more than just ourselves. We also influence others. What do you think it looks like to communicate the earthly benefits of following God (such as health, success, or fulfillment) without shifting the emphasis away from what matters most?

SECTION 4

CHAPTER 8

The Kingdom of Affabel: The Day of Judgment II

*. . . I am He Who searches minds (the thoughts, feelings, and
purposes) and the [inmost] hearts, and I will give to each of you
[the reward for what you have done] as your work deserves.*
—Revelation 2:23 AMP

Let's return to the allegory of the kingdom of Affabel to discover the outcomes of Selfish and Charity. Through them we'll learn about important aspects of the believer's judgment, one of which is that not all believers will be rewarded equally.

The Believer's Judgment

This judgment took place in the morning soon after the Endelites arrived at the Great Hall. Approximately five hundred Endelites waited in the Hall of Life, anxiously anticipating their first meeting with King Jalyn. Charity and Selfish had found friends both old and new and were in the process of conversing when suddenly, the Royal Guards entered the hall. All conversations ceased as the Chief Guard addressed the group.

"Shortly you will face your king. He has always loved you and has yearned for this day when you will be united. Though you've never met, he has seen you. He has beheld your heart and discerned your fruit. He knows your heart, your motives, your thoughts, and your feelings as well as your works. Nothing has been hidden. Know his judgment is just. None will be slighted or misrepresented."

The Chief Guard proceeded to instruct them as to how they would be ushered into the Great Hall, as well as to the necessary protocol once within. Once the briefing was complete, he announced, "The first to go before King Jalyn is Selfish. Step forward so we may escort you to the Great Hall."

Selfish and His Judgment

Selfish surmised he had been summoned first because of his position as the mayor of Endel. He was confident he would be rewarded handsomely for his leadership in the king's outer realm. He remembered how the teachings from the ancient writings spoke of rewards and ruling positions in Affabel for those deemed faithful in Endel. He had seen the community thrive during his two-year term as mayor. He was confident as he went to face the king.

The doors of the Great Hall were opened and Selfish was escorted into the presence of the king. He was overwhelmed by the grandeur of this massive auditorium. He noticed it was almost completely full. All in attendance were standing. Selfish wondered why there were random seats vacant but quickly dismissed the thought by reasoning that it was due to the citizens arbitrarily seating themselves.

There, at a great distance, was the throne of Jalyn. It was more majestic than Selfish ever could have imagined. He also noticed the smaller thrones that he correctly assumed belonged to the underrulers of Jalyn. His heart skipped a beat—there were a couple seats yet unoccupied. He felt certain he would be assigned a vacant throne.

An Old Friend

As Selfish proceeded, he was taken aback by the glorious transformation in the appearance of former Endelites who now held citizenship in

Affabel. After taking just a few steps toward the throne, he recognized an old friend in the very back of the auditorium. His name was Social. He had owned a restaurant that Selfish frequented. He looked to the Chief Guard as if to ask if it was all right to speak. The guard nodded his approval.

Selfish approached, and the two embraced. "How have you been, Social?" asked Selfish.

"I've been very well," replied the old friend, "but my name is no longer Social. It is Content. Lord Jalyn gave me this new name just as he does with all his servants once they appear before his throne.

"Affabel is more wonderful than we ever could have dreamed," Content continued. "This Great Hall is but an entrance to realms of beauty, splendor, and grandeur in the magnificent city. The king is more personable, loving, and majestic than anyone you have ever met or known. I am so thankful to know and serve him. It is an honor to be in his kingdom. It is better than anything we ever knew. If I had known in Endel what I know now, I would have lived differently. I would have focused more on pleasing the king. I would have lived as a better citizen in my short stay in Endel. If I had, I would be closer to him now."

Selfish countered, "What do you mean? You were a great citizen in Endel! You ran one of the best restaurants and sponsored numerous community events. You frequently contributed both finances and free meals for fundraising campaigns. You even sacrificed evenings of revenue to do this!"

Content shook his head. "I did those things to gain recognition and acceptance. I also knew it would draw more patrons. My motive was not to bless but to ensure my success. I should have listened to the words of Jalyn. He told us, 'When you give a dinner or a supper, do not ask your friends, your brothers, your relatives, nor rich neighbors, lest they also invite you back, and you be repaid. But when you give a feast, invite the poor, the maimed, the lame, the blind. And you will be blessed, because they cannot repay you; for you shall be repaid at the resurrection of the just.'[1] I donated those dinners for my benefit, not for the good of the community. I wanted to move among the influential of Endel."

Selfish probed deeper. "But you frequently contributed to the School of Endel. Didn't this win you favor in the eyes of Jalyn?"

Content countered, "I did indeed contribute to the School of Endel, but not in proportion to the success of my business. I actually only gave a small percentage. I hoarded much of the restaurant's profits because I was afraid of failing. This was coupled with a desire to live the good life. My true intentions were to protect myself. The little I gave was to ease my conscience. I was compelled because our teachers frequently discussed the importance of giving to the kingdom and to those in need. I ended up giving out of guilt and compulsion rather than out of compassion and love."

Content continued, "I forgot Jalyn's illustration of the widow who loved the kingdom of Affabel. Remember, he said, 'I tell you that this poor widow put more in the offering box than all the others. For the others put in what they had to spare of their riches; but she, poor as she is, put in all she had—she gave all she had to live on.'"[2]

Selfish pondered the social gatherings and dinners he held at his home. There were no poor or even less fortunate people there. Then he remembered the five thousand entrustments he gave to appease those who were disappointed with his choice to grant the land to the department store rather than to the school. At the time he had thought it was quite a bit, but now he was embarrassed by how little he had given. How would this fair before Jalyn?

These reflections were interrupted by Content's further comments. "If I had been truly passionate for Jalyn and his people," he said, "I would have given my time and served at the school. If all do their part, the burden is lifted, but if not it is borne by the few. If Jalyn's design was implemented, none would be overburdened. The few who took the heavy loads have been greatly rewarded. Bottom line: the little I gave I did to ease my conscience for my lack of commitment to Jalyn's kingdom.

"When my life was reviewed, it was clear to all that I lived more for my comfort, security, and reputation than for his glory. Now I'm one of the lowest citizens in this city. Even though this is the case, I am still overwhelmed by Jalyn's goodness and how much he loves me. I really didn't deserve anything I received from him, but as you will shortly discover, his love and generosity are beyond comprehension. I am in debt to his extravagant kindness for the rest of my life."

Shocked, Selfish cried out, "Lowest citizen! Do you mean there is a class system here?"

Content smiled and said, "Yes, of sorts. We were taught this in Endel, although many of us never considered it seriously. But deep within we knew it. In fact, you even considered this truth when you walked into this auditorium. I heard your thoughts; you anticipate being assigned a throne. You knew this was possible from the ancient writings taught in class, though I doubt you would have acknowledged your belief regarding your future position while in Endel.

"Those who were faithful to Jalyn during our short stay in Endel are the leaders and citizens who hold the most interesting positions in this society. They live in the most beautiful section of the city and have the privilege of frequent interaction with the king. Those of us who lived more for ourselves while in Endel are assigned positions in the outer parts of the city. This is seen in this auditorium as well. Those in the rear of this hall are those who live in the flatlands. We have been assigned the labor-intensive jobs. We are the least in the kingdom. Those who occupy the midsections make their homes in the mountains and hold more creative positions, while those in front and upon the thrones live in the Regal Center where the king lives. They are privileged to live and work alongside him. These are the greatest in the kingdom."

Content concluded, "My friend Selfish, know that Jalyn is a just and loving leader. Anything he gives you will be a reward. None of us would have a life such as what is found in the least parts of this city had it not been for him."

Having said this, Content stepped back into his place. The Chief Guard then motioned for Selfish to continue his progress toward the throne.

A Popular Teacher

Selfish took a few more steps and noticed another he knew and admired whose name was Motivator. He was formerly a teacher at the School of Endel, one Selfish considered outstanding. He was informative and articulate, and he always inspired Selfish when he spoke. This fabulous instructor taught in such a way that the students were uplifted and felt good about themselves. The other teachers were uplifting, but at times they seemed a bit stern and their words brought painful conviction. Not so with Motivator; you always felt great coming out of his class. In fact, he was Selfish's favorite teacher by far.

Selfish again glanced at the Chief Guard, seeking permission to speak to his former teacher. The guard again nodded his affirmation. Selfish approached Motivator, and the two greeted each other warmly.

Selfish couldn't help but ask, "Why are you here in these back rows?"

"This is my position and place. I am one of the least of the citizens of Affabel. I live in the flatlands and work as a plumber."

"What?" cried Selfish. "You were one of Jalyn's finest teachers! How can you be one of the lowest citizens? You should be on one of the thrones."

"There are several reasons I'm not further up in the ranks of this great assembly or ruling with Jalyn," Motivator said. "For time's sake, I'll only share the root of my folly. Remember how all who pledge their lives to Jalyn are likened to builders? We were taught this all through school. One of our chief responsibilities in Endel was to build the lives of others. This was done by the messages we communicated, whether through speech, conduct, or our works.

"As an instructor, I was given both great privilege and great responsibility. I taught students the principles and ways of Jalyn. Yet I failed as a teacher in so many ways.

"My teachings were unbalanced. I emphasized only the positive aspects of serving Jalyn. I motivated many of my students only to pursue success without considering the long-term effects. I didn't teach them that the truest goal of life was to please Jalyn. I taught them how to use his ways to succeed in life. Consequently, I never warned them of the pitfalls and snares of our society.

"The ancient writings clearly stated I was to preach the whole counsel of Jalyn. This included 'warning every man and teaching every man in all wisdom, that we may present every man perfect in Jalyn.'[3] I taught but neglected to warn. By being an exclusively positive teacher and never giving healthy warnings, I built numerous lives that brought little glory to Jalyn." Here he dropped his head. "A good number of them are in perdition."

Seeing the shock on Selfish's face, the teacher emphasized his point. "Yes, they fell into perdition. Many now inhabit the forsaken land of Lone due in part to my unbalanced teaching. I didn't give the students what they needed—I gave them what they wanted. I didn't want to lose their acceptance or my popularity. This caused me to build improperly. I didn't uproot the weak and faulty areas in their lives. I covered them with insights that only served to fuel their self-seeking desires.

"Remember the warning given to instructors in the ancient writings: 'Because they lead my people astray, saying, "Peace," when there is no peace, and because, when a flimsy wall is built, they cover it with whitewash, therefore tell those who cover it with whitewash that it is going to fall.'[4] Many of my students erected and sheltered their lives with temporal things. I knew deep in my conscience that these were flimsy walls, but I didn't warn them. I said all was well when it wasn't. I encouraged their course and solidified their deception.

"I yet grieve for my former students now in Lone. There are some who made it to Affabel. But many of those who embraced only the positive teachings"—looking over his shoulder, Motivator dropped his voice to a whisper—"are found in these back rows. Their lives were wastefully spent and their efforts consumed with fire before this Judgment Seat."

Selfish questioned, "Burned up before this Judgment Seat?"

"Yes," replied the teacher. "Do you not remember the ancient writings? 'Now anyone who builds on that foundation may use gold, silver, jewels, wood, hay, or straw. But there is going to come a time of testing at the judgment day to see what kind of work each builder has done. Everyone's work will be put through the fire to see whether or not it keeps its value. If the work survives the fire, that builder will receive a reward. But if the work is burned up, the builder will suffer great loss. The builders themselves will be saved, but like someone escaping through a wall of flames.'"5

The famous teacher continued, "The foundation the ancient apostle spoke of is the lordship of Jalyn, upon which we both know is the only way a person can enter this kingdom. However, once we truly belong to Jalyn, we should build upon this foundation.

"When measured by the ancient writings, my life fell short of Jalyn's righteous standards, and I failed in the area of my influence on those I taught. I didn't use my authority to impact these students for the cause of Affabel and, inevitably, I lost my reward. Remember what the great teacher of old, Paul, said concerning those he'd been called to influence. 'After all, what gives us hope and joy, and what is our proud reward and crown? It is you! Yes, you will bring us much joy as we stand together before our Lord.'6

"I knew the truths of Jalyn well when I first began to teach, but I allowed insecurity, the desire for the approval of others, and pride to sway me. It wasn't long before I strayed from what I knew. Eventually I started living what I preached. As I drifted, I lost sight of the warnings of Jalyn in my own personal life. I was deceived. The perspective on popularity and favor is very different here than in Endel. Much of what we considered great there is considered least here."

Selfish soberly asked, "Motivator, my friend told me Jalyn changes our names. What is your new name?"

The teacher smiled. "My name is Humbled." With that he inclined his head and stepped back to his place. Selfish turned to the Chief Guard, who nodded, affirming everything he had heard from Humbled was true.

Selfish continued toward the throne. He wasn't as confident now as when he was first called into the hall. He reflected on his life. What were his motives? Did he rule for Jalyn's glory or out of selfish ambition? How had he conducted his life? Was it in line with the words of Jalyn, or was he likewise deceived? Did he build others, or did he use them to build his own success?

A Ruler

Selfish was passing through the midsection of the Great Hall. He noticed the citizens here looked even more regal, if that were possible. Each looked at him with such love and acceptance. He drew comfort from their eyes and facial expressions. This helped immensely because he was feeling quite unsure about himself and what he was about to face.

It seemed to take ages for Selfish to make it to the throne. With each step he reviewed so many aspects of his years in Endel. He still was hopeful that he might be commissioned as a ruler with Jalyn because of his success as mayor.

Now Selfish was in the midst of the underrulers of Jalyn. He noticed their royal apparel and the crowns upon their heads. Each of them held a scepter. They were truly the most regal of all the citizens of this great city. He was amazed that any human could appear so glorious.

Among these underrulers Selfish noticed a former secretary to one of the city council members. *Why is she seated on one of the thrones?* wondered Selfish. She never stood out to him at school. She'd graduated a year before him. He really didn't know her personally because she was of a more reserved nature.

The woman stepped forward, and the Chief Guard stopped and bowed to her. She greeted Selfish with an embrace and a warm smile. "Welcome to Affabel, Selfish. I'm Patient. Jalyn asked me to speak with you before you come before him. I am one of his rulers in Affabel."

Selfish spoke without thinking. "A ruler? How could you be a ruler? You never did anything in Endel." He blushed at the realization of how out-of-line and insensitive his statement was.

Patient nodded as though she understood. "Don't be embarrassed by your statement. Deception cannot hide within this hall or in the great city. You are only being honest. In Endel, you were concerned with both image and reputation. This trains many to speak deceptively while being unaware of their folly. Here words are very important, but motives and intentions are even weightier, as they are always apparent here. You will learn this soon enough as you are judged for every word you spoke in Endel."

"Every word!" cried Selfish. "Do you mean every single word of every conversation?"

"Yes," replied Patient, "Every word. Remember the statement of Lord Jalyn in the ancient writings. 'You can be sure that on the Judgment Day everyone will have to give account of every *useless word* he has ever spoken. Your words will be used to judge you—to declare you either innocent or guilty.'[7] Useless words are vain, idle, or careless, all of which are contrary to the nature of Jalyn."

Selfish questioned, "I always thought we'd have to give an account of the huge lies or great truths we'd spoken, along with the good deeds and major accomplishments we achieved." He pondered a moment, then finished, "What am I about to face?"

Patient replied, "The ancient writings clearly state, 'Your reward depends on what you say and what you do.'[8] So you will be judged not only for everything you did but also for every word you spoke. This includes evil, good, and even idle language that proceeded out of your mouth. However, not only your words and works will be examined. The motives behind them will be judged as well. You will also be judged by the thoughts you embraced. Do not forget that Jalyn's judgment is righteous, 'testing the mind and the heart.'[9] As he himself stated, 'I, Jalyn, search all hearts and examine secret motives. I give all people their due rewards, according to what their actions deserve.'[10] He examines not only every action and word but the intentions behind them as well."

Patient continued, "This is why you are so shocked to see me on a throne. Your judgment of me was according to my accomplishments in the light of Endel. Jalyn's judgment was in a different light; it is the one that you are beginning to see now and will shortly see vividly. My dear brother, you will receive a just reward for your life in Endel."

Selfish had never experienced this kind of hard truth. Yet it was saturated with such love, a love he had never known. He now knew Jalyn must be a loving, compassionate ruler, for he had just experienced a measure of this from an underruler. Patient's words were correction encased in love. He realized love was not about pleasing others; it was about truth.

Patient inclined her head. "Your king awaits you." With that, she stepped back to her throne and the Chief Guard motioned Selfish on to walk alone before the throne. The guard would wait on the lower tier of the platform where the thrones of the underrulers were located.

Selfish before Jalyn

As he had been instructed, Selfish cautiously climbed the steps to the plateau just below the majestic throne. He then looked up and beheld the king himself. No one in this entire assembly was as handsome, regal, and majestic as Jalyn. His splendor was both captivating and awesome. Selfish had never seen anyone like this man. He knew immediately no one could resist his wisdom and strength.

Gazing into Jalyn's eyes for the first time, Selfish recognized that the king was more tender and terrifying than he could have imagined. His eyes gazed right through Selfish, who felt naked. It was clear nothing about him was hidden here. Selfish lost all confidence of a favorable judgment, but he no longer cared. He now desired truth more than anything else.

Jalyn said, "Welcome to my kingdom, Selfish. I've longed for this moment. You were a ruler of my people in Endel. Are you worthy to rule and sit upon one of the thrones in Affabel?"

This normally confident man, who was never at a loss for words, was now speechless. He once felt he could do a great job of leading in Affabel, but after all the conversations he'd had in the Great Hall, he imagined his thoughts were most likely deluded.

Jalyn asked an underruler who was close in proximity, "How many citizens did Selfish impact for my kingdom?"

Very few were named. Selfish was shocked and speechless at this revelation.

The king then asked the same ruler, "What is the number of citizens Patient impacted for this kingdom?"

"Just over five thousand, my lord," replied the ruler.

"How can this be?" blurted out Selfish. "She was just a secretary, and I was the mayor. How could my number be so few and hers so vast?"

Jalyn firmly replied, "I didn't ask how many were influenced but how many were influenced for the kingdom!"

His tone softened but remained resolute. "Even your former teacher, Motivator—now known as Humbled—had more influence on people's lives than you did. However, very little of that influence extended into this realm. This is why he is not a ruler in the city. The influence that endures this Judgment Seat is in accordance with my ways and my kingdom."

Jalyn continued, "Allow me to share with you some of the ways Patient influenced over five thousand people. She cheerfully gave to the school, both financially and through service. Therefore, all who were benefited by the school's ministry were credited to her."

Selfish countered, "But I too gave to the school."

Jalyn replied, "Your contributions were motivated by the desire to appease your conscience or maintain or repair your reputation. For this you received your full reward in Endel. Patient, on the other hand, gave out of passion for the kingdom and love for people.

"Patient led a man named Brutal to my service. At this moment he is in the Hall of Life awaiting his judgment. He will be renamed Evangelist because he became a great communicator of my ways. He personally influenced over a thousand lives for the kingdom. All those lives he built were credited to Patient's account because she led him to my service and supported the school that trained him."

Selfish remembered Brutal from Endel. He had thought Brutal too zealous in his beliefs. He was a contributing writer for the community newspaper and frequently shared in his columns about the citizens' lack of commitment to Affabel. He also rallied numerous Endelites to contact council members and request their support for the school's expansion. He made known his displeasure when Selfish swayed the vote and denied the school the land. For these reasons Selfish had disliked Brutal. Now he felt ashamed as he realized that all Brutal stood for was in line with Affabel's advancement. How could Selfish have been so blind?

Jalyn continued to show other ways Patient had influenced the lives of Endelites for the kingdom. There were many little things that added together to count for so much. She treated everyone kindly out of a pure heart of love. She was generous to those in need, and she was resolute in her firm stance for truth.

When the king was through discussing Patient, he reviewed Selfish's life extensively. As Patient foretold, every motive, word, and deed was evaluated.

Selfish saw the good he had done in the king's name but was overwhelmed by how many of his works were motivated by self-protection, reputation, and selfish motives. By the time the review was complete, Selfish felt certain he was doomed.

He cried out before the king, "I deserve to be punished the rest of my life. I deserve Lone! I've wasted so much and produced so little in return for the talents and responsibilities I had." The pain Selfish felt was indescribable; tears were streaming down his face. This man who'd been so confident before entering the Great Hall was now grasping for a thread to hang onto. All he had left was the hope of mercy, but even this he didn't really believe he deserved. He braced himself in anticipation of hearing the king pronounce his sentence to Lone.

After moments of heavy silence, the king finally spoke. "Selfish, you are my servant. You believed in me and submitted to my lordship, even though you wasted so much. I love you, and I welcome you into my kingdom for the rest of your life."

Selfish was stunned. He looked up, then burst into tears—not of sorrow but of tremendous joy. He was overwhelmed by the mercy and goodness of this great king. In a split second, much of what he'd heard of Jalyn's character became clear. Only seconds earlier, he had felt such doom and pain as he never imagined could exist. He deserved nothing except to be an outcast. He deserved to be condemned; the examination of his life showed it. Now, with the most tender and kind words imaginable, this awe-inspiring king was welcoming him to the majestic city. What mercy! What amazing love!

Selfish had watched as just about everything he had done in Endel was burned up, but still he heard the words, "I love you, and I welcome you into my kingdom." He understood that what his friend Content said was true. Anything he would receive was much more than he deserved.

The king spoke again, "Selfish, you shall no longer be known by your former name. Behold, I give you a new name. In my kingdom you shall be known as Unpretentious. I've prepared a residence for you in the flat-lands, and your occupation will be that of landscaper. Though you will not be a ruler in this city, you will assist me in ruling the outer realms."

Selfish questioned, "Rule with you in outer realms?"

Jalyn responded, "All who live in this city are rulers. My realm spreads to the farthest corners of the planet; there are many other cities in my kingdom. The citizens of these outer cities have not gone through training in Endel as the citizens of Affabel did, nor did they face the judgment. Consequently, they do not have the superior abilities the citizens of this city have. Though you will not be a leader in the city of Affabel itself, you will assist me in administrating my rule globally. Your specific assignment will be to lead through serving and training all the landscapers in the twenty cities on the continent of Bengilla."

Selfish bowed his head and wept. The kindness of the king was overwhelming.

The king walked over to a table and picked up an object, then turned and headed back toward Unpretentious. He walked down to the plateau and said, "Now, take and eat this piece of fruit."

Unpretentious took the fruit from Jalyn's hand and partook. It was the most delicious food he had ever tasted. It seemed to clear his mind and heart. His thoughts overflowed with great love and a desire to serve. As he ate, he was cleansed from his former pain and dark thoughts. He felt invigorated, happy, and full of hope and faith. It didn't take long for him to conclude the fruit was from the famous Tree of Life the teachers spoke of in class. A huge smile came over Unpretentious's face as Jalyn watched in pleasure.

Jalyn then said, "Turn and face your family."

Unpretentious cautiously turned. He still felt a slight amount of shame, knowing everyone had heard and seen the details of his life. When he had turned completely, the crowd roared with applause and shouts of joy. Music played, and some citizens even danced. Unpretentious could hardly believe the love and acceptance he felt from these regal citizens. It was the medicine that brought complete healing from all his errors in Endel.

Unpretentious turned and saw the most glorious and joyful smile on Jalyn's face. It was then he noticed the king's eyes. They looked at Unpretentious with love and warmth such as he had never seen before. Now he could hear Jalyn's thoughts, as Patient and the others had heard his. They were thoughts of acceptance, delight, and anticipation of years of bliss to come for this citizen he loved so much. Unpretentious fell to his knees and thanked the king. The king raised him to his feet, gave him a huge hug, and with a smile said, "Welcome, friend."

Then Unpretentious was escorted to his place toward the rear of the auditorium, where he would await the judgment of his fellow Endelites. Every tear had been wiped away. There was no more sorrow, pain, or crying. The former things had passed.

Charity and Her Judgment

The morning progressed, and all the citizens were called out of the Hall of Life—with the exception of Charity. She remained alone. This was not a burden because the room was filled with several beautiful books by authors from the city. She was reading the *Second Chronicle of Affabel* when the Chief Guard came to call her. He spoke tenderly. "Charity, your king awaits you."

Her heart raced with joy. She would now have the privilege of beholding the one she longed to see and loved. She had waited years for this moment, and now it was upon her. The guard smiled as she approached, and they walked together to the Great Hall.

Once the Great Hall's doors opened, Charity was overwhelmed by the magnificence she beheld. Her focus, however, was the distant throne of Jalyn. At this point all she could see was his outline. Her eyes swept the audience of the regal citizens of Affabel. *Oh what exceptional people*, she thought. *How could I ever call these regal men and women my peers?*

She noticed the citizens all bowed as she passed. Why would these stately men and women bow to her? They were handsome and beautiful, in outfits of increasing glory as she approached the throne. They looked as though they were superhuman. How could people such as these bow, especially to her?

Charity recognized several people she knew from Endel. Their smiles were full of excitement and love for her. She wanted to stop and embrace each but sensed it was not the proper time. She noticed Ruthless and couldn't help herself. She ran over and gave him a huge hug. The two rejoiced together.

After their embrace, Ruthless bowed to her and said, "Welcome to your new home."

Charity said, "Why do you bow to me, Ruthless? I'm not a god to be worshipped."

The regal citizen replied, "There is a difference between worship and honor. Only our lord is to be worshiped, but in this kingdom we honor those who served us well in Endel. We honor as well those who rule among us. We didn't understand the importance of honor in Endel.

"Charity, you served me in Endel. If it had not been for your obedience to the king, I would never be here; I would abide in the forsaken land of Lone. I am first and foremost indebted and grateful to the king, but I am also grateful and indebted to you. It will be my pleasure to serve and honor you the rest of my life."

He continued, "Charity, my name is no longer Ruthless. Lord Jalyn changed my name to Reconciled at this Judgment Seat. I'm one who was shown possibly the greatest mercy before our king."

Charity replied, "Reconciled. What a magnificent name. Dear friend, I didn't reach out to you in Endel so that you would serve me in return. I did it because I loved you and cared about your life and destiny."

"Your motives are exactly the reason I will honor and serve you. You will be greatly rewarded by the king. You labored out of love for Jalyn. You never reached out to gain the recognition of your fellow followers or to receive a reward. Jalyn delights in those who reach out to others with his love. It was so important we caught his heart, not just his vision, while in Endel. You did both, dear sister, and your heart motives were imparted to me. This is why I reached out so passionately to so many my last week in Endel. Now I've been rewarded handsomely for my labor even though it was brief."

Charity smiled. "Reconciled, I am so happy for you. I will serve you the rest of my life."

"Charity, you already speak as one who has lived in Affabel for years," Reconciled responded. "We live to serve one another in this great city. In fact, those of us who lead are the greatest servants here. We have the heaviest responsibilities, and it's our delight to bear them. It's different than in Endel. The leaders here don't seek to be served but rather rejoice that they are given greater opportunities to minister. The greatest joy of any citizen here is to serve first our king, second our fellow citizens—especially those who influenced us in Endel—and finally the citizens of the outer realms, of whom you shall soon learn."

Reconciled concluded, "My dear sister, I'm proud of you. Go to your king. He longs to see and reward you for your service to him." With that, the two embraced. Charity rejoined the guard, and they proceeded toward the throne.

Charity before Jalyn

Jalyn's features were now in clear view, for Charity was roughly seventy-five feet from the throne. As she passed the underrulers, she didn't even notice them bowing; her gaze was on Jalyn. She was awed by his majestic splendor.

Charity climbed the steps and, upon reaching the plateau, fell prostrate before her king. Jalyn stepped down and raised her to her feet. He spoke affectionately. "Charity, my dear servant, welcome to my kingdom. I've longed for this moment, to meet you in person."

Charity responded, "Sir, it is I who've greatly longed for this moment. You are my king. I hope now to be in your presence the rest of my life that I may serve you more fully."

The king then said, "Come and possess the kingdom which has been prepared for you ever since the creation of the world. I was hungry and you fed me, thirsty and you gave me a drink; I was a stranger and you received me in your home, naked and you clothed me; I was sick and you took care of me, in prison and you visited me."

Charity responded in shock, "When, Lord, did I ever see you hungry and feed you, or thirsty and give you a drink? When did I ever see you a stranger and welcome you in my home, or naked and clothe you? When did I ever see you sick or in prison and visit you?"

The king replied, "I tell you, whenever you did this for one of the least important of these brothers or sisters of mine, you did it for me!"[11]

Jalyn then showed Charity how she had so greatly ministered to him by serving his people and obeying his laws. Her life was reviewed: each word, deed, thought, and motive of her heart. Everything was revealed— her service, her giving to the school, the love she showed fellow citizens, her refusal to take part in careless or inappropriate activities and discussions, the persecution she received for her passion for Jalyn, her labor to serve others through the restaurant, her reaching out to wayward souls, the hours of sighing and weeping for the lost, the stances she took in strictly adhering to Jalyn's ways, her being excluded from social gatherings because of her zeal for Jalyn, her refusal to speak against fellow citizens or partake of gossip, and the list extensively continued.

Charity was shocked at all the ways she had affected and influenced others. Much of what she did to bring glory to Jalyn wasn't consciously planned or thought out. She was just following closely the manner of life taught in the ancient writings.

There were some things Charity did that were burned up. These brought her great sorrow and remorse for the missed opportunities or the errors she'd committed. However, only a small fraction of her life's labor was lost.

Charity's Reward

After the review of her final words and thoughts, the king looked to an underruler sitting close by and asked, "How many lives did Charity influence for my kingdom?"

The ruler replied, "My lord, 5,183. A little more than one-sixth of the population of the community."

Charity was surprised. "How could it be so many?"

Jalyn replied, "Recall in the ancient writings that I promised to 'multiply the seed you have sown and increase the fruits of your righteousness.'[12] Charity, my kingdom works on the multiplication principle."

The king then showed in greater detail how her obedient efforts multiplied to influence the masses, even though she wasn't a leader in the community. The ripple effects were staggering. Jalyn added, "As it is written, '[The benevolent person] scatters abroad; he gives to the poor; his deeds of justice and goodness and kindness and benevolence will go on and endure forever!'[13] A life submitted to me will result in a scattering effect of which no citizen is fully aware until he or she stands before this Judgment Seat. For this reason, many did not obey in the small matters because they saw them as insignificant. Yet most often it is the seemingly insignificant matters that produce the greatest harvest in this kingdom. The key was your obedience no matter the circumstances."

Jalyn then said, "Charity, do you see the unoccupied throne to your left, which is near mine?"

She replied, "Yes, my lord."

"This will be your throne on which to sit, and you will rule with me for the rest of your life."

Charity was in complete shock. "Lord, I'm not worthy to rule. I was simply a restaurant owner. There are so many who are more gifted than I. How could I rule with you in such a magnificent kingdom? Selfish was a great leader in our community. How about him? Please give me a job that just serves you or your people."

Jalyn responded, "Selfish is in the rear of the Great Hall and will be a landscaper in the sections of our city called the flatlands. He will also serve landscapers in selected outer cities. However, you shall be a ruler because of the love you showed me and my people. Your endurance, loyalty, and humility have secured you this honor. Do you not recall my words from the ancient writings? 'For everyone who exalts himself will be humbled (ranked below others who are honored or rewarded), and he who humbles himself (keeps a modest opinion of himself and behaves accordingly) will be exalted (elevated in rank).'[14] Not only shall you rule with me, but I've prepared a glorious home for you on the coast of the Great Sea, near my home in the Regal Center. I know how much you love water and the sound of waves, so I've granted your desire and delight. I grant all faithful servants their hearts' desires."

Charity was speechless.

The king continued, "You shall be governor over ten districts in the city. There are eleven other governors along with you, overseeing a total of 120 districts in the city of Affabel. You'll work closely with me along with the other seventy-seven rulers in our city who sit upon these thrones. The other rulers have governing authority over areas such as education, manufacturing, entertainment, the arts, and various other fields. The seventy-seven rulers, my Father, and I are the ones who plan, forecast, and oversee life in Affabel. You will be one of my trusted advisors and liaisons between my citizens and me.

"Not only shall you rule with me in this city, but as do the other seventy-seven rulers, you shall also have leadership over the cities of the outer realm. I give you charge over the twenty cities on the continent of Bengilla. You shall be prime minister of this continent. All those who live and lead there shall report to you. You will only report to me."

As Jalyn spoke these words to Charity, Unpretentious stood in the back, full of joy for his fellow classmate. However, his joy was mixed with a twinge of regret as he thought of how he'd had the opportunity to influence thousands of lives for the kingdom and did not. He could have been one of these underrulers privileged to work directly with Jalyn. He was thankful for his acceptance in the kingdom of Affabel, but he realized he had wasted time in his short stay in Endel and it would affect the rest of his 130-year life.

The king then said to the Chief Guard, "Bring the Crown of the Overcomer and the Scepter of Rulership to me."

Once Jalyn received them, he placed the crown on Charity's head. "Well done!" the king exclaimed. "You are a trustworthy servant. You have been faithful with the little I entrusted to you, so you will be governor of ten districts and twenty cities as your reward."[15]

Then the king handed her the scepter and said, "You shall no longer be called Charity, for I give you a new name. You shall be called Cherished Overcomer. For did I not foretell all the citizens of Endel, 'To him who overcomes and does my will to the end, I will give authority over the districts and nations—he will rule them with an iron scepter, just as I have received authority from my Father'?"[16]

Jalyn walked over to the table that contained one last piece of fruit. He brought it to Cherished Overcomer and said, "My dear friend and fellow ruler, you may partake of the fruit from the Tree of Life."

As Cherished Overcomer ate, she experienced a powerful cleansing and purifying, just as the others had experienced when eating this most delicious food. Her thoughts overflowed with even greater love, and her desire to serve expanded to a magnitude she had not previously known. She was cleansed from any former pain or dark thoughts of Endel. All things were made new. She felt totally invigorated, happy, and full of hope and faith. She looked up to Jalyn and smiled. Then, without knowing exactly why, they laughed joyously together. This was the beginning of a lifelong companionship.

Jalyn escorted Charity up to his throne and said, "Cherished Overcomer, turn and face your family."

She turned to thunderous applause. Great sounds of joy and dancing overtook the audience. It was more than had been witnessed at any other judgment. The atmosphere was filled with exuberant rejoicing and celebration. A radiant smile filled the face of Cherished Overcomer, and the outpouring of such love amazed her. Her king put his arm around her and with great joy proclaimed, "Well done, good and faithful servant. Enter into the joy of your lord!"[17]

Thus concludes our story of the great king, his servants, and the kingdom of Affabel.

A Word of Instruction and Caution

In this chapter we've glimpsed what the judgment of saints will look like. I cannot overstress the fact that the glory of Christ's Judgment Seat will be much greater than any glory depicted by this story. However, this allegory illustrates many truths reflected in the kingdom of God.

The details of this story are not meant to establish truth, rather to amplify and convey it. When Jesus told parables, you saw the points He made through the stories and did not stumble over the minute details that had no real relevance to the truth He was communicating.

Even so, I've attempted to carefully stress the important points of this story that have relevance to the eternal kingdom of Christ. By the time you are finished with this book, you will be able to reread the allegory and most likely glean even greater depths from the teachings of Scripture relayed in the surrounding chapters.

CHAPTER 9

HEAVEN

As for me, I will see Your face in righteousness;
I shall be satisfied when I awake in Your likeness.
—Psalm 17:15

Let's now discuss the passing of the righteous. Just as there is a temporary abode for the unbeliever, called Hades, and later a final home, called the Lake of Fire, there are two residential locations for believers who have died. The present home is referred to by most as *heaven*, but it is scripturally referred to as *the heavenly Jerusalem*. The final home of the righteous will also be called Jerusalem, but it will be located on earth. This is the city that will come down from heaven after the final judgment. It is called the *New Jerusalem* (see Revelation 21:2).

Jerusalem Above

You have come to Mount Zion and to the city of the living God, the heavenly Jerusalem, to an innumerable company of angels, to the general assembly and church of the firstborn who are registered in heaven, to God the Judge of all, to the spirits of just men made perfect, to Jesus the Mediator of the new covenant . . . (Hebrews 12:22–24)

The heavenly Jerusalem, or "Jerusalem above" (see Galatians 4:26), is a city, as depicted by Affabel in our allegory. It is built on a mountain called Zion. The Father and Son live there, as do countless angels. The general assembly and the church of the firstborn reside there along with the Old Testament saints and those in Christ who have passed on.

Notice that "the *spirits* of just men made perfect" are found in this city as well. Who are these people, since the writer has already listed both the Old and New Testament saints who've gone on to their reward?

Recall that when we are reborn through the Spirit of God, we become brand-new creations. Our spirits are made perfect in the likeness of Christ and we are found in Him. In this verse the writer does not refer to people's souls or bodies, only their spirits. I personally believe this refers to the saints serving Jesus here on earth. Think of it! The writer of Hebrews compels us, "Let us therefore come boldly to the throne of grace" (Hebrews 4:16). The throne of grace is located in the midst of the city of God, and this invitation is spoken to us who are on earth. Could it be that many who yet live here on earth are well known in the throne room because they come often through prayer?

We are spirits with souls—the soul is a combination of intellect, will, and emotion—who now live in physical bodies. Jesus said the only way we can truly worship God is in "spirit and truth" (John 4:24). Paul reemphasizes this: "For God is my witness, whom I *serve with my spirit* in the gospel of His Son" (Romans 1:9). Because our spirits have been created in the image of God and we have been born again, we have the ability—through the blood of Jesus and the power of the Holy Spirit—to go into the throne room of God anytime we have need or desire to worship.

Visits to Heaven

The Jerusalem above is presently located in a place called the third heaven. It is a real place the apostle Paul visited before his death. He wrote:

> I will go on to visions and revelations from the Lord. I know a man in Christ who fourteen years ago was caught up to the third heaven. Whether it was in the body or out of the body I do not know—God

knows. And I know that this man—whether in the body or apart from the body I do not know, but God knows—was caught up to paradise and heard inexpressible things, things that no one is permitted to tell. (2 Corinthians 12:1–4 NIV)

Bible scholars agree Paul was talking about himself. In fact, in the New Living Translation, verse two is recorded as, "I was caught up into the third heaven fourteen years ago." Notice that Paul was unaware whether he was in his body or out of it. This could only be explained by heaven being a real and physical place. I find there are many who think it is an invisible area where people float around as ghosts. No, it is a physical place with streets, trees, animals, buildings, water, and the like.

I know several people who have been to heaven and back, just like Paul, but let me share one of my favorite stories. I have a friend, a pastor named Greg. In October 1979, on his first evening of ministry, he came home from the meeting to find his wife crouched down on their staircase and weeping uncontrollably. He knew immediately something was seriously wrong. He soon learned that his ten-year-old son Justin[1] had brought a small television set into the bathroom to watch a football game while taking a bath. He accidentally pulled the TV into the bathtub and was electrocuted.

When Greg found his son, Justin had no pulse, his flesh was cold and blue, and his eyes were fully dilated, which indicated there was no brain activity. Greg had received paramedic and first aid training while working as a deputy sheriff for the Los Angeles County Sheriff's Department and had witnessed many deaths. If he had walked into a similar situation as a police officer, he would have pronounced the victim dead and called the coroner.

But Greg was a believer who knew the power of prayer. He started praying and doing CPR on his son. After a few minutes the paramedics arrived, so Greg left the medical work to the experts while he continued to pray. They were there for forty-five minutes without any success in bringing Justin back. The EKG machine had been a flat line the whole time. The paramedics were becoming restless waiting for what they thought was a fanatic to give up.

Greg finally prayed, "Father, I don't have any more faith. I've exhausted mine, but I know in Your Word You speak of another faith." (He was referring to the gift of faith spoken of in 1 Corinthians 12:9.)

Greg said he felt something like a hand on the top of his head. Once he did, he sensed a very strong force and authority rising up from within his spirit, and he shouted at his son, "You will live and not die, in the name of Jesus!"

All of a sudden the EKG machine started beeping with pulse motions appearing on the screen. The paramedics jumped with excitement. By the time they got Justin down the stairs and into the ambulance, he had gone from blue to pink, his eyes were fully restored, and his body was warm.

Greg was so excited. His son was alive and well. He also had a great miracle story to tell all his friends what God had done. What he didn't realize was that the fight for his son's life had only begun.

The doctors reported that the boy was in a coma. After examination, they found kidney tissue coming out of the catheter. This meant, in layman's terms, that his body had had a meltdown. They told Greg that if his son lived, he would be a vegetable. Later on, they reported that his socially functional age would be that of a three-month-old baby, having an IQ of 0.01.

To make a long story short, after seven months of his family's praying and refusing to give up, Justin suddenly came out of the coma. His father was by his bedside when this occurred and started firing questions at his son, to which he received immediate answers. Justin went on to graduate from high school, UCLA, and Bible school, all with honors. He was even the senior class president of his high school. Today he is happily married and has two children.

"Dad, I've Been with Jesus"

Three days after Justin got out of the hospital, Greg noticed his son's face was glowing. He asked, "What's going on, Justin?"

Justin replied, "Dad, I've been with Jesus. When the TV hit the bathtub, I didn't feel a thing. A huge angel grabbed my right arm and took me right out of my body. We flew through a tunnel at an amazing rate of acceleration. We hit the speed of light before landing on one of the streets of heaven."

Justin went on to tell his father that the streets were not golden. They were made of pure gold; he could see through them. On earth, gold cannot be refined as wholly as it is in heaven, but it is transparent in its purest state. Even on earth, it is often used in windows to give them a gold color (think of the shields on older astronaut helmets, the cockpit windows of some jets, or the windows of certain buildings).

Justin shared that the first people to greet him on the heavenly street were relatives who had died. He named each of them, some of whom he had never met or whose names (which his mom and dad recognized) he had never even known. There was also a lady named Phyllis in this welcoming group. She was a neighbor Justin's mother had prayed with to receive Jesus a month before Justin was electrocuted. She had died two weeks after her conversion.

Justin was conversing with all these people when suddenly he heard rustling and the group around him split apart. There stood Jesus.

The Lord took Justin on a tour of heaven. There were many streets and buildings; it was definitely a large city. The flowers, grass, and even rocks were all alive and singing in harmony. Justin said it seemed as if they were praising God. If he stepped on grass or a flower, it wouldn't be crushed. It immediately rebounded to its previous position. Justin noticed the colors were vibrant and bright, much more so than he'd seen on earth. There were even colors he'd never seen before. He also got the privilege of seeing His mother's, father's, and two siblings' mansions.

Then came the shock: Jesus told Justin he had to go back to earth. Justin didn't want to leave heaven, but Jesus brought him to a place where He pulled open a veil. Justin could see his father calling him back. Jesus said, "He is your father and has the authority to call you back."

Since that time, Justin has told his father to never call him back if he happens to die again—I found that part of the story amusing when Greg shared it with me. But heaven is so much better than earth that I've found those who experience it always have a very difficult time returning.

Paul also struggled with this, as he said to the Philippian church, "My yearning desire is to depart (to be free of this world, to set forth) and be with Christ, for that is far, far better" (Philippians 1:23 AMP). Not just better or far better but far, far better! Paul had experienced the City of God and wanted to return, but he chose to stay for the good of the kingdom.

Justin later shared with his father that he wasn't ten years old when he was in heaven. He had the body of a grown man. Many, including Justin, believe we will all be thirty-three years old when we are in our glorified bodies. That makes sense because this was Jesus's age when He was crucified, and Scripture says, "Yes, dear friends, we are already God's children, and we can't even imagine what we will be like when Christ returns. But we do know that when he comes we will be like him" (1 John 3:2 NLT).

This is just one of many real stories I could share. It, along with Scripture, shows the reality of heaven. Those who are faithful servants of Jesus shall enter this city upon leaving this earth.

Salvation of Spirit, Soul, and Body

As already stated, people's spirits become brand-new creations the moment they receive Jesus as their Lord. They are instantaneously remade in the likeness of Jesus. This is affirmed by the apostle John's statement: "As He is, so are we *in this world*" (1 John 4:17). As you can see, John distinctly addresses believers who are here on earth rather than those who have already gone on to their reward. A person who is truly born again by the Spirit of God is made perfect in spirit here and now.

Once our spirit is saved, then starts the process of the saving of our soul. As indicated earlier, the soul is comprised of our mind, will, and emotions. Our soul is saved or transformed by the Word of God and our obedience to it. The apostle James confirms this by stating, "So then, *my beloved brethren* . . . lay aside all filthiness and overflow of wickedness, and receive with meekness the *implanted word*, which is able to *save your souls*. But be *doers* of the word, and not hearers only, deceiving yourselves" (James 1:19, 21–22). It is important to note James is speaking to *brethren*, not unbelievers, regarding their souls' salvation. He emphasizes both hearing and obedience to the Word of God.

The soul is the only part of man whose rate of salvation we help determine. We cooperate by hearing and obeying God's Word, which in turn speeds up the process—or, conversely, we slow salvation's progress by disregarding what God has said. The transformation of our souls is crucial to our finishing well as believers.

Finally, there is one last part of us that must be saved: our bodies. Read carefully what Paul writes on this matter.

For we know that when this earthly tent we live in is taken down— when we die and leave these bodies—we will have a home in heaven, an eternal body made for us by God himself and not by human hands. We grow weary in our present bodies, and we long for the day when we will put on our heavenly bodies like new clothing. For we will not be spirits without bodies, but we will put on new heavenly bodies. Our dying bodies make us groan and sigh, but it's not that we want to die and have no bodies at all. We want to slip into our new bodies so that these dying bodies will be swallowed up by everlasting life. God himself has prepared us for this, and as a guarantee he has given us his Holy Spirit.

So we are always confident, even though we know that as long as

we live in these bodies we are not at home with the Lord. That is why
we live by believing and not by seeing. Yes, we are fully confident,
and we would rather be away from these bodies, for then we will be at
home with the Lord. (2 Corinthians 5:1–8 NLT)

Reading these words gives us great hope and even purifies our souls.
Notice Paul doesn't just mention but dwells on the fact that we will have
eternal bodies. In another place he states, "For the perishable must clothe
itself with the imperishable, and the mortal with immortality" (1 Corinthians 15:53 NIV). Our bodies will be no different than Jesus's, for
Scripture states, "We also shall be in the likeness of His resurrection"
(Romans 6:5), and, "Beloved, now we are children of God; and it has
not yet been revealed what we shall be, but we know that when He is
revealed, we shall be like Him" (1 John 3:2).

Let's consider Jesus's body after His resurrection. Any trait His physical body possessed, we'll have once we experience the salvation of our
bodies. Let's begin with what happened right at the tomb the morning
He arose. Mary Magdalene first discovered the empty tomb and wept,
thinking the Lord's body had been stolen.

. . . She turned around and saw Jesus standing there, and did not
know that it was Jesus. Jesus said to her, "Woman, why are you weeping? Whom are you seeking?"
  She, supposing Him to be the gardener, said to Him, "Sir, if You
have carried Him away, tell me where You have laid Him, and I will
take Him away." (John 20:14–15)

Jesus wasn't different in appearance from a normal man. He didn't
look like an alien from a sci-fi movie. Mary didn't recognize Him, for
she couldn't dare believe He was alive. She saw Jesus brutally murdered,
carried away, and buried. It wasn't until He spoke to her personally that
she could believe it was really Him. So she mistook Him for the gardener.

He therefore had a body that is very similar to the ones we possess.

Jesus's body didn't appear different than a normal man's. But we must ask, was Mary seeing a vision of His spirit, or did He actually have flesh? This question is answered clearly in a later story when Jesus appeared to His disciples. He said, "Why are you troubled? And why do doubts arise in your hearts? Behold My hands and My feet, that it is I Myself. Handle Me and see, for a spirit does not have *flesh* and *bones* as you see I have" (Luke 24:38–39).

Jesus has flesh and bones! So we too will have them. But notice Jesus says nothing about blood. That's because His blood was sprinkled on the Mercy Seat of God. Now what flows through His veins is, I believe, the glorious life of God.

Jesus was also able to eat physical food. We read, "But while they still did not believe for joy, and marveled, He said to them, 'Have you any food here?' So they gave Him a piece of a broiled fish and some honeycomb. And He took it and ate in their presence" (Luke 24:41–43).

Jesus's eating in His disciples' presence didn't happen just that one time. There were two other recorded incidents: one in the home of certain men He met on the road to Emmaus, and the other when He cooked breakfast for His eleven disciples by the sea. Therefore, we will be able to eat in our eternal bodies.

In His glorified body, Jesus could speak, sing, walk, hold objects, and so forth like a normal man, but He could also walk through walls and disappear in a flash!

You may question, "He had flesh and bone, but He could walk through walls and disappear?" Oh yes. See what John recorded: "That evening, on the first day of the week, the disciples were meeting behind locked doors because they were afraid of the Jewish leaders. Suddenly, Jesus was standing there among them!" (John 20:19 NLT)

In this encounter with His own, Jesus asked Thomas to put his fingers in His hands and his hand in His side. So again we definitely see Jesus had flesh and bone. How was it that He was suddenly standing among them when the doors were locked? He came through the wall and simply appeared—and He could just as easily disappear, which is recorded as well. After He broke bread with the men He met on the road to Emmaus, we're told, "Then their eyes were opened and they knew Him; and He vanished from their sight" (Luke 24:31).

We too will have the ability in our resurrected bodies to vanish and reappear in a different location. This explains how we'll be able to travel great distances in the new heaven and the new earth. We'll have to do this, because the City of God is 1,400 miles long and wide, saying nothing of the distance involved in travel to other galaxies. We'll also be able to drift in the air; recall that Jesus floated up to heaven after forty days of interacting with His disciples. One of the things Justin reported to his father (as has also been reported by others I know who've been to heaven) is that you can walk, float, or immediately translate somewhere. There were parts of Justin's tour with Jesus where he walked and other parts where he hovered and floated to locations.

The Millennial Reign of Christ

We need to turn our attention to the relocation of the City of God, but first let's discuss the events that will transpire beforehand. At the conclusion of the Church Age, there will be a seven-year tribulation. The man of lawlessness, the antichrist, will be revealed and will deceive many. He will oppose and exalt himself above all that is called God or worshipped. He will persecute the saints and lead many nations into great darkness in rebellion against God.

During this time period, the Lord will come for His saints. Some believe it will happen before the seven years begin, others midway, and still others at the end. That is a matter I will not discuss in this work. What's important is whether we are ready.

Paul discusses this "catching away" of the church a few times in the

New Testament. One such passage reads:

> For the Lord Himself will descend from heaven with a shout, with
> the voice of an archangel, and with the trumpet of God. And the
> dead in Christ will rise first. Then we who are alive and remain shall
> be caught up together with them in the clouds to meet the Lord in
> the air. And thus we shall always be with the Lord. (1 Thessalonians
> 4:16–17)

This is not the Second Coming of Christ because Jesus will not come
to the earth but will meet His faithful in the clouds. The Second Coming
occurs at the conclusion of the seven-year tribulation with Jesus returning on a white horse, leading the armies of heaven, a multitude of His
saints in their number (see Jude 14).

The antichrist, false prophet, world leaders, and armies of nations
will gather to fight against the Lord and His army. Jesus shall smite them
with His sword in a single day of battle, and the birds of the air will consume their flesh. This is commonly referred to as Armageddon because
it will occur at a place in the valley of Megiddo, which extends from
Mount Carmel southeast to Jerusalem (see Revelation 16:16; Revelation
19:11–21).

There will be multitudes of people throughout the world who neither rebelled against the Lord in this battle nor gave their allegiance to
the antichrist. Many theologians believe these people will survive and
go on living into the next age, commonly referred to as the millennial
reign of Christ. They will remain in their nations and will be subject to
Christ's global rule. They'll have natural bodies and continue to populate
the earth.

So in essence, two types of people will inhabit the earth after the
years of tribulation: those who survived the battle of Armageddon and
the saints who return with Jesus. The saints will have glorified bodies in

the likeness of King Jesus, and they will be the ones who rule with Him on the earth. It is not difficult to understand how the two groups will relate; it will be no different than Jesus's interaction with His followers after His resurrection. The glorified saints will be able to talk, walk, eat, and socialize with those inhabiting natural bodies.

Scripture shows that during this time there will be global peace—in fact, universal peace—because Satan and his cohorts will be bound for a thousand years. There will be no wars, prejudices, hatred, shame, crime, sickness, and so forth because of the great turning to God by all the nations. The prophet Micah states:

> In the last days, the Temple of the Lord in Jerusalem will become the most important place on earth. People from all over the world will go there to worship. Many nations will come and say, "Come, let us go up to the mountain of the Lord, to the Temple of the God of Israel. There he will teach us his ways, so that we may obey him." For in those days the Lord's teaching and his word will go out from Jerusalem. The Lord will settle international disputes. All the nations will beat their swords into plowshares and their spears into pruning hooks. All wars will stop, and military training will come to an end. Everyone will live quietly in their own homes in peace and prosperity, for there will be nothing to fear. The Lord Almighty has promised this! (Micah 4:1–4 NLT)

There will be global prosperity and a secure financial system because the nations will abide by the laws of God. It will be an amazing time!

The Great White Throne Judgment

After the thousand years end, Satan will be released from his prison for a short while. He will be given permission to go out and deceive the nations. This will not include the saints in their glorified bodies, only those in natural bodies who populate the nations, the ones who lived through Armageddon or were born during the Millennium.

Rebels will assemble together and surround the city of Jerusalem to make war, and then the fire of God will proceed from heaven and devour them. The devil will be cast into the "lake of fire and brimstone" and tormented day and night forever and ever. He will never be released again (see Revelation 20:7–10).

The Great White Throne Judgment will immediately follow. Hades will surrender the dead of every generation, spanning from the days of Adam to this final battle. All who did not enter into Jehovah's covenant in Old Testament times or submit to the lordship of Jesus thereafter will stand before the King and give an account, just as we saw in the judgments of Independent, Deceived, Faint Heart, and Double Life. Anyone whose name is not written in the Book of Life will be cast into the Lake of Fire with Satan and his cohorts forever.

The New Heaven and Earth

Once the existing heavens and earth are purged by fire (see 2 Peter 3:10–13), the new heaven and new earth will emerge. The apostle John writes, "I saw a new heaven and a new earth, for the first heaven and the first earth had passed away" (Revelation 21:1).

The apostle John then described the New Jerusalem's descent from above to be eternally located on earth. This city is referred to as the Lamb's wife or bride because it will be home to all the ransomed of the Lord, stretching from Adam to those received into glory at Christ's second coming. John gives an overall description of this New Jerusalem:

> So he took me in spirit to a great, high mountain, and he showed
> me the holy city, Jerusalem, descending out of heaven from God. It
> was filled with the glory of God and sparkled like a precious gem,
> crystal clear like jasper. Its walls were broad and high, with twelve

gates guarded by twelve angels . . . There were three gates on each side—east, north, south, and west . . .

The angel who talked to me held in his hand a gold measuring stick to measure the city, its gates, and its wall. When he measured it, he found it was a square, as wide as it was long. In fact, it was in the form of a cube, for its length and width and height were each 1,400 miles. Then he measured the walls and found them to be 216 feet thick (the angel used a standard human measure).

The wall was made of jasper, and the city was pure gold, as clear as glass. The wall of the city was built on foundation stones inlaid with twelve gems . . . The twelve gates were made of pearls—each gate from a single pearl! And the main street was pure gold, as clear as glass. (Revelation 21:10–21 NLT)

This city is breathtaking, a wonder like no earthly city we have ever seen. It will emanate opulence, radiance, and splendor. There will be no corruption whatsoever because it is utterly pure.

John continues his description:

And the angel showed me a pure river with the water of life, clear as crystal, flowing from the throne of God and of the Lamb, coursing down the center of the main street. On each side of the river grew a tree of life, bearing twelve crops of fruit, with a fresh crop each month. The leaves were used for medicine to heal the nations.

No longer will anything be cursed. For the throne of God and of the Lamb will be there, and his servants will worship him. And they will see his face, and his name will be written on their foreheads. And there will be no night there—no need for lamps or sun—for the Lord God will shine on them. And they will reign forever and ever. (Revelation 22:1–5 NLT)

Notice Scripture clearly reveals we will see God's face. What Moses longed for and was denied, we will behold. How awesome and exciting!

Also notice that the leaves of the tree of life will bring healing to *the nations*. This raises some interesting questions. Who will comprise these nations, since the saints will dwell in the city? Who will the saints reign over forever and ever? Will there be natural-born people alive during this time as well? Isaiah answers this.

> "Look! I am creating new heavens and a new earth—so wonderful that no one will even think about the old ones anymore. Be glad; rejoice forever in my creation! And look! I will create Jerusalem as a place of happiness. Her people [the redeemed saints] will be a source of joy. I will rejoice in Jerusalem and delight in my people. And the sound of weeping and crying will be heard no more." (Isaiah 65:17–19 NLT)

Now Isaiah turns to speak of people outside the New Jerusalem:

> "No longer will babies die when only a few days old. No longer will adults die before they have lived a full life. No longer will people be considered old at one hundred! Only sinners will die that young! In those days, people will live in the houses they build and eat the fruit of their own vineyards. It will not be like the past, when invaders took the houses and confiscated the vineyards. For my people will live as long as trees and will have time to enjoy their hard-won gains. They will not work in vain, and their children will not be doomed to misfortune. For they are people blessed by the Lord, and their children, too, will be blessed. I will answer them before they even call to me. While they are still talking to me about their needs, I will go ahead and answer their prayers! The wolf and lamb will feed together. The lion will eat straw like the ox. Poisonous snakes will strike no more. In those days, no one will be hurt or destroyed on my holy mountain.

I, the Lord, have spoken!" (Isaiah 65:20–25 NLT)

Many incorrectly apply this passage to the millennial reign of Christ. However, it clearly speaks of the age when the *new heaven* and new earth are in place. By examining the writings of both the apostle John and Isaiah, we learn that there are people who live outside the City of God during this period. They build their own homes in an everlasting time of universal peace and prosperity. These couldn't be the saints residing in the holy city, for they will have already had mansions prepared for them by Jesus Himself (see John 14:2–4).

Notice as well that there will be children born to these people. This also couldn't refer to the glorified saints, because Jesus made it clear that those with glorified bodies will not give birth to babies, for they'll not marry. He said, "For in the resurrection they neither marry nor are given in marriage, but are like angels of God in heaven" (Matthew 22:30). This was another fact Justin confirmed in his tour of heaven.

These nations will inhabit the new earth, enriching it with planting, harvesting, and building. They will multiply and replenish the Earth unhindered, just as Adam and his descendants would have done if he had not fallen.

How can this be logically explained? One possibility that can be argued is that once the Millennium begins, natural human life will be extended because our final enemy—death—will be destroyed (see 1 Corinthians 15:26). Jesus will have destroyed the curse of death, both spiritual and physical. Therefore, mankind could potentially endure the thousand-year period.

At the end of the Millennium, it may be that those in natural bodies are granted this gift of life forever if they didn't rebel against God when Satan was briefly loosed. The psalmist writes, "Therefore, the nations will praise you forever and ever" (Psalm 45:17 NLT). One way to bring understanding to this possibility is to view these people as being like Adam and Eve before the fall. Adam was not created for death but to live forever. This gift was lost through his disobedience; he brought the curse of death and decay onto his race.

Only the redeemed of Christ with glorified bodies will reside in the New Jerusalem. However, it appears from Scripture that those in natural bodies will be able to travel through the city, partake of its fruit, and worship the Lord. This is seen in John's writings:

> The nations of the earth will walk in [the New Jerusalem's] light, and the rulers of the world will come and bring their glory to it. Its gates never close at the end of day because there is no night. And all the nations will bring their glory and honor into the city. (Revelation 21:24–26 NLT)

In the beginning, man fell to the temptation of sin. The penalty was death, both physical and spiritual, resulting in eternal death. However, the Fall didn't deter God from His original *eternal plan* for man on earth.

Can God suffer a failure to His design because of man's disobedience? No. God instead reversed man's defeat into a blessing through Christ's redemption by gathering out of fallen mankind a *glorified heavenly people* who will eventually *reign* over humanity in the new earth. This helps us in understanding Jesus's words in the story of the faithful steward: "Well done, good servant; because you were faithful in a very little, *have authority over ten cities*" (Luke 19:17). Could these be cities in the Millennium and the eternal era of the new earth?

If the Fall hadn't occurred, God wouldn't have had a glorified class of people to help Him administrate and rule over the affairs of earth and the universe forever and ever. He foresaw this in His eternal wisdom; for this reason, Jesus is referred to as the "Lamb slain from the foundation of the world" (Revelation 13:8).

After the Millennium begins, and on into the eternal era of the new earth, God's original purpose—to populate this earth with natural men who will live forever—will be fulfilled. Jesus's words will be completely fulfilled: "Your kingdom come. Your will be done on earth as it is in heaven" (Matthew 6:10). It will be on earth just as Justin witnessed in heaven: beautiful new colors, living plants and rocks that sing praises to God, perfect architecture, living water, and so on. A truly perfect world!

Isaiah concludes his prophetic book by saying this of the new earth age:

> "As surely as my new heavens and earth will remain, so will you always be my people, with a name that will never disappear," says the Lord. "All humanity will come to worship me from week to week and from month to month. And as they go out, they will see the dead bodies of those who have rebelled against me. For the worms that devour them will never die, and the fire that burns them will never go out. All who pass by will view them with utter horror."
> (Isaiah 66:22–24 NLT)

The thought is rather sobering, but throughout all eternity, we will be able to go to a certain place and view the horrible fate of Satan, his angels, and mankind who rebelled against the Lord. Perhaps this is the wisdom of God to always keep before every creature the terrible consequence of sin and rebellion. Think of it: Satan fell into rebellion without a tempter. If God keeps this scene before His entire creation throughout eternity, it will be a strong deterrent from falling into the terrible sin Lucifer and his angels fell into.

As already stated, the glorified saints will live in the city of God, the New Jerusalem. They'll receive their rewards and eternal positions of service to the Eternal King prior to the Millennium at the Judgment Seat of Christ, which we will explore in depth in the next chapter.

CHAPTER 10

The Judgment Seat of Christ

But why do you judge your brother? Or why do you
show contempt for your brother? For we shall all
stand before the judgment seat of Christ . . . So then
each of us shall give account of himself to God.
—Romans 14:10, 12

W e shall all stand before the judgment seat of Christ." Who is Paul referring to, believers or unbelievers? In examining these scriptures in context, there's no misunderstanding: he is speaking to believers. Paul addresses the seriousness of a Christian judging or showing contempt for a fellow brother, saying those who do so will have to give an account.

Therefore, not only will unbelievers stand before God in judgment—as seen in earlier chapters—but all Christians will also stand before the throne of God to give an account of their lives here on earth. This is further emphasized in Paul's letter to Corinth, which we examined in the previous chapter:

> . . . We would rather be away from these bodies, for then we will be at home with the Lord. So our aim is to please him always, whether we are here in this body or away from this body. For we must all stand before Christ to be judged. We will each receive whatever we deserve for the good or evil we have done in our bodies. It is because we know this solemn fear of the Lord that we work so hard to persuade others. (2 Corinthians 5:8–11 NLT)

Again, it is evident Paul is not talking about the judgment of sinners but of Christians. His statement, "We would rather be away from these bodies, for then we will be at home with the Lord," gives no room for doubt as to whom he's addressing. No unbeliever will be at home with the Lord once he leaves his body. He will be immediately transported to Hades, and his eternal home is the Lake of Fire.

As stated earlier, the ungodly will stand before the judgment that has come to be known as the Great White Throne Judgment, which occurs long after the believer's judgment referred to in the above passage.

Let's quickly review what we observed in the previous chapter. Jesus will return to this earth with the armies of heaven, conquer the antichrist, throw Satan into prison, and then set up His rule in Jerusalem for a thousand years. Afterward, Satan will be released from the bottomless pit and will be permitted to deceive the nations for a short time. Fire from heaven will consume them, and the devil will be hurled into the Lake of Fire for all eternity. Then all the ungodly and unbelievers will be raised up from Hades to stand before the Great White Throne. Jesus refers to this as the resurrection of condemnation (see John 5:29). All those whose names are not written in the Book of Life will be cast into the Lake of Fire.

On the other hand, the believer's judgment will occur long before the Great White Throne Judgment. The timing of it is not made clear in Scripture. However, we do know it will take place sometime after the church is caught away in the clouds and before the thousand-year reign of Christ commences. So there are roughly a thousand years separating the two major judgments. (This is one of the points not reflected in our allegory of Affabel.)

Echoing the words of Romans, 2 Corinthians 5:10 says, "For we must all appear before the *judgment seat* of Christ." In both Romans 14 and 2 Corinthians 5, the English words *judgment seat* are translated from the single Greek word *bema. Strong's Concordance* defines this word as "a step, foot-breath, a rostrum [an elevated platform], i.e. a tribunal [a court of justice]."[1] The *UBS Commentary* states, "The judgment seat was the judicial bench of a city court in the Roman Empire. Paul uses this imagery to refer to the judging activity of Christ."[2] Based on all this, we will refer to the believer's judgment as the *Judgment Seat of Christ.*

The Judgment Seat of Christ is literally the divine tribunal of God. Scripture declares that the Father has committed all judgment to the Son (see John 5:22). Jesus Christ is not only our Savior. He is also our Judge and will soon judge His own household. The simplest way to define the original word for judgment is to say it is a decision resulting from an investigation—a decision *for* or *against.*

Numerous individuals in church are unaware that they will give an account of what they've done during their short stay on earth. Many have the erroneous idea that all future judgment is eradicated by their salvation. Indeed, Jesus's blood cleanses us from the sins that would have kept us from the kingdom; however, it does not exempt us from the judgment of how we conducted ourselves as believers, whether good or bad.

Eternal Decisions

The judgments or decisions rendered over us at Christ's judgment seat will be *eternal;* they will last forever, never being altered or changed.

Pause a moment and reflect back to our discussions in the first chapter when we tried to mentally grasp eternity. James states our temporary life on earth is a passing vapor (see James 4:14). This is his figurative way of comparing a lifetime of eighty to one hundred years with eternity. If he possessed the mathematical knowledge we have today, he could have been more exact in his portrayal. As a student of mathematics, I learned early in my education that anything divided by infinity is zero.

$$80 \text{ years} \div \text{infinity (eternity)} = 0$$
$$\text{or}$$
$$100 \text{ years} \div \text{infinity (eternity)} = 0$$

Any finite number divided by, or compared to, infinity is zero. It doesn't matter how long you live on earth. Even if you were to make it 150 years before dying, life on earth is zero compared to eternity. That means as believers in Jesus Christ, everything we do here in this zero window of time will determine *how* we spend eternity. Remember, *where* we spend eternity is determined by what we do with the cross of Jesus and His saving grace. But *how* we will live for eternity in His kingdom is determined by the way we live here as believers.

Do you recall in our allegory how Selfish and the others he met in the back parts of the Great Hall regretted the way they wasted their short time in Endel? A good part of their five years in Endel was spent on their own desires and benefits rather than being given entirely to the will of Jalyn. They faced the rest of their lives at a level far below their potential, for each had the opportunity to work with and live close to Jalyn, even to reign beside him in the city. They may or may not have enjoyed the brief time that followed their graduation from the school. Either way, their futures were now set. For the next 130 years, their lifestyle would be a direct result of how they lived those five short years. Think of it: 130 years compared with five years. That is a very long time. Few people even come close to living that long on earth. If only Selfish and the others would have considered this before their time in Endel expired, they most likely would have lived differently.

As sobering as the example in this allegory is, it doesn't come close to comparing with what we are discussing. So let's try another scenario. Imagine this. You are given one day, and how you spend that single twenty-four hour period will determine how you spend the next thousand years. Try to imagine a thousand years. That would date back before the birth of the United States of America, before Christopher Columbus set sail to discover the new world, even before the Norman conquest of England.

A thousand years is a very long time. Yet the rewards you receive— the position you hold, the job you do, the people you work with, the neighborhood you live in, the type of house you dwell in, the views you have from your house, and everything else about your life for a thousand years—will all be determined by how you spend that single day.

Do you think you would give it your best? How would you live? Would you live differently than you're living now? Would your priorities change? Would obeying the Master take absolute precedence? Would you read His words with greater care and seek to obey them more diligently? Would you seek to influence people's lives for the kingdom? Would you treat people differently? The list of possible lifestyle changes is endless. Yet this is nothing in comparison to what we are discussing here, for one day divided by 365,000 days (the equivalent of one thousand years) is still a finite number—not zero.

Let's go further. Let's say the way you spend that single day will determine how you spend the next one million years—your possessions, your job, the people you work with, they type of house you live in, your neighborhood, the car you drive, and so forth! Try to imagine this amount of time. We have no reference point, for mankind has only been on earth approximately six thousand years. So this would be over 150 times longer than mankind has been on earth. That in itself is almost unfathomable. Yet this also is nothing in comparison to what we are discussing, for one day divided by 365,000,000 days (the equivalent of one million years) is still a finite number—not zero. It makes no difference if I was to say a billion or a trillion years; you would still have a finite number when comparing it to one day.

So no matter how long we live on this earth, our time here compared to eternity is zero. Could this be why the apostle Paul tells us with urgency to live in such a way as to receive our maximum reward? In his letter to the Corinthians, he tells us that anyone who competes in athletics does so to win, then says to all of us:

> You also must run in such a way that you will win. All athletes practice strict self-control. They do it to win a prize that will fade away, but we do it for an eternal prize. So I run straight to the goal with

purpose in every step. I am not like a boxer who misses his punches. I discipline my body like an athlete, training it to do what it should. (1 Corinthians 9:24–27 NLT)

According to Paul, we live this life with a purpose: to receive an eternal prize that will never fade. In this life, we are to run to win. In order to win, we must develop tenacious discipline and self-control and live single-mindedly.

I've been active in athletics for years. When I played in the United States Tennis Association Circuit, Junior Davis Cup, and NCAA Division One tennis, I trained hard. I was on the courts as many as six hours per day, hitting sometimes hundreds of specific shots with my coach and fellow players. I read books about mental toughness on the court. I physically trained off-court by weightlifting, running, jumping rope, juggling to improve hand-eye coordination—the list is almost endless. I was so single-minded and full of purpose that my mother threatened to move my bed down to the tennis courts in our neighborhood. I steered clear of any activity or other sport that would hinder my progress. Why did I do this? To win. To be a champion. To be the best. And to receive the rewards of being the best.

It's slightly different in the kingdom. We are not competing against others, only ourselves, and our goal is to be well-pleasing to Jesus in everything we do (see 2 Corinthians 5:9). When we read the Scriptures carefully, we find out what our Lord desires in the way we treat people, what we pursue, what we give our time to, who we affect for eternity, how we give to His kingdom and to others, how we forgive others, and more. We will discuss this in more depth later. Bottom line: we should live to win!

A Wide Range of Rewards

Scripture shows that the eternal rewards and positions given to believers will not only differ but will span a wide range. They will vary from seeing everything lost and burned up all the way to reigning beside Christ for all eternity (see 1 Corinthians 3:15; Revelation 3:21).

Many flinch when they hear the terms *lost* and *burned up* in regard to their lives. They find it hard to believe this could ever happen in heaven. However, this is made crystal clear to us in Scripture.

Before I share these verses, let me preface by explaining that many times in Scripture, the metaphor of building is used to represent individual lives. Other times, Scripture speaks of the church as a single building or temple. In both uses of the metaphor, we are depicted as the builders in regard to how we affect our own lives, others' lives, or the overall church. I'll reference this metaphor frequently throughout the rest of this book. On that note, Paul clearly states:

> You are also God's building. . . . But each one must be careful how he builds. For God has already placed Jesus Christ as the one and only foundation, and no other foundation can be laid. Some will use gold or silver or precious stones in building on the foundation; others will use wood or grass or straw. And the quality of each person's work will be seen when the Day of Christ exposes it. For on that Day fire will reveal everyone's work; the fire will test it and show its real quality. If what was built on the foundation survives the fire, the builder will receive a reward. But if anyone's work is burnt up, then he will lose it; but he himself will be saved, as if he had escaped through the fire. (1 Corinthians 3:9–15 TEV)

We determine how we will build, and we have two major choices in our construction every moment of our life. One is to gravitate toward the temporal, that which appeases the flesh (wood, grass, or straw). The other is to live in line with our born-again spirit's desire, following the eternal Word of God (gold, silver, and precious stones). How we build, or how we live our lives, will determine how we fair when the fire of God's presence examines our work.

Not only will our works be examined but our thoughts, motives, and intentions will be exposed as well. This is why it is so crucial for believers to carefully listen to, heed, and hide in our hearts the Word of God, for it is continually "exposing and sifting and analyzing and judging the very thoughts and purposes of the heart" (Hebrews 4:12 AMP). Nothing else can get to the depths of our hearts like His Word.

If we *listen* to human reason, logic, psychology, or wisdom, we will gravitate in our thoughts and heart motives toward the temporal, and we will most often be completely unaware, just as Selfish was before he came into the Judgment Hall. For this reason, Jesus warns:

> "Whatever is hidden away will be brought out into the open, and whatever is covered up will be found and brought to light.
>
> "Be careful, then, how you listen; because whoever has something will be given more, but whoever has nothing will have taken away from him even the little he thinks he has." (Luke 8:17–18 TEV)

Jesus tells us it is what we *listen to* or *heed* that sinks into our hearts and shapes our inner thoughts and purposes, which in turn determine how we build our lives. We must carefully heed the Word of God because it is a light to our path. Without it we will certainly stray, just as anyone would stray from a path in a dark night. You may happen to stay on course for a short while, but eventually you will wander.

Once we stray, the way we build can easily become motivated by the temporal. This will not be exposed until the light of God's Word shines on it. Paul amplifies this by saying, "But when anything is exposed and reproved by the light, it is made visible and clear" (Ephesians 5:13 AMP).

If we stray, two things can happen. First—and the better of the two options—is that as we hear the Word of God (as it is preached, read, or spoken by a friend or leader), it convicts us in our consciences. This is why it is so crucial for us to maintain a steady diet of the Word of God. If we are wise, we will be quick to repent and ask forgiveness for our thoughts, motives, or intents. However, if our consciences are dull from our repetitive erring, it is harder to hear God's Word—and if our consciences are seared, it becomes practically impossible. For this reason, Scripture speaks of the importance of keeping one's conscience pure (see Proverbs 4:23; 2 Timothy 1:3). If we protect and keep our consciences clear, we can easily sense the dealings of the Living Word in our hearts.

The second option, which is not preferable, is to have our motives exposed at the Judgment Seat. If this happens, we lose our potential reward. So you must ask, is it worth it to resist the conviction of the Word of God? Each time you do, your heart becomes harder and enters a state of greater deception. We will not realize our own condition and will have it exposed by the light of God's glory at the Seat of Judgment.

Preparing for Our Eternal Future

The judgment of our lives will leave nothing unknown. Everything will be made visible and clear. This is why Paul refers to the Judgment Seat as the "solemn fear of the Lord." It will be a thorough investigation of our motives, intentions, thoughts, words, actions, and so forth. Paul's words in 1 Corinthians 3:9 and 12–15, as stated in *The Message* Bible, are so powerful in regard to building and judgment:

> Or, to put it another way, you are God's house. . . . Take particular care in picking out your building materials. Eventually there is going to be an inspection. If you use cheap or inferior materials, you'll be found out. The inspection will be thorough and rigorous. You won't get by with a thing. If your work passes inspection, fine; if it doesn't, your part of the building will be torn out and started over. But you won't be torn out; you'll survive—but just barely.

I don't know about you, but I don't want to just barely survive the Judgment Seat of Christ. We're speaking about our eternal destiny here.

Can you imagine how shocked many people are going to be? In our allegory, every character was caught completely off guard by what they faced—except for Charity, the one who was prepared. The others didn't take seriously the elementary doctrine that they should have been aware of from the beginning.

I constantly see wise people in this world preparing for their futures. It starts out with working hard in school to open the door to a good career. Once in their careers, they strive to purchase houses in order to build equity. They also develop some sort of savings and IRAs (Individual Retirement Accounts). Some will take their excess money and invest so it will work for them. All this is done to prepare for their futures; they don't want to be found lacking, especially when they hit their retirement years. If these people prepared for their retirement years like many are preparing for eternity, they would not only be headed for huge trouble. They, unlike many in the church, would be very concerned and frightened.

So let me give you a hypothetical scenario. Can you imagine this situation on the precise day a man retires? First, Social Security goes bankrupt and has no funds left to give him on a monthly basis. Not only this, but the bank that holds all his money also closes its doors and goes out of business. All his savings are lost. Then, on that same day, this man wakes up to flames. His house is burning. He escapes his home with nothing more than the clothes on his back, only to watch it burn to the ground, destroying everything he owns.

This would be a very sad day in that man's life. Yet this is the exact picture Paul paints, which will actually happen to some Christians at the Judgment Seat of Christ. Hear again his words: "But if the work is burned up, the builder will suffer great loss. The builder will be saved, but like someone barely escaping through a wall of flames" (1 Corinthians 3:15 NLT). Those who are wise in the kingdom realize we are not working to provide a future in retirement years. We are preparing for eternity!

The wise I speak of are those who are planning their eternal futures.

They live with purpose and know their eternal destiny is being written by how they live on earth. This will provide for them a grand entrance into the kingdom of God, rather than their slipping in with all they've done burned up and destroyed. See what Peter says in regard to this:

> Therefore, my brothers, be all the more eager to make your calling and election sure. For if you do these things, you will never fall, and you will receive a rich welcome into the eternal kingdom of our Lord and Savior Jesus Christ. (2 Peter 1:10–11 NIV)

A rich welcome is to hear the Master say to us, "Well done, good and faithful servant; you were faithful over a few things, I will make you ruler over many things. Enter into the joy of your lord" (Matthew 25:21).

Recently the Lord gave me a vision. I saw the champions of the kingdom come marching into the City of God. They were parading through the streets of gold with multitudes of men and women cheering them on the sidewalks. King Jesus was high up on a platform, visible to the entire city. The faithful soldiers marched up the steps, carrying to Jesus His spoils while the crowds rejoiced. In the vision it was as if the Lord was saying to those warriors, "Well done."

Then the Lord spoke to my heart. "Do you want to be one of these soldiers who bring the fruit they've harvested for Me, or do you want to be one of these on the sidewalks cheering?" I determined, more than ever before, to make my calling and election sure. I was resolute in the knowledge that I wanted to see a smile of pleasure on my Lord's face when He reviewed my life—not a look of sadness, knowing the potential He had given to me was lost.

I'm also determined to make this truth known to all who love God in my generation, in order that they will walk with me into His great presence with His well-deserved spoils and see our Father's glorious smile. We determine whether or not we will have a rich welcome through our service here. That is the main reason for the upcoming chapters.

To Come

The upcoming chapters will contain discussions of the major areas we'll be judged in and rewarded for. Though room will not permit all to be covered extensively, we will address some of the more important issues. A good foundation will be laid upon which you can further build to make your life count for eternity.

In closing, read these words of Peter slowly and allow them to speak to you regarding all you've read in this chapter. You'll see key words and phrases that will make what we've said more alive. Peter's words will also prepare us for what we'll soon discuss in the chapter to come:

> Everything that goes into a life of pleasing God has been miraculously given to us by getting to know, personally and intimately, the One who invited us to God. . . . So don't lose a minute in building on what you've been given, complementing your basic faith with good character, spiritual understanding, alert discipline, passionate patience, reverent wonder, warm friendliness, and generous love, each dimension fitting into and developing the others. With these qualities active and growing in your lives, no grass will grow under your feet, no day will pass without its reward as you mature in your experience of our Master Jesus. . . . So, friends, confirm God's invitation to you, his choice of you. Don't put it off; do it now. Do this, and you'll have your life on a firm footing, the streets paved and the way wide open into the eternal kingdom of our Master and Savior, Jesus Christ. Because the stakes are so high, even though you're up-to-date on all this truth and practice it inside and out, I'm not going to let up for a minute in calling you to attention before it. This is the post to which I've been assigned—keeping you alert with frequent reminders—and I'm sticking to it as long as I live. (2 Peter 1:3, 5–8, 10–13 The Message)

DISCUSSION QUESTIONS

SECTION 4: CHAPTERS 8–10

1. Perhaps one of the most powerful moments in the judgment of a citizen of Affabel is when they receive their new name. Think about who and how you were before you came to Christ and how Jesus has transformed your life. What do you think might be the story told by your own name change thus far?

2. Why do you think it is that even though believers may suffer great loss because of the way they lived, heaven can be a place of joy where every tear is wiped away?

3. In your own words, explain what set Charity apart from her peers at the judgment. What does her example teach us about how we should live?

4. Did anything about the biblical descriptions of heaven in chapter nine surprise you? How so?

5. Chapter ten contains the statement, "Jesus's blood cleanses us from the sins that would have kept us from the kingdom; however, it does not exempt us from the judgment of how we conducted ourselves as believers, whether good or bad." What was your initial reaction to this assertion? What are your thoughts after studying this section?

SECTION 5

CHAPTER 11

God's Custom Home

. . . You also are being built together
for a dwelling place of God . . .
—Ephesians 2:22

We'll divide the believer's judgment into two major categories. First, our involvement in building the kingdom of God in accordance with our callings and gifts. Second, how we built individual lives—which certainly would include our own. In regard to building others, the focus is our influence upon them; in building our own lives, it's how we cooperated with God's grace in developing Christlike character. The latter would certainly be a byproduct of how we responded to God's Word, and of what we believed and our obedience to it. Our actions and works, words, thoughts, and motives will all be examined in all cases.

We'll first examine the judgment of our roles in building God's kingdom; after that, we'll discuss our personal lives.

"What Can You Do for Me?"

Our ability to build the kingdom is entirely based upon our obedience to the Holy Spirit because we can do nothing of eternal value unless it is by the grace of Jesus Christ. We are told, "Unless the Lord builds the house, they labor in vain who build it" (Psalm 127:1). This verse clearly points out that we can build apart from the Spirit of God, yet that labor is worthless in the light of eternity. It will be burned up at the Judgment Seat. It is crucial we understand this.

God tells a group of people in the Old Testament who were busy serving Him:

> "Heaven is my throne, and the earth is my footstool. What kind of house, then, could you build for me, what kind of place for me to live in? I myself created the whole universe! I am pleased with those who are humble and repentant, who fear me and obey me." (Isaiah 66:1–2 TEV)

Simply put, the Lord is saying, "I'm God. Are you fully aware of Who I really am? So what is it you think you can do for Me?" The idea that we can create something God is in need of could be compared to a bunch of ants saying to a human being, "We are going to build a house for you." How ridiculous! We can do nothing in our own strength to serve and please our majestic, unfathomable, and awesome God. He really doesn't need us.

On the other hand, God then identifies who can please and benefit Him: those who are humble, repentant, and fear and obey God. They are the ones He privileges to build His house. How can they benefit such an awesome God? "'Not by might nor by power, but by My Spirit,' says the Lord of hosts" (Zechariah 4:6). It is a human being cooperating in obedience to the Holy Spirit that brings results. Only then is a laborer's work not in vain.

Co-laborers

Here is the staggering fact: as majestic and awesome as the Lord God is, He—by His own choice—restricted Himself in what He does on the earth when He gave man the authority over our planet in the beginning. Consequently, God can be restricted.

This may shock you, but there are examples throughout Scripture. The descendants of Abraham "limited the Holy One of Israel" (Psalm

78:41). And Jesus said to the spiritual leaders of His nation, "Thus you are nullifying and making void and of no effect [the authority of] the Word of God through your tradition" (Mark 7:13 AMP). We are responsible to cooperate with God to fulfill His desired goal, which is chiefly to have a people conformed to Jesus's image and likeness whom He can inhabit for all eternity. For this reason, we are called co-laborers:

> We are fellow workmen (joint promoters, laborers together) with and for God; you are God's garden and vineyard and field under cultivation, [you are] God's building. (1 Corinthians 3:9 AMP)

Almost every time you hear the New Testament reference eternal labor, you will see it likened to working in a field or on a building. Why a field? Because the earth is the field where the growth of the kingdom of God presently occurs. All of heaven cheers while watching the saints build the kingdom on earth. Why a building? Because God is looking for a permanent habitation, and we are the living stones that compose His place of residence.

Peter writes, "Now God is building you, as living stones, into his spiritual temple" (1 Peter 2:5 NLT). Paul writes, "Together, we are his house . . . carefully joined together in him" (Ephesians 2:20–21 NLT). So in essence, our reason for being on the earth is to build up God's glorious temple or *house*, whether it's by getting others saved, teaching, serving, ministering to others, or something similar. We each have a role as a pure, living stone and as a builder, one who causes the living stones to be fitted and joined together into a glorious house for God. This illustrates the personal and kingdom responsibilities we will all give an account for.

The Custom House

If I'm a custom home builder, I will design and plan the construction of a house before any work on it begins. Drawings will be prepared detailing how to assemble the house and the materials needed. But that's not all. Every home builder knows that one of the most crucial parts of his job is scheduling the subcontractors at the proper times. These are the framers, concrete men, plumbers, tile layers, electricians—the list goes on extensively. They are the ones who actually do the labor of putting up the building. If they are not scheduled properly, chaos is inevitable. An example would be scheduling the sheetrock sub before the electrical wiring and insulation were installed.

If a subcontractor does a bad job or misses his assigned time, then the builder will call on someone else who can do the job. The newly appointed worker will have to come in on short notice and will possibly have to rip out the bad job done by the previous sub. Even though a subcontractor might miss his assigned job, the builder will make sure the work is finished.

I've also observed that when the builder is working on *his own house,* he is quite particular in finding choice subcontractors. He makes sure they have the finest materials and anything else they require to get the job done right. He will oversee the work with great care. God is the Custom Builder of *His own house,* but His house is a city made up of people!

Frequently on earth, special homes are given names. For example, the queen of England's home is titled Buckingham Palace. In the United States, the president's home is called the White House. Others you may not be so familiar with. The actress Phyllis Calvert's home is called Hill House. Actor/director Charles Ivan Vance's house is called Oak Lodge. The novelist Charles Dyer's home is called Old Wob. And the list continues. However, God started this long before any of us did. He refers to His eternal house, which is still under construction, as *Zion.* We read:

> For the Lord has chosen Zion; He has desired it for His dwelling place: "This is My resting place forever; Here I will dwell, for I have desired it." (Psalm 132:13–14)

If you've had the privilege of designing your dream house, you know the excitement and anticipation of finishing it. You desire to rest there, for it will be where you will find joy and peace.

Lisa and I had the privilege of building a custom home in the mid-1990s. While we were living in Orlando, Florida, an award-winning custom home builder named Robert loved our ministry and approached us declaring, "I want to build you a home." At the time we were living in a very small house and assumed his prices would be far too high. When we hedged, he blurted out, "I'll do it for a God price." As it turned out, he didn't take one cent of profit from the house.

We had owned two homes prior to this one. They were both tiny tract houses; this meant we had nothing to do with their design. I'll never forget when Robert came to our tract house a few days after our initial conversation, sat down with us at our kitchen table, laid out a blank piece of paper, and enthusiastically said, "Draw your dream house!"

We were stunned. We didn't realize you could do such a thing. Immediately my wife got to work and started drawing. She had been dreaming of this opportunity for years. Eventually I got into the process. It was exhilarating, and our excitement grew more and more as we discovered we could actually design the house however we desired. There were no limitations.

Then we watched our dream house, scribbled on that blank piece of paper, go to the architects and designers. Several days later Bob showed us the blueprints. We could hardly wait for work to start.

When Robert's subs broke ground and started building, we went to the job site every day—sometimes twice a day—through the entire construction process. We were so eager. We couldn't wait for another facet of the house to be built. It seemed those few months lasted years, and days seemed to last weeks, because of the anticipation of something new being done on our house and the ultimate expectation of one day moving in. We were amazed to behold the dream we'd drawn on a blank piece of paper come to life before our very eyes!

In a tiny way, this resembles God's emotions and anticipation for His dream home, but He's been waiting a lot longer than a few months. He's been looking forward to His home's completion since the foundation of the world. We are told, "For the Lord shall build up Zion" (Psalm 102:16), and, "Out of Zion, the perfection of beauty, God will shine forth" (Psalm 50:2).

God has been working on His house for a few thousand years. He laid out the plan before man was placed on earth. He knew in His omniscience that man would fall, even though that wasn't His design or doing. So from His foreknowledge, He planned to build Zion out of redeemed mankind.

God had to start out with the foundation and chief cornerstone, who is none other than Jesus, the Redeemer Himself. Of Him the Father says, "See, I lay a stone in *Zion*, a tested stone, a precious cornerstone for a sure foundation" (Isaiah 28:16 NIV). Because the Father designed and planned His house before creation, Jesus is called "the Lamb slain from the foundation of the world" (Revelation 13:8), and Peter states, "He indeed was foreordained before the foundation of the world" (1 Peter 1:20).

Not only is Jesus the foundation and chief cornerstone, but He is also the chief subcontractor. Jesus didn't miss His assignment; He fulfilled it perfectly. In prayer, He spoke these words to the Father just before His crucifixion: "I have *finished* the work which You have given Me to do" (John 17:4).

God the Father began the whole design of His home by scheduling Jesus at the appointed time (see Galatians 4:4). Then He scheduled the rest of the subcontractors. These subs are you and me. However, as stated earlier, we were to be not only subcontractors but also the materials of His house. As Paul says, "He chose us in Him *before the foundation of the world*, that we should be holy and without blame before Him" (Ephesians 1:4). This speaks of our being the materials of the house; we are the living stones.

God also chose us as subcontractors, for we read, "For we are God's workmanship, created in Christ Jesus *to do good works, which God prepared in advance for us to do*" (Ephesians 2:10 NIV). Notice He prepared our assigned tasks in advance. It doesn't say anywhere in Scripture that our assignments were given from the foundation of the world—although that is certainly possible. We do know that "the works were finished from the foundation of the world" (Hebrews 4:3). However, in regard to our personal assignments as subcontractors, the only thing we find written is that they were given before we were born. David says, "You saw me before I was born. Every day of my life was recorded in your book. Every moment was laid out before a single day had passed" (Psalm 139:16 NLT).

Our life's work was foreordained before we were formed in our mother's wombs. This truth is captured in God's word to Jeremiah. He said, "I knew you before I formed you in your mother's womb. *Before you were born I set you apart and appointed you as my spokesman to the world*" (Jeremiah 1:5 NLT). The apostle Paul also writes, "But when it pleased God, who separated me from my mother's womb and called me through His grace . . ." (Galatians 1:15–16). These testimonies only confirm David's words, that all of us were set apart to do specific work for God before we were born.

So here is the amazing truth: God wrote a book about you prior to your birth, and in it every moment of your life was laid out before a single day passed! The question is, will we fulfill what was planned for us? Solomon states:

> I know that whatever God does, it shall be forever. Nothing can be added to it, and nothing taken from it. God does it, that men should fear before Him. That which is has already been, and what is to be has already been; and God requires an account of what is past. (Ecclesiastes 3:14–15)

There is so much in these scriptures. First of all, God has a plan. Nothing can take away from its being accomplished, and mankind cannot add anything to it. However, Solomon goes on to say that the things that are presently being accomplished were in the mind of God beforehand. What is to be accomplished in the future was also in the plan of God beforehand. However, we will have to give an account for that which has already been done! Did we walk in what God ordained for us to fulfill? Did we mess it up or miss our assignment altogether? Did He have to assign another to do what we were called to do in the master plan?

At this juncture I need to make an important statement. Everyone has a divine calling on his or her life. Each of us is an important part of the master plan of God's house. So it is good for us to know this truth:

> In regard to your calling, you'll not be judged according to what you did but rather according to what you were called to do!

Let me give you an example. At the Judgment Seat, Jesus may say something like, "Evangelist Anderson, please step forward and give an account of all the souls I called you to impact for Me."

That man may come before Jesus a bit confused and trembling, saying, "Sir, You mean Accountant Anderson, right? I was an accountant with my own firm. This was my occupation. In fact, I set up many churches and non-profit organizations. Those ministries influenced many souls into Your kingdom. Do you have me mistaken for someone else?"

The Master may reply, "No. I called you before you were born to influence and win multitudes in Asia to Me. Give an account of where they are. If you had obeyed Me, you would have been rewarded greatly for all the fruit you harvested for My kingdom. Now as a result, your works will be burned up, for they were not in obedience to Me."

Then we may see this scenario. Jesus may say, "Accountant Jones, please step forward and give an account of what I called you to do."

That man may step forward also very confused and trembling saying, "Sir, You mean Pastor Jones, right? I was a pastor of a church that had nine hundred members. I built that church from the ground up."

To which the Master may reply, "No, I called you to work in the marketplace as an accountant and build a strong firm that would help many of My churches and ministries effectively fulfill what I ordained them to accomplish. If you would have sought Me earnestly, I would have shown you this. Then all the multitudes of people those ministries eternally impacted would have been credited to you; you would have been rewarded for each soul. But now you will receive nothing for what you did, for it was not in obedience to Me.

"I also ordained you to be the head usher in a church across town from where you started your church. Even though this church's membership totaled just over five hundred, their members impacted many lives in the community. Had you obeyed, all twenty thousand souls they eternally touched also would have been credited directly to you because you would have been a vital part of this body I called you to. Since you were not there, you will receive no reward for those twenty thousand souls."

Allow me to give an actual example. Our ministry has a board member who is a dear friend and pastors a thriving church in the southeastern part of the United States. He started the church in 1991 with twenty-two people, and it is now pushing four thousand members. It is one of the easiest churches to preach in because of the hunger of the people. Multitudes have been saved and discipled in this church.

The church grew rapidly through much prayer, strong preaching, and hard labor, and they built a beautiful building to accommodate the large numbers of people. After several years, my friend observed a distinguished white-haired gentleman, always well dressed, attending the services. He also noticed that this man would sit and watch service after service with tears running down his face. The pastor felt that these weren't tears of joy.

Finally, the gentleman approached one of the associate pastors and shared that in 1981, the Lord spoke to him clearly that he was to start a church in that city. A few days later he had a dream about the building this church he was to pastor would meet in. The dream was so vivid that he got a professional to draw a rendition of the building he saw. He then said that he ran into some resistance and backed off from starting the church. After a while, he traveled and ministered in other cities for a short time and eventually ended up back in the business world.

He then opened a carefully folded paper and told the associate it was the artist's rendition of the building he had drawn up in 1981. When the associate looked at the drawing, he almost went into shock. It was the building my friend had built years later, in which they were now meeting. My friend has since ministered comfort to this man, but the gentleman has shared the difficulty he's had in getting over it. (Of course God does not intend for him to live in condemnation but to learn, grow, and find out how he can effectively serve the Lord the rest of his life.)

Several years ago I was speaking on this very topic at a large conference. After the service a pastor, who was quite shaken and a bit miffed, approached one of our team members. This leader said, "He's not serious about what he said tonight, right?"

My team member responded, "Of course he meant what he said. It's the Word of God. Why, what's wrong?"

The pastor, who was over fifty years old, replied, "When I was young, I had a vivid dream of living in and ministering to the people of the Philippines. The dream was so real I believed I was to one day move there. However, it never happened, and now I've been pastoring my church for over thirty years."

Our team member gently responded, "Well, what are you going to do about it?"

The pastor was speechless and walked away.

A year later our team member heard from the former pastor. This leader had given the church over to an associate and was now living in the

Philippines and loving it. The former pastor's report was, "I feel for the first time in my life I'm doing exactly what I was created to do."

Allow me to share another story that affirms this truth. A short time ago, a friend of mine set up a dinner for me to meet a Navy SEAL. To protect his identity—because at the time of this writing, he's still in active service—I'll give him a fictitious name, Paul. For two hours I was gripped with awe listening to his testimony.

Back when Paul was in his late teens and early twenties, he'd completed two years of Bible college and was interning in the youth department of a church. After the second summer of his internship, Paul was accused of having sex with one of the girls in the church. Paul said, "John, I didn't sleep with her. In fact, I didn't even find her attractive! However, the leadership not only believed the report, they perpetuated it, and I lost everything. They took away my credibility. My reputation was tarnished, and I was asked—without actually being asked—to leave."

Paul then said, "I sought God like I've never sought Him before. One day in prayer I heard God clearly speak, 'I didn't call you to ministry. I called you to the military.'"

Paul went to the recruiting offices of the Army, Marines, and Air Force and had no witness that he was to enlist. All that was left was the Navy.

As Paul was applying to the Navy, the recruiting officer went down a list of jobs he could enlist under. Paul was greatly discouraged because none of them resonated in his heart as being in line with God's direction. Seeking desperately to sign a new recruit, the officer then offered some special programs within the Navy. When he said the word *SEALs*, my new friend said he knew that was it. He signed the contract.

The recruiting officer tried to discourage Paul because very few make it through the SEALs training program. In fact, Paul was informed that no one from that office had ever made it through and that it was considered the toughest military training in the world! However, Paul was filled with an overwhelming, almost euphoric, sense of taking that first step into a God journey. He emphatically insisted this was what he should enlist to do.

There were, however, a couple large problems. First, Paul didn't know how to swim. He had to pray and ultimately teach himself. Second, to make matters even more interesting, he had tubes in his ears many times as a child and had had multiple surgeries to open his ear canals. Because of this, even as a young man, if so much as a small amount of water entered his ears, Paul would experience excruciating pain often followed by intense ear infections. But he truly believed that if something was attainable by his own power, it wasn't what God had called him to.

Paul taught himself to swim and prayed earnestly that his ears would be healed. Every day of this water training was painful, but he would not quit. One day, after about four months of persevering through daily agony, not only could Paul swim, but he could dive to great depths completely pain-free! He was healed and ready to embark on the journey to the SEAL teams.

Paul experienced tremendous hardship and resistance in passing the program, but he finally did so and was initiated into that hardened brotherhood forged by war. He's been in the SEALs for over fourteen years and has stories of divine intervention on missions so miraculous that they caused the hair on my arms to stand up.

I knew that evening that I was sitting with a great man of God, yet he was not called to stand behind a pulpit. He was called to reach people in the military and serve our nation in that capacity. Today, Paul is not just a SEAL but a Navy SEAL instructor. He allowed God to correct his course so he could enter into the good work planned for him.

I've heard many examples of people who, unlike Paul, missed their destinies. I've seen examples of it as well. In over twenty years of traveling to churches worldwide, I have seen senior pastors who I knew in my heart were called to be associate pastors, businessmen who I knew were supposed to be in full-time ministry, and even pastors whose calling I knew was to be in the marketplace. I've seen people out of place in the corporate or business worlds; they worked for someone else out of fear of failing on their own. And then I've seen those who were not faithful to someone else just because they wanted to be their own bosses.

I've seen people marry out of the will of God; their calls have been thwarted. Others have been influenced by or entangled with certain friends who kept them from their callings. I've seen those entangled in recreation, sports, lust for money or power, or various other scenarios. The examples are endless, but whatever the situation, it kept a believer from fulfilling their role in the master plan of building God's house.

These are sobering thoughts, but the good news is that none of us has to veer from the path God has placed before us. God is the Author of our stories, and He is well able to lead us in fulfilling them. The question we should now ask is, how do I find out what I'm called to do as a subcontractor? We'll discuss this important question in the next chapter. We'll also give some insights on how to return if we've veered off the path.

CHAPTER 12

CALLED BY GOD

For God's gifts and his call can never be withdrawn.

—Romans 11:29 NLT

Many would find the thought that one can stray from God's plan— even by deviating into things that look good or godly—to be terrifying. That's an understandable response! But remember, we're called not into the fear of failure or punishment but the fear of God. The fear of the Lord keeps us in the counsel of the One of whom it is said, "Your own ears will hear him. Right behind you a voice will say, 'This is the way you should go,' whether to the right or to the left" (Isaiah 30:21 NLT). So let's turn our attention now to the issue of how we can know our place as builders of God's Custom House.

First: Have You Sought God Earnestly?

When asked if you are fulfilling your destiny, you may think, *I want to. But I don't know what I'm called to do!* There could be a couple reasons for this. The first question to ask yourself is, have you sought God earnestly? We are told that God rewards those who diligently seek Him in faith (see Hebrews 11:6), not those who casually seek Him in wonder or doubt. If anyone earnestly seeks God, fully expecting an answer, that person will be shown what they've been put on the earth to do.

After I was saved in my college fraternity at Purdue University, I immediately started seeking God's desire for my life. I was a student of engineering and worked every other semester at IBM. One of the things that motivated me to know my calling, in addition to a simple desire to obey God, was something that happened just a few months after I was saved. I was in an office with a group of eight to ten engineers celebrating a man's thirty-eighth year of service to the company. We were casually chatting, and the man said to all of us, "I've hated coming into this job every day for thirty-eight years." Everyone else in the room either agreed or snickered, except me. I was in shock.

As a rookie among these seasoned professionals, I wondered why no one else commented differently. So I blurted out, "Why have you done this for thirty-eight years if you've hated it?"

He looked back at me and said, "It's a job."

I, too, had started having an aversion to coming into work. My dad was an engineer, and he said it was a good profession that was secure and paid well. But this encounter caused me to change my outlook. I thought, *No money, security, or anything else is going to keep me from my reason for being placed on earth.* I made up my mind right there that I would find out what I was called to do and what the next step was to move toward it.

I've learned that God will give you the overall picture of your life's calling if you seek Him early in your walk with Him. In other words, He'll show you the end from the beginning. As a young boy, Joseph was shown that he would be a great leader; even his father and brothers would serve under him. It wasn't until years later that this was fulfilled. Moses knew he would lead Israel at least forty years before his time came. David was shown that he was to be king while he was still a young boy watching sheep. It was years afterward that he became ruler of Israel. And the list continues.

My plans were to finish my engineering degree at Purdue, pursue an MBA at Harvard, and move up into high-level management in corporate America. I would marry and take several vacations a year and give a tenth of all I made to God. That was my idea of serving Him.

The more I sought God, the more I felt drawn to ministry. I didn't like the sound of that either, but I was smart enough to know that in obeying God I would find fulfillment and satisfaction. Once I made the commitment to Him that I would obey no matter what, God began to show me an overall picture of what He had called me to do.

By the early 1980s, God had already shown me I would one day influence many nations with the Word of God as long as I stayed in obedience to Him. Needless to say, it blew my mind. I saw no way this could ever be accomplished. I was a small-town boy who didn't know anyone on a national or international level in ministry.

In the same manner as He did in Joseph's or David's example, God will show us the final picture but not all the steps to accomplish it. This keeps us in faith rather than reasoning. We need to seek to obey what He tells us, then move toward that goal. Often, however, our next step may not look as if we are headed toward the goal but rather in the opposite direction. Being sold as a slave for ten years after receiving a dream of leadership (as in Joseph's case) isn't exactly a logical step. This is why we are told, "Trust in the Lord with all your heart; do not depend on your own understanding. Seek his will in all you do, and he will direct your paths" (Proverbs 3:5–6 NLT).

A few months later, during my senior year of college, I stayed at the school in my fraternity house while every other student went home for a four-day Thanksgiving break. I fasted and prayed, seeking God's direction and will for my life. A couple months later I received the direction for the next step, and it seemed totally opposite the natural direction to take toward ministry. It only seemed logical for me to go to Bible school, but the Lord showed me I was to interview for a position as an engineer. This is why God tells us to not lean on our own understanding!

I met with many companies on our campus and knew almost immediately I was to work for the Rockwell Corporation in Dallas, Texas. This didn't make sense at all because there were no Bible schools in Dallas that I was aware of. I had thirteen job offers in various other cities—some of which had Bible schools—and every one offered more money than Rockwell. However, I just obeyed.

Once I arrived in Dallas, I walked into a church, and the Lord showed me I was to plant myself there. It was in this church that I was raised up through serving, which was the start of the path that brought me where I am right now.

Second: Have You Planted Yourself?

This brings us to the second reason why many don't find the will of God for their lives. They don't plant themselves in the local church. God's Word tells us, "Those who are planted in the house of the Lord shall flourish in *the courts of our God*" (Psalm 92:13).

Those who plant themselves in the house of God—which in this life would be the local church—shall flourish in the *courts of our God*. One aspect of *the courts of our God* is the Judgment Seat of Christ. So we will flourish both now and at the judgment if we've been firmly planted in a local church. This is God's design.

The Lord, not men, ordained the church. Jesus says, "I will *build* My church, and the gates of Hades shall not prevail against it" (Matthew 16:18). Notice the word *build*. How can Jesus build His church without physically being here? The answer is, through His body—which is us. Again, this is why we are called co-laborers (subcontractors). The grace, ability, and gifts are given by Him, and He is the One who supplies the supernatural power. But He must have yielded and obedient vessels to fulfill His work. The question is, are we erecting His church in cooperation with Him, or are we motivated by our own agendas?

Jesus has a global church subdivided into local churches. One of the numerous examples of this would be His words to each of the seven local churches in the book of Revelation: the churches of Ephesus, Smyrna, Pergamos, Thyatira, Sardis, Philadelphia, and Laodicea.

The church is also referred to in Scripture as the body of Christ. Just as the overall church is subdivided into local churches, so the overall body of Christ is subdivided into local bodies as well.

The Lord is the One who places His people. Paul tells us, "But now God has set the members, each one of them, in the body just as He pleased" (1 Corinthians 12:18). This may be a shocking statement to you: *we are not the ones who choose where we go to church. God is!*

Stop and ponder that for a moment. Many people pick churches like they select grocery stores rather than asking God where He desires them. But how can you fulfill your destiny if you aren't in the right location of His body? Each part of a human body is carefully connected by God's design. A hand would have a difficult time if it was connected to a knee cap. Even so, we should seek God's agenda in moving to a city or joining a local church.

Every one of us has a role in the local church. We read:

Now you are the body of Christ, and members individually. And God has appointed these in the church: first . . . (1 Corinthians 12:27–28)

Paul then gives a list of some of the major positions within the local church. Even though he doesn't give an exhaustive list, we know from other New Testament references that every believer is a part of the body of Christ, and each of us plays a vital role, no different than the members of our physical body do. If we are not functioning in our assigned body, then the local church is crippled—just as your body would be if one or more of your physical members (such as a leg, eye, or kidney) worked independently, didn't work at all, or became disconnected.

The sad fact is that much of the ministry of Jesus Christ is not being accomplished in our communities because local churches are severely disabled. Why are they crippled? Often it's not because of ineffective leaders but because of professing believers who live independently. Can you imagine if my eyes—or my legs or feet or any other part of my body—

decided they were going to do whatever they wanted? It's amazing what God has been able to do in America considering the state of our local churches.

Why did the early church, by contrast, explode in growth so quickly? Let's examine and see:

> They joined with the other believers and devoted themselves to the apostles' teaching and fellowship, sharing in the Lord's Supper and in prayer. . . . And all the believers met together constantly. . . . They worshiped together at the Temple each day, met in homes for the Lord's Supper, and shared their meals with great joy and generosity— all the while praising God and enjoying the goodwill of all the people. And each day the Lord added to their group those who were being saved. (Acts 2:42–47 NLT)

Do you see that the believers were planted in the local body? They worshiped together, heard the same messages, had a common vision and did life together. This resulted in healthy church growth. People served the Lord through their local church, and this service affected their home lives as well.

For the early believers, being a part of the local church was their life. In fact, a problem arose later where some widows were neglected in being served food. The apostles summoned the local body of believers and told them it wasn't good for the leaders to leave the ministry of the Word of God to serve tables. "Look around among yourselves, brothers," the apostles said, "and select seven men who are well respected and are full of the Holy Spirit and wisdom. We will put them in charge of this business" (Acts 6:3 NLT).

Notice the leaders didn't say, "We need some volunteers. Would anyone mind giving their time to serve these ladies?" No, all the believers were committed to service because they were planted in the local church.

I personally believe each member was hoping he would be selected to serve. Seven men were chosen . . .

> . . . whom they set before the apostles; and when they had prayed, they laid hands on them.
> Then the word of God spread, and the number of the disciples multiplied greatly in Jerusalem, and a great many of the priests were obedient to the faith. (Acts 6:6–7)

The apostles laid hands on these seven men. This anointing wasn't to minister from the pulpit, teach a home group, lead praise and worship, or go out on a ministry trip. It was to serve food to widows at the church. Wow!

However, notice that once the seven men took their place of service in the body—as insignificant as it seemed—the *word of God spread* and the number of the disciples *multiplied* greatly in Jerusalem. Here we find an amazing fact. In Acts chapters 1 through 5, the word *added* is used several times in describing the growth of the church in Jerusalem. Here are some occurrences:

> . . . And that day about three thousand souls were *added* to them. (Acts 2:41)

> And the Lord *added* to the church daily those who were being saved. (Acts 2:47)

> And believers were increasingly *added* to the Lord, multitudes of both men and women . . . (Acts 5:14)

Up to this point, only the apostles were doing the work of the ministry in the local church, and Peter was the only recorded communicator. However, at some point the believers realized everyone had two major responsibilities. First, to proclaim and teach the gospel to other individuals. Second, to play a role in the local church.

The discovery that all believers were to tell the amazing story of Jesus's resurrection is found in Acts 5:42–6:1: "And daily in the temple, and in every house, they did not cease teaching and preaching Jesus as the Christ. Now in those days, when the number of the disciples was multiplying . . ." There was no possible way for Peter to communicate in every house because there were no radios, televisions, or Internet connections. So we know that all the believers had begun proclaiming and teaching the gospel of Jesus Christ to their neighbors. Notice the church was now growing not by addition but by multiplication. This is the first time in the book of Acts you will find multiplied growth.

However, the dynamic of multiplication doesn't stop there. Once believers took their places of serving in the church (the example given being that of the men serving widows in need), we read that the number of the disciples wasn't just multiplying but was *greatly* multiplying. Greatly multiplying is *exponential growth*!

Let me share with you the difference between addition and great multiplication or exponential growth. Let's consider a pastor who wins 10,000 people to the Lord every month. Would you consider this a fairly effective ministry? Probably so. But do you know how long it would take him to reach the world? The answer is a staggering 50,000 years—and that is provided nobody was born or died in that time! That is over eight times the span of years mankind has been on earth. Impossible!

Now let me give you an example of great multiplication. Let's say you win two people to the Lord and get them plugged into your local church. Then the next month, each of those two people lead two others to the Lord and get them plugged into the church. The next month each of those four do the same, and the following month each of those eight lead two people each to the Lord and get them plugged in. If this trend continues, do you know how long it would take to reach the entire earth's population with the gospel? The answer is a mere thirty-three months. Yes, that's right, less than three years! This is great multiplication.

Now do you understand how we can read this in the Bible?

This continued for two years, so that *all* the inhabitants of [the province of] Asia, Jews as well as Greeks, heard the Word of the Lord . . . (Acts 19:10 AMP)

All the inhabitants! If Scripture says *all*, it means *every* person. We are not talking about a city but an entire region. They didn't have satellites, televisions, radios, social media, cars, or even bicycles. This is exponential growth.

It takes a healthy body of believers to experience great multiplication. A healthy body is made up of believers planted in a local church, which includes serving in that local church (by doing things such as waiting on widows' tables, ushering, working in the parking lot, greeting, doing prison outreach, participating in children's ministry—the list is huge). Those who serve are also reaching people where they work or live and getting them plugged into their local church. Remember, Jesus tells us to make disciples, not just converts, of all nations. We must get those we reach plugged into our churches for them to be taught all of the things Jesus commanded us (see Matthew 28:20). It takes the entire local body, and all the gifts within it, to make people mature in Christ.

The key is being planted in the local church. Here we will flourish. If you notice, Philip was one of the seven who were chosen to wait on widows' tables. However, later in the Book of Acts, he is called Philip the evangelist. His work of ministry was now expanded to include many cities: "On the next day we who were Paul's companions departed and came to Caesarea, and entered the house of Philip the evangelist, *who was one of the seven*, and stayed with him" (Acts 21:8).

Even though Philip was now a great evangelist and had been moved by the Lord to a different city, he was still recognized as one of the seven men who served the widows. Serving in the local church played a crucial role in getting him into his life's calling. I tell people this: "You may have a life calling to do something great, but it will not mature properly if it's not first birthed from being planted in a local church."

Let me repeat the psalmist's words: "Those who are planted in the house of the Lord shall flourish in the courts of our God" (Psalm 92:13). Think of the word *planted*. To understand the operation of the kingdom, you must consider the law of seedtime and harvest. Jesus told His disciples that if you don't understand the principles of the seed, ground, and harvesting, you cannot understand all His parables (see Mark 4:13). Simply put, the entire kingdom of God is:

> ". . . as if a man should scatter seed on the ground, and should sleep by night and rise by day, and the seed should sprout and grow, he himself does not know how. For the earth yields crops by itself: first the blade, then the head, after that the full grain in the head. But when the grain ripens, immediately he puts in the sickle, because the harvest has come." (Mark 4:26–29)

Let's say I have a handful of various seeds, all of which are from fruit trees, but I'm not familiar with them. The only way I'll be able to discover their kind is if I plant them. Once each seed is planted, as time progresses, I'll discover its nature.

God places in each of us a predetermined calling and the gifts to accomplish it: "He has created us anew in Christ Jesus, so that we can do the good things he planned for us long ago" (Ephesians 2:10 NLT). And "the gifts and the calling of God are irrevocable" (Romans 11:29). According to Jesus, my calling and gifts are in seed form. If I plant myself in the church, I will reach my God-given destiny. If not, I may use the gifts in my life for a different purpose than my Creator intended. So don't be deceived by success according to the world's standards. You may be very successful with your gifts, but their use may not be in obedience to the Master's plan.

Allow me to give examples. You'll see many in the world who have great voices and can move people to tears. Their gifts were given to glorify God and stir people to pursue His heart and desires. They never fulfilled their destinies because they didn't get saved or were not planted in a church.

That is one example of many I could give of those who never came to Jesus in their lifetimes. However, there are also people who have given their hearts to Jesus but attend church irregularly. They are not fulfilling their highest kingdom calling because they've not been planted. They may have been called to influence lives outside the church, and they may be doing it to a degree, but their impact would be much greater if they planted themselves in the church.

A person can perceive certain gifts and use them in the way deemed best, but just as you will never know the exact type of a tree—its form, shape, strength, and so forth—if it remains in seed form, even so you will never know your true, God-given destiny unless you've been planted in the church. This is God's design, not man's.

Another problem occurs with believers transferring churches when problems arise. Today, men and women readily leave churches if they see something wrong, especially in their leadership. Perhaps the issue is the way the leadership and team run the church. Maybe it is the way the offerings are taken or how the money is spent. If people don't like what the pastor preaches, they leave. He is not approachable, or he is too familiar. Or the problem could be the lack of attention given to someone by fellow congregation members. This list goes on and on. Rather than face the difficulties and maintain hope, these people run to where there appears to be no conflict.

Let's face it. Jesus is the only perfect pastor or member of the church. So why do we run from difficulties in our Western society instead of facing them and working through them? We then go from church to church looking for a place with flawless leadership or members.

But remember, the place where God places us is the place the devil wants to offend us and get us out of. Our enemy wants to uproot men and women from where God plants them. If he can get you out, he has been successful. If you will not budge, even in the midst of great conflict, you will spoil his plans and fulfill God's.

Again, "Those who are *planted* in the house of the Lord shall flourish in the courts of our God." What happens to a plant if you transplant it every three weeks? Its root system will begin to diminish, and it will not blossom or prosper to its potential. If you keep transplanting it, it will die of shock.

Many go from church to church trying to develop their ministry callings. If they are not recognized in the places where God sets them, offense is easily perceived. If something is done in a manner with which they do not agree, they are offended and leave. They go while blaming the leadership. They are blind to any of their own character flaws, and they do not realize God was refining them with the pressure they were under. (This is not just limited to ministry but extends to marriages, employment, and other such relationships.)

Let's learn from the examples God gives with plants and trees. When a fruit tree is put in the ground, it has to face rainstorms, hot sun, and wind. If a young tree could talk, it might say, "Please, get me out of here! Put me in a place where there is no sweltering heat and no windy storms!"

If the gardener listened to the tree, he would actually do the plant harm. Trees endure the hot sun and windy rainstorms by sending their roots down deeper. The adversity they face is eventually the source of great stability. The harshness of the elements surrounding them causes them to seek another source of life. They will one day come to the place that even the greatest of windy storms cannot affect their ability to produce fruit. Knowing this, we should not resist the very things God allows us to live through in order to strengthen us in our callings.

Third: Are You Entangled?

The final reason we'll discuss regarding why people don't find and fulfill their callings is entanglement. Weights hold people back from running and completing their races.

Paul said of himself, "But I reckon my own life to be worth nothing to me; I only want to complete my mission and finish the work that the Lord Jesus gave me to do" (Acts 20:24 TEV). Paul was keenly aware of his life's mission. He had a job to finish, and he was also aware it wasn't yet complete. How did he know? Just as Jesus knew. Just as Peter knew (see 2 Peter 1:14). And just as others know who seek God, plant themselves in the church, and endure. The Lord reveals this to anyone who does not count his life more valuable than the will of God. In this lies the final key: when we wholly lay down our lives to fulfill God's desired plan for us, then we will not only discover our calling but fulfill it as well.

An example is seen in the Gospels. On a certain day, Jesus was traveling from one town to another. We read, "Now it happened as they journeyed on the road, that someone said to Him, 'Lord, I will follow You wherever You go'" (Luke 9:57).

The man who says this is excited, passionate, and sincere. He wants to follow Jesus all the way. However, Jesus has a way of seeing through enthusiasm and going right to the true motive or snares of the heart. He saw an entanglement that would hinder this man in fulfilling his destiny, so Jesus addressed it by saying, "Foxes have holes and birds of the air have nests, but the Son of Man has nowhere to lay His head" (Luke 9:58).

This man most likely took comfort in the earthly securities that he had in place. He probably had a good job, sizable equity in his home, and a retirement program set up for his latter years. Jesus hit this desire for earthly security head-on by saying He had no secure place to lay His head.

I can just see this man, as well as many others in the crowd, beginning to back up slowly to the rear of the crowd and eventually slipping away. The man is most likely saying, "Jesus, I'll usher for Your meetings, play in the band, or even park cars for the elderly who attend Your convention in my town." The glamour of following Jesus just lost its luster and the good intentions of serving Him quickly faded. So this man and many others drift off with the intention of still supporting Jesus but not committing all.

Then Jesus looked at another who was still eager and said, "Follow me."

> But [the man] said, "Lord, let me *first* go and bury my father."
> Jesus said to him, "Let the dead bury their own dead, but you go and preach the kingdom of God." (Luke 9:59–60)

Wow. What a strong reply. Some may think Jesus was being insensitive and a bit harsh. However, we must understand the culture of that day. Scholars tell us tradition was that when a father died and the firstborn fulfilled his obligation to bury him, that child would receive a double portion of the inheritance—with the other sons receiving a single portion. However, if the firstborn didn't fulfill his duty to bury the father, the double portion would go to the second son.

This man had money on his mind. He most likely had a love of being well-off, which eventually would have hindered him from following Jesus. He would have been distracted or made decisions based on finances rather than on the plan of God.

With this instruction from the Master, I'm almost certain this man, along with a slew of others, began to back up. His reply was something to this order: "Jesus, I'll serve in the conferences You hold in my city. I'll sing in the choir or play the drums. I can do that. I'd love to do this and won't charge You a thing for my services." The excitement of following Jesus lost its appeal to this man and to a good number of others.

Notice this man didn't say he would not follow Jesus. He said he would follow, but the key to his loss is found in the words "let me *first*." He wanted to make sure what he desired was accomplished before he yielded his life to Jesus.

Nothing can come before the will of God if we are going to discover and fulfill His plan for our lives. I've seen countless believers who drew back from obedience because of the intent of attending to their priorities first. How sad that they missed their callings. Someone else had to come in and fulfill their roles. How will they fair at the Judgment Seat?

Back to our story. The crowd was getting smaller, and another eager volunteer stepped up.

> And another also said, "Lord, I will follow You, but let me *first* go and bid them farewell who are at my house."
>
> But Jesus said to him, "No one, having put his hand to the plow, and looking back, is fit for the kingdom of God." (Luke 9:61–62)

Again, notice the word *first*. Obviously this man was very close to his family, or he had friends or a girlfriend back home. He just wanted to run his decision to follow the Man from Galilee by them. His tight-knit relationships would have been the final determining factor in how he served Jesus. So the Lord directly confronted this by saying he would not be suited for kingdom service.

I can just see this man backing up with still another large group. I can almost hear him saying, "Jesus, I'm good with public relations and human resources. I can be a consultant for Your ministry and get You hooked up with some really good employees. I can also help secure the local conference center for Your next meeting in our city. And when You come, I'll be in charge of all the greeters and ushers who work Your meetings. I'll even usher for You if you need me. I'm there for You!"

More than likely, at this point Jesus had witnessed the large crowd of enthusiastic followers whittled down to just around seventy. There were probably thousands to start with, but He had directly dealt with three major areas of entanglement that hinder people from fulfilling their destinies: security, money, and relationships. (There are other areas of entanglement—such as pleasures, the desire for other things outside the purposes of God, and so forth—but in my years of experience, these are the major ones.)

When reading the Gospels, most miss Luke's next crucial statement because of a transition into a new chapter. However, let me remind you that the book of Luke is one long letter. The church added the chapter and verse designations later for easy reference. Hear what Luke says next:

> After these things the Lord appointed seventy others also, and sent
> them two by two before His face into every city and place where He
> Himself was about to go. Then He said to them, "The harvest truly
> is great, but the laborers are few . . ." (Luke 10:1–2)

There is so much in these verses. First of all, look at the words "after these things." We must ask, after what things? The answer is, after Jesus witnessed the crowd whittled down to a remnant of people, the ones who were still standing there saying to themselves, *I don't care what it costs to follow Him. I'm willing and will do it!* They heard Jesus's response to security, money, and relationship issues, and they were determined not to allow anything to keep them from fulfilling their destiny in God.

Then Jesus *appointed* seventy new team members, who were most likely the only ones remaining. The words *appointed* and *chosen* are used synonymously in the New Testament. A person who is appointed is one who has been chosen, and one who is chosen is one who's been appointed. Jesus makes a particular statement in two different places in the Gospel of Matthew. If He repeats a statement exactly in two places in the same gospel, then we need to pay close attention. Here it is: "For many are called, but few chosen" (Matthew 20:16; 22:14).

Many are called. How many? Everyone to be exact. All believers have a call upon their life and possess the gifts to accomplish it. However—and this may shock you—only few are chosen or appointed to fulfill that call. Why are only a few appointed? Because only a few will forsake all their own desires, securities, lust for money, hindering relationships, and so on to fulfill the call upon their lives.

Notice Jesus said, "The harvest truly is plentiful, but the laborers are few" (Matthew 9:37). It is not God's fault our generation is not being reached, for God "desires all men to be saved and to come to the knowledge of the truth" (1 Timothy 2:4). We are the ones who will have to stand before His Judgment Seat and give an account for why our generation wasn't reached. If we fulfilled our call, then we will not be judged. However, if we allowed entanglements to hinder us, then our judgment will be sobering.

You may say, "I'm only one of many." What if your liver said, "I'm an insignificant member of the body, and nobody notices me or my work, so I'm going to do my own thing rather than what I'm created to do"? As you know, without a liver, a body is in serious trouble. What if the lungs said this—or a leg or foot or any other part of the body? Just as every member of the body is significant, so every member of the church is significant.

Here is the sobering fact. Jesus tells us that only a few will fulfill their destinies as subcontractors in the house of God. Every believer will have a call to build, but few will fulfill it. This means that the majority who stand before the believer's judgment will suffer loss and not gain glorious rewards.

I know this is not happy news. However, here is the good news: you can start now. You can get on your knees and pray and ask God to forgive you for all that you have allowed to keep you from obeying His will for your life, then move forward step by step. Smith Wigglesworth, a great evangelist of the twentieth century, didn't start his ministry until he was in his fifties. It is not too late for you.

Remember, the keys to building well are: First, seek God in faith.

Second, get planted in the local church God shows you—and stay submitted and obedient to the leadership of that local body. And third, forsake the entanglements of your life. As God shows you the weights that hold you back, ask for His sword to sever the ties they have on your soul or flesh. His grace is sufficient to free you.

The Full Reward[1]

One final word before we move into the next chapter. There are many who have never started, or have even veered off from, building God's house. They've been distracted by temporal glories: the riches of this world; lust for influence, power, or pleasure; or man's approval, all of which fade. Don't be fooled, sidetracked, and misled. Stay focused. You have a task to do in Christ. Your work must be finished.

There will be those whose seasonal or even lifelong labor will not endure. It will be torn out and therefore will not be a part of God's eternal home. Can you imagine this?

To help you envision the gravity of this statement, allow me to return to the story of our family's custom home. Since I went to the home site daily, the subs came to know me quite well. They called me "the preacher."

Each day when I drove to the construction site, the workers' acid rock was blaring away. Upon seeing me, one of them would quickly run over to the portable stereo and shut it off. I'd smile inside at the reverence they held for the things of God. Then we'd all chat for a while. I had some interesting conversations with those guys—and some great ministry opportunities.

On one of these occasions, I recall that the subs told me about some of the magnificent homes they'd been a part of building. They lit up as they relayed their contributions. You could see the enormous satisfaction and pleasure they held in being a part of such glorious works. There was no shame at all, only joy over the labor that was benefiting other families and was well known to observers of fine homes.

Let's take it a step further. Can you imagine how the men who built the White House in Washington, D.C., felt? Imagine the day one of them sees their very own child come home from school and report that they learned in class about the most famous house in the nation. Then their son or daughter enthusiastically announces the upcoming school field trip to see it.

Can you imagine the thrill that man experiences in telling of his involvement in building that very house? Can you imagine his emotions when he accompanies his child's class to 1600 Pennsylvania Avenue for the field trip? Can you imagine how he felt observing the excitement and pride on his child's countenance when his or her fellow classmates discover he had a part in building the house where the president of the United States resides?

Something similar is true of us. But we are not working on a house that will eventually be torn down and replaced. We are working on the house that will be the central focus of the entire universe forever and ever. Oh, yes! Recall the words of Micah the prophet: "Many nations shall come and say, 'Come, and let us go up to the mountain of the Lord, to the *house* of the God of Jacob; He will teach us His ways, and we shall walk in His paths.' For out of *Zion* the law shall go forth" (Micah 4:2).

All the affairs of the universe will revolve around this house. The wisdom and laws governing all creation will flow out of it. And here is the amazing fact: it will be just as beautiful ten trillion years from now as it will be on the day of its completion.

There's a great minister of the gospel who was faithful to the end. He ministered effectively for over sixty years and entered his reward close to the turn of the millennium. A year after his departure, I traveled to a large church in the Midwest where the worship leader shared that God had given him a vivid dream. In it, he was in heaven and he saw and conversed with this great minister. The minister said to the worship leader, with a large smile, "It's much better than I'd ever imagined."

They talked of truths and events, and then this minister turned and pointed out his portion of the work in Zion. It was massive. The impact of his faithfulness went so much farther and wider than he dreamed, and it was right there before him. He was able to point out his work, just as those construction subs relayed their contribution to me. What an eternal reward!

Just imagine, throughout all eternity, your being able to show not only your descendants, but the myriads of nations and peoples who come to behold the glorious house of God called Zion, your part in constructing His home. Can you imagine people coming and looking at the beauty of God's house and discussing your contribution throughout all eternity?

Let's contemplate the flip side. Consider the scenario of not having any representation of your work because you didn't finish well. Can you imagine your descendants or ancestors coming to observe your labor, yet your being unable to show them anything? Can you imagine the nations coming to see what you did, and your having nothing to show throughout all eternity because your intended portion was torn out and replaced? Recall Paul's words from *The Message*:

> If your work passes inspection, fine; if it doesn't, your part of the building will be torn out and started over. (1 Corinthians 3:14–15)

That is truly eternal loss. Sadly, it's a reality. But oh, dear friend, I don't want it for you. God doesn't want it for you. And you can determine now that it won't happen to you. God's given you grace to build up Zion. As the apostle John says:

> Watch out, so that you do not lose *the prize* for which we have been working so hard. Be diligent so that you will receive your *full reward*. (2 John 8 NLT)

The Lord Himself has made it so that every one of His children will have the opportunity to receive a full reward for building His house. Your labor need never fade out, never grow old, never have to be replaced. If you rely on God's grace and build well, what you contribute will be admired by myriad angels and people forever and ever.

DISCUSSION QUESTIONS

SECTION 5: CHAPTERS 11–12

1. We know that God doesn't need us to do anything for Him—but He does want us to labor with Him. What does this tell us about Him? About His kingdom? About ourselves?

2. Psalm 139:16 tells us that God wrote a book outlining every moment of our lives before we were even born. What are some ways we can know what God scribed for our unique stories?

3. It's possible (perhaps even easy) to spend our lives on seemingly good things and still miss out on what we were called to do. Is there anything you've allowed to go dormant because of fear or discouragement that you might now seek God to renew in your life?

4. In chapter twelve, we discussed three keys to establishing lives in line with God's will: seeking Him earnestly, planting ourselves in His house, and freeing ourselves of entanglements. Which of these stood out to you as areas of personal opportunity? How can you grow in them?

5. In eternity, we can be rewarded fully, partially, or not at all. What to you is the full reward?

SECTION 6

CHAPTER 13

MULTIPLICATION

*"The harvesters are paid good wages, and the fruit they harvest
is people brought to eternal life. What joy awaits both the
planter and the harvester alike! You know the saying, 'One
person plants and someone else harvests.' And it's true."*
—John 4:36–37 NLT

*The one who plants and the one who waters work as a
team with the same purpose. Yet they will be rewarded
individually, according to their own hard work.*
—1 Corinthians 3:8 NLT

Those who serve faithfully in the kingdom by building God's house receive handsome eternal wages. We will be rewarded for our work individually, according to our own labor. Each of us has different responsibilities, but all our different callings produce one result: lives impacted for eternity.

Many believe only the ministers who've publicly touched millions of lives will stand in the front lines of heaven receiving the greatest rewards. However, this is not true. God does not reward as man does. He rewards according to righteous works of obedience. If He did reward according to human standards, entrepreneurial accomplishments would be the focus of ministry. As we saw in the last two chapters, this is absolutely not the case. God judges and rewards according to what we've been called to do—what He's empowered us to accomplish.

Empowered by Grace

In AD 56, roughly ten years before he finished his course, Paul wrote that he was the "least of the apostles" (1 Corinthians 15:9). This would seem odd to those who've studied church history. Paul had impacted the entire known world and accomplished more for the kingdom than anyone else in his day. There was no doubt he was the greatest apostle of his time. So how could he make such a statement? Could he have been exaggerating? That's not possible; you cannot lie when writing Scripture. The only way the Holy Spirit would allow such a statement is if he really believed he was.

The answer is found in what he continued to write: "But *by the grace of God I am what I am*, and His grace toward me was not in vain; but *I labored more abundantly than they all, yet not I, but the grace of God which was with me*" (1 Corinthians 15:10).

Interestingly enough, Paul acknowledged his accomplishments were more than any other apostle's, yet he still considered himself the least among them. The explanation of this oxymoron is found in his words, "By the grace of God I am what I am." Paul was able to separate himself from all God did through him. He was completely aware that he could not add to God's calling on his life nor accomplish anything beyond the ability given him. This is all summed up in one word: *grace*. And this dynamic applies to all believers regarding their calling.

Let me comment on my own experience in ministry. The books I've written are now in over ninety languages worldwide. They number in the multimillions, and the testimonies of changed lives are countless.

Often people approach me asking for the secret to how I write. I laugh inside and think of how terrible an English student and writer I was before God's grace manifested in my life. It would take me hours to write a two-page English paper, and it seemed I would go through half a notepad before coming up with the first paragraph. Now when I write, the words fly out of me. I'm more aware than anyone else Who it is that writes these books. I'm really just the first guy to get to read them.

Once I was interviewed on a national television talk show, and the focus was to be the messages of the books I've written. However, as the interview progressed, the host became more focused on me and my accomplishments than on the messages. I became very uncomfortable and looked within to seek the Holy Spirit's counsel on how to change the focus.

Within moments, there was a break in our discussion, and it was a perfect time to interject the comment the Holy Spirit gave me. I quoted Solomon's words, "I know that whatever God does, it shall be forever. Nothing can be added to it, and nothing taken from it. God does it, that men should fear before Him. That which is has already been, and what is to be has already been; and God requires an account of what is past" (Ecclesiastes 3:14–15).

I then said, "There are untold multitudes of pastors and ministers out there doing what God has called them to do. Some are overseeing churches of three hundred members in rural areas. Others are ministering to the lost and hurting in developing nations; they've sown their lives into the mission fields. Others are working in the inner city, placing their lives on the line daily to help those whom many consider worthless. Still others are serving God faithfully in the marketplace. The list is endless. You will most likely never have any of these people on this program, but many will stand on the front lines of heaven because they've been obedient to what they've been called to do, and they've done it out of pure motives."

I proceeded to say, "In regard to me, God has called me to do a specific work for Him, and its scope has touched many lives. This is why you've asked me on this program. However, I cannot add one thing to what He's called me to do. I can't enlarge, enhance, or make it go further in my own ability. The only thing I can do is mess it up, and that causes me to fear!"

The atmosphere of that interview immediately became solemn. The man who was interviewing me, who also has an international ministry, registered what I said and changed the focus of the remainder of the interview back toward ministering to people.

This is true for anyone. Maybe you've been called to be a wife and a mother of children, serve in the nursery at your local church, and intercede in the prayer closet. If you've done this faithfully to the end, then you will be rewarded greatly for your obedience. Or you may have been called to serve in prison ministry in your church, touch lives in the marketplace, and give largely to the work of the ministry. If you've faithfully done this to the end, doing it from your heart as unto the Lord, you'll be rewarded just like an evangelist who faithfully won multitudes will.

The list goes on. I personally believe that on the front lines of heaven, we will see far more mothers, businesspeople, blue-collar workers, and the like receiving the greatest rewards from the Master.

God's Army on Earth

The church of Jesus Christ is God's army on earth. We all have positions of rank and gifts to accomplish our missions. Years ago, my wife was awakened by the Lord and shown this great army in the Spirit. It was four in the morning, but she immediately woke me up to report what she had seen in the vision.

"John," she said, "it was a military in which everyone knew their rank, position, and responsibilities. They marched in perfect order, and there were open positions throughout the ranks, which I saw people slipping into. I saw you and me move into our two places of service. No one had to look at another to see where to march. They were all in perfect unison because their eyes were on the Master."

Then she made a comment that particularly caught my attention. "No one coveted another's position. Everyone was content to serve in the place the Lord created for them." Did you catch that? No one in the army was envious of any other person's place of service. Everyone was content and happy to labor in his or her position.

Keeping this in mind, let's return to our custom home example. Recall that Scripture says, "Through wisdom a house is built" (Proverbs 24:3). There are two types of wisdom through which we can build, one of which is from above and the other of which is not.

> Who is wise and understanding among you? Let him show it by his good life, by deeds done in the humility that comes from *wisdom*. But if you harbor bitter *envy* and *selfish ambition* in your hearts, do not boast about it or deny the truth. Such *"wisdom"* does not come down from heaven but is earthly, unspiritual, of the devil. For where you have envy and selfish ambition, there you find disorder and every evil practice. (James 3:13–16 NIV)

No matter what we do or how good it appears, if it is fueled by the motive of envy or selfish ambition, we are building with fleshly, unscriptural, and demonic motives that will certainly not be rewarded.

Webster's defines envy as "a feeling of discontent or covetousness with regard to another's advantages, success, possessions, etc."[1] If we view the call of God through the eyes of the world, then envy is unavoidable. There were preachers who envied Paul's life assignment. He wrote, "It is true that some preach Christ out of *envy* and rivalry, but others out of goodwill. The latter do so in love, knowing that I am put here for the defense of the gospel. The former preach Christ out of *selfish ambition*" (Philippians 1:15–17 NIV).

These ministers were not content in the callings God had placed on their lives, and they desired Paul's success. This *envy* was fueled by their *selfish ambition*. Ambition is an eager and strong desire to accomplish something. When it is selfish, the focus is on ourselves rather than on the good of others. This motive will only produce disorder and strife and will open the door to every evil thing.

Godly wisdom, on the other hand, will fuel *kingdom passion*, not *selfish ambition*. It will build according to the Master Planner's wishes with

His heart's desires motivating the labor. We read of this wisdom: "But the wisdom that comes from heaven is first of all pure; then peace-loving, considerate, submissive, full of mercy and good fruit, impartial and sincere" (James 3:17 NIV).

The wisdom of God is first pure. In other words, it is not two-faced, having an outward appearance of godliness mixed with an envious or selfish motive. Its motives are to be faithful to the Master, accepting His assignments with joy. Its goal is not to be the greatest but to be obedient to the call. It will cause us to rejoice at the advancement of the kingdom whether it occurs through us or another.

Godly wisdom always focuses on the good of others, not itself. It's peaceable, not quarrelsome, overbearing, critical, or dominating. Its root motive is to see others walking in godliness and fulfilling their destinies. There are those who love the ministry and endure people, and then there are those who love people and view their ministry as a vehicle to serve them. The latter do so motivated by godly wisdom.

Another trait of godly wisdom is *submission*. When we are content in our calling, we will be submissive to God's direct and delegated authority. We see the big picture of God's house being built, and there is only one Architect, Designer, and Builder in charge. He's delegated His authority, abilities, and assignments to various individuals in His church. Those who will be rewarded greatly at the Judgment Seat are those who've stayed submitted to those in positions over them. Associate pastors who've split churches, employees who've built their own businesses while being paid by their employers, and so on—all will suffer tremendous loss at the judgment, even if they did produce great results in their rebellion.

Don't allow results to deceive you. We can have great results and still be in rebellion to God's authority. Consider Moses. The Lord told him to speak to a rock and water would miraculously come out. He didn't obey. Rather, out of anger he struck the rock. Water still came out, enough to give three million people a drink in the desert. The people were probably saying to each other as they drank, "Wow, God sure listens to Moses. What power!"

Yet after they all drank, God called Moses aside and told him he would not enter the Promised Land because he had not obeyed. Moses had results—miraculous results, in fact. But results are not the indication of success. Obedience is. Godly wisdom is rooted in the fear of the Lord, which places God's will above anything or anyone else. Those who fear God are completely submitted to His authority.

Let's return to my wife's vision. She reported to me that morning, "John, all the warriors had the exact same faces." In other words, it was a faceless army. This shows God doesn't have superstar positions. Understanding this will keep us from coveting another's place in the church or rebelling against authority in order to gain greater positions. Our promotion will come from above only if we stay planted.

Different Levels

In the Gospels we find two similar parables that each illustrate a different truth related to the Judgment Seat. These are the parables of the talents and the minas. The first parable, that of the talents, emphasizes that not all believers are given the same level of calling and gifts. Jesus says:

> "For the kingdom of heaven is like a man traveling to a far country, who called his own servants and delivered his goods to them. And to one he gave five talents, to another two, and to another one, to each according to his own ability; and immediately he went on a journey." (Matthew 25:14–15)

The man who travels to the far country represents Jesus, and the servants represent us. A talent is a measure of money; however, since this is a parable, the talent likely represents something else.

One possibility, which I personally believe to be true, is that the talents stand for the level of our call and gifts. For example, there are certain individuals who have levels of ministry that reach nations, others that reach cities, and still others who reach home groups within the church. Some writers reach millions, others reach thousands, and still others reach hundreds. One person possessing an administrative gift could bring a ministry to a megachurch level, while others can only handle churches of intermediate or smaller sizes. There are businessmen and women whose entrepreneurial abilities enable them to grow businesses that net hundreds of thousands for the kingdom. Others grow businesses that make millions, and still others have the ability to grow several companies that produce millions or billions to give to the work of the kingdom.

Back to the parable. Notice two important points in it. First, all the servants are given something, which tells us there isn't one person in the church without a call (accompanied by gifts) on their life. Second, the different levels of calls and gifts given to each servant were according to their ability. However, we must remember God gives us our abilities. We have nothing of value that wasn't given to us, for Scripture states, "For who makes you differ from another? And what do you have that you did not receive?" (1 Corinthians 4:7)

In this parable, the man with the level-five calling and gifts doubled his invested effort. The man with two talents did the same. I personally believe this shows that even if God gives us gifts, we must cooperate with our labor in order to create the return He desires.

However, the man with the level-one calling and gifts could have felt his entrustments were insignificant. He viewed his master as unfair, unreasonable, and austere. He may have thought, *Why was I given less than the others? Why did they get national or citywide influence? Why did they get the ability to preach, sing, or write and not me? Why didn't my company grow in such a way that I could give as the others did?* And so forth. So he hid his talent. He didn't fulfill his calling. He used his gifts for himself or in arenas that did not profit the kingdom.

After a long time, the lord of the servants came and settled accounts with them. The two individuals who doubled what they were entrusted with were rewarded with the same praise: "Well done, good and faithful servant; you were faithful over a few things, I will make you ruler over many things. Enter into the joy of your lord" (Matthew 25:21). The level-five individual was not praised any more than the level-two servant because they were both faithful and diligent. This again affirms that God only requires us to be faithful to what He's given us.

The man with the single talent was sternly rebuked, and his lord commanded that what he was entrusted with be taken and given to one of the other men. The unfaithful servant suffered great loss, while the man who was faithful gained even more.

In hearing this, I reflect on 1992, when God instructed me to write. I almost laughed in unbelief of what I'd heard in my heart in prayer. I hated English! If anyone had said I would write a book, I would have laughed them out of the room.

However, ten months later, two women came to me within two weeks of each other and gave me the same prophetic word: "John, if you don't write what God has given you to write, He'll give the message to someone else and you will be judged." I trembled and stepped out in faith, and the rest is history. If I had not obeyed, someone else would have written the messages, and I would have lost the talent entrusted to me.

Multiplying What We've Been Given

We've extensively discussed that you can't add to your calling or gifts. Now let's turn our attention to *multiplying* what every believer has. The parable of the minas, which is similar to that of the talents but different in a huge way, shows this truth. Jesus says:

> "A certain nobleman went into a far country to receive for himself
> a kingdom and to return. So he called ten of his servants, delivered

to them ten minas, and said to them, 'Do business till I come.'"
(Luke 19:12–13)

A mina, like a talent, is a measure of money. But in this parable each man is given the same amount, a mina each. Therefore, the mina doesn't represent the level of our calling or gifts as the talents do. Rather, the mina represents the truths of God's Word, our foundational faith, the love of God shed abroad in our hearts, and the covenant blessings that are given to each believer. Each individual has the same measure; no one is given extra to start.

This parable speaks of what every one of us as believers possesses in Christ. Scripture states, "Therefore let no one boast in men. For all things are yours" (1 Corinthians 3:21). And again, "Blessed be the God and Father of our Lord Jesus Christ, who has blessed us with every spiritual blessing in the heavenly places in Christ" (Ephesians 1:3). These blessings are ours in Christ, but it is our faith that appropriates and manifests them here on the earth. And it's our obedience, prayers, and giving that cause them to multiply. This is why the nobleman, who represents Jesus, says to his servants (who represent us), "Do business till I come." We are to take what we've been given and *multiply* it to the glory of God.

Examine the results produced by these servants:

"And so it was that when he returned, having received the kingdom, he then commanded these servants, to whom he had given the money, to be called to him, that he might know how much every man had gained by trading. Then came the first, saying, 'Master, your mina has earned ten minas.' And he said to him, 'Well done, good servant; because you were faithful in a very little, have authority over ten cities.' And the second came, saying, 'Master, your mina has earned five minas.' Likewise he said to him, 'You also be over five cities.'

"Then another came, saying, 'Master, here is your mina, which I have kept put away in a handkerchief.'" (Luke 19:15–20)

The nobleman sternly rebuked the final man, and the mina he had was taken away and given to the man who multiplied his mina to ten. The Master said, "For I say to you, that to everyone who has will be given; and from him who does not have, *even what he has will be taken away from him*" (verse 26).

In this parable, Jesus only addresses three of the ten servants. Again, the important difference in this parable is that each individual started with exactly the same amount; however, one man increased it tenfold, another fivefold, and the third not at all. We also see that the rewards differ according to how effectively the servants did business. Their success directly determined how many cities they ruled over.

The manner in which we multiply what is entrusted to us will directly determine how much authority is entrusted to us in the Millennium and in the new heaven and new earth. The faithful will rule with Christ, but not all will have the same authority. Our diligence here will determine the scope of our rule with Him throughout eternity. This is based on all of us starting at an equal place with a mina each, so the faithful wife and mother who serves diligently in the church has the same opportunity to gain a reward as does the evangelist who wins hundreds of thousands.

This parable shows that each man had the potential of multiplying his mina many times over. In our personal lives, we can affect and build the kingdom of God as much or little as we desire; the choice is ours. In fact, in certain ways we are unlimited. You may hedge at this comment, but allow me to expound through examples. There are many I can give, but just a few will open the door of your heart of this spiritual principle. But before we dive into them, let's first look at the apostle Peter's words:

Grace . . . be multiplied to you in the knowledge of God and of Jesus our Lord, as His divine power has given to us all things that pertain to life and godliness . . . (2 Peter 1:2–3)

Grace can be *multiplied* in our lives. James says, "But He gives us more and more grace" (James 4:6 AMP). It's by grace we can do anything of worth in the kingdom. This ability is multiplied through knowing God intimately. This is why every believer should spend quality time with God. We should pray, read the Scriptures, read inspired books, and listen to anointed messages, all the while looking for and listening to the Holy Spirit and His revelation. As we do this, grace is multiplied in our lives, which gives us the ability to do more.

I've discovered that the more intimately I come to know God and His ways, the more effective I become. If I possess an ax that has a very dull blade, chopping down a tree may take all day. However, if I sharpen it, I can chop down five trees in one day using the same energy. This is what happens when grace is multiplied in our lives. We labor with greater efficiency.

I recall street witnessing at a gay pride parade in Dallas, Texas, years ago. For two hours I told these lost souls about Jesus, and they just looked at me as if I were from another world. Some fired scriptures back to me as fast as I was speaking them. I sensed that somehow I was beating my head against a wall. It was like casting seeds on concrete.

Then the Lord whispered to me, "Look to Me, and I will show you what to do." In the thirty minutes following, God led me to people and gave me the words to speak. The words were now sinking in, and three men gave their lives to Jesus Christ. Looking to the Holy Spirit and listening to His word spoken in my heart multiplied my efforts.

I've seen this in all areas of life. As I've grown in the Word of God, I've had the ability to do more in less time. I've discovered paths of truth that saved me hours, days, and even months of time. Prayers become more powerful, God's presence stronger, the impact on lives more efficient. Scripture promises this:

> Fear of the Lord is the beginning of wisdom. Knowledge of the Holy
> One results in understanding. Wisdom will multiply your days and
> add years to your life. (Proverbs 9:10–11 NLT)

Two things are promised in this passage: more years, which means a longer life, and multiplied days. The latter doesn't also mean more years, as that would be redundant. It means the ability to accomplish more in the same amount of time. This is described in another place as length of days: "For length of days and long life and peace they will add to you" (Proverbs 3:2). The writer of this verse speaks of adhering to the Word of God, as Peter discussed above. Notice not only long life but also length of days is given. Hearing and heeding God multiplies our time.

Multiplication through Giving

Anyone who comes to know God intimately becomes a joyful and generous giver because God Himself is an extravagant giver. He gave the greatest gift of all, His only Son. Nothing was of more value to Him than Jesus. The Lord never gives a halfhearted, insignificant gift. He gave Jesus looking for a multiplied harvest—which would be many sons and daughters coming into His family—and the harvest is still coming in.

Giving in faith is another sure way to multiply what we have; it can multiply what we possess to eternally affect lives, just as was the case when the Father gave Jesus for us. Jesus pointedly tells us, "I tell you, use worldly wealth to gain friends for yourselves, so that when it is gone, you will be welcomed into eternal dwellings" (Luke 16:9 NIV). Our money, used properly, can affect our quality of life in heaven and in the New Jerusalem long after the money is gone. "As it is written, He [the benevolent person] scatters abroad; He gives to the poor; His deeds of justice and goodness and kindness and benevolence will go on and endure forever!" (2 Corinthians 9:9 AMP)

The poor are not only the financially poor but also those who are poor in spirit. A person can have millions of dollars and still be poor in spirit. One example is the man Zacchaeus. In describing His mission, Jesus had said, "The Spirit of the Lord is upon Me, because He has anointed Me to preach the gospel to the *poor*" (Luke 4:18). Later He enters a city, finds the wealthiest man, and then addresses him in front of a large crowd by saying, "I must be a guest in your home today" (Luke 19:5 NLT). Even though Zacchaeus was the richest man in the city, he was obviously the poorest. In other words, he knew more than anyone else how much he needed God. Jesus ministered to many people who were financially wealthy, but they were well aware of their need of the Word of God.

Ministries are raised up to do the work of Jesus, to proclaim and teach the Word of God to the poor. In giving financially to the work of God, we sow into the poor, and our deeds endure forever. It makes no difference how much or little you have financially. As long as you have a seed—which God says He will give you—you can multiply your efforts in building the kingdom.

How does your gift multiply? Consider an apple seed. If you plant it, you'll eventually receive a crop of apples. But even more important is that within all those apples will be many more seeds. If all of those seeds are planted, they will yield many times more, and the cycle continues. It is exactly the same with our finances. See what Paul says to the Corinthians regarding their giving:

> Remember this: Whoever sows sparingly will also reap sparingly, and whoever sows generously will also reap generously. Each man should give what he has decided in his heart to give, not reluctantly or under compulsion, for God loves a cheerful giver. (2 Corinthians 9:6–7 NIV)

Our multiplied harvest will be in direct proportion to how much we sow. Notice that sowing is not as God decides but according to what we decide to give. If we purpose in faith and love to be generous, then our giving is greatly multiplied: "Now he who supplies seed to the sower and bread for food will also *supply* and *increase* your *store of seed* and will enlarge the *harvest of your righteousness*" (2 Corinthians 9:10 NIV).

The Lord will increase our store of seed, similar to the example of the apple seed just given. If we sow what we have, we will get many more seeds. The process continues until we find in our possession a storehouse of seeds, giving us greater ability to bless others.

Through our giving, God will also enlarge the *harvest of our righteousness.* This is where it gets very exciting. This speaks of increasing our harvest of eternal rewards from the lives we've touched through our giving. So in essence, we are multiplying our minas, just like the men in the parable.

Partnering with Others

Our giving to others, especially those in need who can't repay us, brings rewards both in this life and at the judgment. In regard to multiplying our efforts to build the kingdom, we can do this through *partnership* in the gospel. See what Paul says to the believers in Philippi who supported his ministry financially:

> But it was right and commendable and noble of you to contribute for my needs and to share my difficulties with me. And you Philippians yourselves well know that in the early days of the Gospel ministry, when I left Macedonia, no church (assembly) entered into partnership with me and opened up [a debit and credit] account in giving and receiving except you only. For even in Thessalonica you sent [me contributions] for my needs, not only once but a second time. (Philippians 4:14–16 AMP)

Notice Paul speaks of the Philippian believers' *partnership* with his ministry. A partnership is defined as "a relationship between individuals or groups that is characterized by mutual cooperation and responsibility, as for the achievement of a specified goal."[2] Healthy, God-given partnership always gives the individuals involved the ability to do more than they could ever dream of doing on their own.

As I've stated, Jesus commissioned us to go into the entire world and make *disciples* of all nations, not just converts. This assignment encompasses every believer. However, if all believers were on the mission field accomplishing this on a full-time basis, how would the gospel be funded? (This again is why God gives different callings and gifts to each individual.) The Lord never intended ministries to receive their necessary finances by the distribution of angels or by money falling from the sky. Rather, He entrusted His body with the privilege of giving, which creates partnership.

God has called and ordained people with ministry gifts to reach the masses. As already stated, He gives special gifting, abilities, and anointing to accomplish this purpose. He didn't give this task to all but to some in the church (see Ephesians 4:11). The rest of the church He commissioned and entrusted with another integral part of His purposes. This includes working, making money or receiving wages, and reaching those within their circles of influence with the gospel. However, if you work full-time, how can you reach the masses? The answer is found by way of partnership.

If you had a life-changing product but you were only able to produce two per month, it would be impossible to distribute this item to your city, your country, or the world. However, if there existed a company with both the ability and special equipment necessary to produce and distribute thousands of these products per month, you would partner with them in order to get the job done. In doing this, you would not only be reaching your two people a month (an example of personal evangelism and discipleship) but also the additional thousands the company reached. You would have effectively multiplied your talents and efforts through simple partnership.

This very same principle applies to Paul's comments to the Philippians. He continues: "Not that I seek or am eager for [your] gift, but I do seek and am eager for the *fruit which increases to your credit* [the harvest of blessing that is accumulating to your account]" (Philippians 4:17 AMP).

Notice the phrase "fruit which increases to your credit." These Philippian believers multiplied their efforts in reaching and teaching souls by sowing finances into Paul's life and ministry through partnership. They gave that which is temporal, thereby converting it to the eternal, and in the process it was multiplied as well.

When you enter this type of partnership, Paul says you will have a "harvest of blessing that is accumulating to your account." This is your heavenly account. When you stand before the Judgment Seat of Christ, you will not only be rewarded for the lives you personally affected in your workplace, neighborhood, school, and so forth, but also for the thousands or millions of others you reached and trained through partnering with God-ordained ministries. For this reason Scripture tells us, "Give generously, for your gifts will return to you later. Divide your gifts among many" (Ecclesiastes 11:1–2 NLT).

As you consistently give to God-ordained ministries (including your local church), you join with them as they touch others through their outreach. You have a part in all they do because you partner with them. Here is the exciting news: the more you invest, the greater your reward.

Know that God does not judge the gift so much by the amount but by your faithfulness to sow. God the Father is looking for quality gifts of the heart. He loves and blesses this heart aspect, not just the amount. For example, someone could be faithful to give a ministry a gift of thirty dollars each month. By doing this, there may be some personal cost to the giver. God would see this gift as more than merely a financial amount, for it is given from the necessities of the giver's life. Then there could be another who gives one thousand dollars each month, but this gift is extended out of the person's abundance. There is no personal cost or sacrifice involved. Both are beautiful and valuable to God, but the one who gave more through God's view is the one who gave the thirty dollars. This dynamic is illustrated by the widow who gave her two mites (see Mark 12:41–44).

We must also keep in mind that God multiplies our gifts in this earthly life as well. This flow gives each of us a greater ability to give more. Scripture states, "There are those who [generously] scatter abroad, and yet increase more" (Proverbs 11:24 AMP). Think of it. Your investment not only grows eternally, but it also expands in the natural world, and this gives you the ability to reach more people. This is a cycle that continually renews itself and increases.

Twenty-two years ago, a group of businessmen I know got together and committed to designate a certain portion of their business profits to the furtherance of the gospel. The effort started small, but with each passing year, it grew. The men remained consistent in their giving and partnership. Their giving has expanded to the point that they gave over $120 million to the gospel in the first twelve years since their commitment was made. They have taken their mina and multiplied it for kingdom purposes; their reward shall be great.

There are a large number of men and women in the church whose businesses are very successful; however, many give a fraction of what they've earned to the kingdom. Even though they are hugely successful in society's eyes, what will be the Master's view of what they've held onto? Even if they made millions, will they be judged like the one who hid his mina? They didn't multiply what was given them for the sake of the kingdom. Those who live in this manner are not *driven by eternity*.

Recently I played golf with a businessman who had given to our ministry on occasion. After the round, he drove me back to my hotel. As we drove he said, "John, I'm almost fifty years old. I've worked extra hard to build my company's net worth to nine million dollars. All is well, the business is running itself, and my wife and children are set for life. Why should I spend the next ten years of my life working my tail off to build my business up to thirty or forty million?"

I realized he didn't see himself as a vital part of building God's house. He saw me as holding an important role in the kingdom, but as a businessman, he didn't see his worth.

I quickly answered his question with another question. "Suppose I said to you, 'I've worked extremely hard and written seventeen books, traveled seven million miles, and preached thousands of sermons. Things are cruising along, the ministry is running itself, and my wife and kids are set for life. Why should I work my tail off to write more books, travel, and preach more messages?' How do you think Jesus would respond to that?"

He laughed and said, "I wouldn't want to be in your shoes when you faced Him."

I immediately responded, "You just said exactly that!"

I let him think for a moment. Then I continued, "The gifts that Jesus has given me to build His kingdom are preaching and writing. The gift Jesus has given you to build His kingdom is making money to fund the kingdom. You have not connected the dots. I'm limited in what I can do for Jesus by your obedience or lack of obedience, just as my mouth would be limited in those it could speak to if my legs decided to stop working in order to get me to the people I needed to talk to." The man was stunned.

Six months later, I called him. I asked how he was doing. He said, "John, I've been haunted in a good way each and every day by the words you spoke to me six months ago. I've been working my tail off to make more so I can give more." I love his humility.

On the flip side, my wife and I know another businessman who was planted in our home church and was very active in it, serving wherever he was needed. He knew he was not called to minister full-time but to work in the marketplace. He set a goal to live off 10 percent of his income and give 90 percent. He hit that goal, yet with that 10 percent, he drove an extremely nice car and lived in a spectacular home. His kingdom partnership caused his businesses to blossom and his 10 percent to expand. He applied the principle of Jesus: those who are faithful in little will be faithful with much.

Another reason for partnering is that it is our chance to give back to the ministries that have touched us. Paul states, "If we have sown [the seed of] spiritual good among you, [is it too] much if we reap from your material benefits? If others share in this rightful claim upon you, do not we [have a still better and greater claim]?" (1 Corinthians 9:11–12 AMP)

This translates into the natural world as well. If you were given a gift from one friend, you would not write a thank-you note to another. You would thank the one who blessed you, and in doing this you would be establishing or strengthening a relationship. God designed partnership this way on purpose, for the more people a ministry reaches and touches, the greater their financial needs to operate become. So if all who are being impacted by the ministry give finances back (even if their contribution is the two mites of the widow), then the expenses needed to continue at that level of ministry, as well as to expand, are covered.

Paul concludes his statement to the Philippians by saying:

> But I have [your full payment] and more; I have everything I need
> and am amply supplied, now that I have received from Epaphroditus
> the gifts you sent me. [They are the] fragrant odor of an offering and
> sacrifice which God welcomes and in which He delights. And my
> God will liberally supply (fill to the full) your every need according
> to His riches in glory in Christ Jesus. (Philippians 4:18–19 AMP)

The promise that God will supply every need according to His riches is made to the ones who partner with ministries. If you tithe and partner with ministries, then you can stand strong on this promise of God. You will never lack.

Multiplication through Prayer

Another way we can multiply is through prayer. Just as we do through the giving of our finances to ministries, we can eternally touch lives of those we'll not meet until heaven by praying for individuals, families, churches, cities, and nations. We can also touch lives by praying for ministries. In our ministry, we have both financial partners and prayer partners. A prayer partner is someone who commits to pray for Messenger International on a daily basis.

People often come to me and say, "I'm praying for you every day." I can always tell if they sincerely do or if they are just saying so. To the ones who sincerely intercede for us, I say, "That is the greatest thing you can do to help us." It's true! If people pray, more lives get touched and with a greater impact. Prayer will also cause God to move on hearts to give toward His work—so if I had to choose between a prayer partner and a financial partner, I'd take the prayer partner first. However, both are very necessary.

Multiplication through Serving

Another way we multiply is by serving ministries. There are many helpers and team members in our organization whom Lisa and I constantly remind that they'll receive credit at the Judgment Seat for every life our ministry touches.

I know this from David's statement to all his men when returning from battle. In 1 Samuel 30, we find the account of David pursuing the Amalekites and recovering what had been captured and stolen from Israel's camp. When David and his men returned to the camp, some of the men who had gone with David didn't want to share the rewards with those who stayed behind to guard the equipment. But listen to David's response:

> "We share and share alike—those who go to battle and those who guard the equipment." From then on David made this a law for all of Israel, and it is still followed. (1 Samuel 30:24–25 NLT)

David is a type or representation of Christ. So the statement, "From then on David made this a law for all of Israel, and it is still followed," tells me that this still applies today with Jesus and His church. At the

Judgment Seat, all a ministry touches isn't credited just to the leader but to all those who faithfully served, gave, and prayed even if they were not on the scene of the battlefield.

Attitude Is Important

An integral part of receiving rewards for your service is your attitude, as we have discussed. It is not just our works that count but also the motives that fuel our works, and our attitude will affect our motives. God says, "If you are willing and obedient, you shall eat the good of the land" (Isaiah 1:19).

I recall a time when I was very dry in my walk with God. I seemed to get nothing from our church services, especially my pastor's preaching. I certainly was not flourishing.

I worked on the staff of this eight-thousand-member church, reporting directly to the pastor, but I had become critical of him. In prayer one morning God spoke to me and said, "The problem is not with your pastor. The problem is with you."

I was stunned. "What's my problem?"

The Lord then asked me what Isaiah 1:19 stated. I quoted the above verse, as I had memorized it. He then said, "There is your problem. You keep saying you are not being fed, and this is correct, for you are not eating the good of the land."

I immediately countered with, "I am obedient. I do everything my pastor requests of me!"

Then the Lord responded, "I didn't say if you were obedient you would eat the good of the land. I said if you are *willing* and obedient." He then said, "Obedience deals with your actions, and *willing* deals with your attitude. And your attitude stinks!"

The Lord went on to reveal how I did obey and even looked submitted, but my attitude was critical, complaining, and judgmental, thus affecting my motives for serving.

I immediately repented, and the next service, the heavens opened. I received from God once again. I shed tears while my pastor preached, thinking of all I had missed for months because of my attitude. Shortly afterward, these words of Paul inspired by the Holy Spirit became very clear to me: "For this was my purpose in writing you, to test your attitude and see if you would stand the test, whether you are obedient and altogether agreeable [to following my orders] in everything" (2 Corinthians 2:9 AMP).

I realized that God will test our attitude of submission to His will for us. I'm not discussing tolerating what the devil tries to throw on us, which Jesus paid the price to set us free from. We are to resist the enemy steadfastly through faith, prayer, and speaking God's Word. Rather, I'm speaking of our attitude toward the path God has chosen for us to walk. Of this Paul says, "Your attitude should be the same that Christ Jesus had" (Philippians 2:5 NLT). Jesus not only drank from the cup the Father prepared for Him but did it willingly. For this reason, Paul tells us to "be constantly renewed in the spirit of your mind [having a fresh mental and spiritual attitude]" (Ephesians 4:23 AMP).

Why? Because our attitude will affect our motives, and at the Judgment Seat we will be rewarded not only for our works but also for the motives that fueled them. Again, let's look at Paul's words:

> For we must all appear and be revealed as we are before the judgment
> seat of Christ, so that each one may receive [his pay] according to
> what he has done in the body, whether good or evil [considering what
> his purpose and motive have been, and what he has achieved, been
> busy with, and given himself and his attention to accomplishing]. (2
> Corinthians 5:10 AMP)

I've grieved in seeing how some have become bitter serving God. They've lost sight of the eternal perspective. They continue to work, but their attitude grows jaded and their motives become envious and self-seeking. This, more than anything else I can think of, has caused people who started passionate to not finish well. That is why we are warned to be "looking diligently lest anyone fall short of the grace of God; lest any root of bitterness springing up cause trouble, and by this *many* become defiled" (Hebrews 12:15).

Notice this verse says *many* may become defiled. I have witnessed this repeatedly in over thirty years of full-time ministry, and it is heartbreaking. In the *Amplified Bible*, this verse encourages us to "exercise foresight and be on the watch to look [after one another]." We should speak words to one another that will prevent this bitterness from setting in, because we don't want to see our loved ones fall or fail to receive their full reward due to a root attitude that was not confronted.

My wife and I have especially looked out for our children and staff in this area. We are called to travel full-time, and our children have grace on their lives for our lifestyle. However, we don't want them to fall short of that grace. We have spoken to them words to encourage, guard their attitudes, and keep them strong.

I recall one day sitting down with our four sons and saying, "Boys, you are well aware that I travel many days a month, and your mother is out several days a month as well. We do this because it is the call of God on our lives. This is how He has ordained us to touch people's lives for His glory and build His kingdom."

I continued, "You can view the call of God on our lives one of two ways. You can see it like your parents are being taken from you and you are being ripped off of normal family life. Or you can see it as *your* ministry, not just your parents'. The way it becomes your ministry is that you are sowing your parents—sending them into the lives of multiplied thousands for God's purposes. If your attitude is this, then every soul we touch, you will be rewarded for at the Judgment Seat. If you see us as being taken, then you will not receive one reward for the lives we touch. So boys, it all comes down to one word: *attitude*."

They grabbed what was said to them, and as a result they have never complained about our traveling. In fact, many times when Lisa and I have hedged over accepting an invitation, our boys have encouraged us to do so. We have fabulous relationships with them. They all love God, and all of them serve with us in our ministry. Thanks be to God for His amazing grace. Now, as a result, our sons are multiplying their minas at a very young age.

I've done the same with our staff. I've told them, "You can see working here as a job, and you will eventually get tired and bitter and not receive a reward at the Judgment Seat. Or you can see it as your privilege to touch millions of lives. With every book you mail out, every email you help us answer, every person you reach out to on social media, every meeting you arrange, and so on, you are a vital part of what God is doing to touch the lives He's ordained this ministry to touch. You are like David's men guarding the equipment." They grabbed this truth and have a great attitude. It's my job as a leader to speak words of life that will help protect that attitude, although the ultimate responsibility for each person's attitude is their own.

Keeping a great attitude helps us to multiply our minas and finish well. God is building His custom home, and what a privilege we have in being co-laborers with Him. So no matter how insignificant your part seems, remember that every part is vital and that you can be as effective or ineffective as you choose. My hope for you is the same as the apostle John's: "Look to yourselves, that we do not lose those things we worked for, but that we may receive a full reward" (2 John 8).

CHAPTER 14

ᑭersonal Influence

But you know…how I live, and what my purpose in
life is. You know my faith and how long I have suffered.
You know my love and my patient endurance.
—2 Timothy 3:10 NLT

In eternity, we'll be rewarded or suffer loss in regard to our influence in other's lives. This will result not only from our ministries but also (and just as importantly) from our personal walks—the manner in which we lived and treated others.

How we view others motivates our treatment of them, either in an edifying or a destructive way. If we see people as below us, we'll treat them as such. We'll take their needs lightly and speak down to them. If we value individuals, we'll seek to build and strengthen their lives out of a heart of compassion and love.

If we see people as sources, then we will use them, especially when our wishes, needs, or desires are placed above their value. If we view people as ones who are created in the image of God and are extremely precious and valuable, then our motive will be to bless others even when it appears to be at our own expense. This is Christlike behavior.

Selfish Strongholds

I was a very self-focused person before I came to know Jesus. After my conversion in 1979, the Holy Spirit had to attack selfish strongholds in my behavioral patterns. Needless to say, my first decade in Christ was a period of strong confrontation.

One of the strongholds in my life was sexual lust. If tempted with pornography, I found it very difficult to resist. After struggling for six years, I was delivered on the fourth day of a fast in 1985. Once I was free, the process of being renewed in the spirit of my mind began.

Over the next few years I discovered the root of this lust. The love of God continued to grow in my heart, and my sense of people's value steadily increased. I realized the extreme selfishness of my former addiction. To look upon a woman in a pornographic or lustful way was to reduce her to a piece of meat, and that grew to be revolting to my heart.

The revelation that women were created in the image of God and crowned with glory and honor grew stronger in me. I had long known this truth, but my understanding was only mental knowledge, not a part of my being. Over a period of time, I discovered the reality of God's transforming process. When pornographic images were flashed before me on a billboard, magazine cover, or television screen, I would feel assaulted. I'd find myself very upset that this person Jesus shed His blood for was being reduced to a piece of meat. How I responded to women changed significantly as this revelation grew.

I'm shocked how women are treated even by some in the church. They are looked down upon, viewed as if they are less valuable, and even scorned. This is absurd. Men and women are equal heirs of the kingdom of God, and as the stronger vessels (which refers to stronger physical bodies, not stronger souls or hearts), men should honor women above themselves. Men should respect, value, esteem, protect, and always seek to build up women. Husbands, you are the head of your unions, but headship in the kingdom means you lay your life down for your family through serving. It does not mean that you lord your role over your wife and children. If you see headship as putting you above your wife, then you will treat her in such a way that will wound and tear down rather than build up. You will give an account for this at the judgment.

Wanting Acceptance

Another area of selfishness God exposed to me was even more deceptive. In the mid-1980s I served on a church staff of roughly four hundred employees. Our church had over eight thousand members and reached thousands of churches nationwide.

I hated confrontation at the time, so I would avoid it at any cost. I was extremely kind and polite to people. At every opportunity, I spoke nice things to people, even if what I said wasn't true. I built a reputation for being one of the nicest guys on staff. These reports were leaking back to me, and I reveled in them.

Then one day in prayer, God asked me, "Where did I say in 1 Corinthians 13 that love is nice?"

I was a bit taken aback and responded, "Nowhere."

Then God said, "Son, do you know the reason you tell others only nice things, even if they are not true?"

I answered, "Why, no, I've not thought about it."

He quickly responded, "You fear their rejection. So who is the focus of your love, you or them? If you really love people, you would tell them the truth whether they like it or not. You would be more concerned for their welfare to help them, even if it meant their rejection of you."

I clearly saw my selfishness masked by politeness; the painful truth was made clear. I used people for my need of acceptance. I wanted affirmation to appease my insecurities and didn't place priority on helping others. I just wanted their acceptance.

This is why there are countless ministers who will only preach the "positive" side of the Word of God. They will refrain from warning, correction, or rebuke. They are more concerned with not offending their members and not seeing the church dwindle than with genuinely loving their congregations.

Who is the focus of such love, others or self? If we saw someone headed for a cliff blindfolded, would we not cry out in order to turn them from harm's way? Yet I've heard some of these "loving ministers" speak in private, and the way they talk about people is alarming. They treat waiters, bellmen, and other service people like they are lower-class citizens. How are such believers impacting people outside their public lives? They will give an account for how they influenced each individual they came in contact with.

From Nice to Harsh

Once this revelation came into my life, the pendulum swung to the opposite side. I became a harsh preacher. I still did not have God's love for people burning in my heart. I was more focused on being right than on the eternal well-being of people. Sometimes I would fry congregations. The focus was still on me, but my selfishness was manifesting in a different way. My behavior was a classic example of this passage: "You think that everyone should agree with your perfect knowledge. While knowledge may make us feel important, it is love that really builds up the church" (1 Corinthians 8:1–2 NLT).

I look back on the earlier days of our traveling ministry now and feel so bad for some of the pastors who had to clean up after my departure. If I were a pastor back then, I certainly wouldn't have invited John Bevere to come and minister in my church. I'm so grateful to these leaders who saw in me a sincere desire to serve God and His people even though I still needed a lot of growth.

At this point, I was no longer flattering to gain acceptance and avoid rejection. I was speaking truth and confronting, but with the same selfish motives that God was purging from me hidden away.

After a few years, a well-known pastor criticized me to some very influential leaders; I heard about his comments from three different continents. I was very angry and devastated at first, but I knew offense would only cause me to drift from God. Eventually this man's attack against me caused me to cry out for more of the love of God like never before. I passionately petitioned God for a greater measure of compassion in my life. Without my realizing it, over time God matured His love for His valued people in my heart.

During this process, the Lord gave me a revelation that changed my ministry. You may think you're going to hear something very deep and profound, but it's really quite simple. You may even think it sounds silly until you ponder it. The revelation was, "A spoonful of sugar helps the medicine go down." I realized medicine's potency is not diminished if it is given with something sweet. It just makes it easier to take, and most times even makes it delightful.

Now numerous leaders have said to me, "John, I'm amazed how you had us all laughing as we were being filleted by the Word of God. You made such a serious subject life-giving." When I first heard these comments, I realized I was being matured by God's grace. I'm so grateful to Him!

Even though the pastor who criticized me to the other leaders most likely didn't intend to bless me, he was actually one of the greatest blessings to my life. You have to remember that sometimes God will use people's ill intent to get you into His will for your life. He used Judas's betrayal to orchestrate Jesus's destiny at the cross. He used Joseph's brothers' evil intents to bring about Joseph's God-given dream. And the list continues.

The Goal Is the Love of God

It all comes down to the way we view people. If we allow the love and compassion of God to grow in our lives, we will not look down upon others. Seeing people as below us fuels critical treatment, judgmental attitudes, harshness in our behavior, etc. See what Paul says to the Roman believers:

> Why do you criticize and pass judgment on your brother? Or you,
> why do you look down upon or despise your brother? For we shall all

stand before the judgment seat of God. . . . And so each of us shall give an account of himself [give an answer in reference to judgment] to God. (Romans 14:10, 12 AMP)

If believers lose sight of the second-greatest commandment—to love one another—we will inevitably fall into the trap Paul discusses above, that of looking down upon others. This mentality is especially found when one possesses biblical knowledge apart from the foundation of the fruit of the Spirit.

Scripture tells us that God is love. It's important to point out that love is not God. There is a huge difference. God's personality, ways, and purposes are not confined to our definition of what love is, for no one knows love until he or she knows Jesus. He is the very essence of love.

Also, nowhere do we read, "God has love." He has power. He has gifts. He has authority. And the list goes on. But Jesus is the very essence of love. Since this is so, we should be no different, for we are reborn in His nature. This is why Paul says:

> If I could speak in any language in heaven or on earth but didn't love others, I would only be making meaningless noise like a loud gong or a clanging cymbal. If I had the gift of prophecy, and if I knew all the mysteries of the future and knew everything about everything, but didn't love others, what good would I be? And if I had the gift of faith so that I could speak to a mountain and make it move, without love I would be no good to anybody. If I gave everything I have to the poor and even sacrificed my body, I could boast about it; but if I didn't love others, I would be of no value whatsoever. (1 Corinthians 13:1–3 NLT)

Love doesn't originate in our words. We can say we care for someone while our actions deny it. Love doesn't begin with our actions either. Paul says in the above passage that we can perform deeds that have the appearance of the highest love (giving everything to the poor and sacrificing our bodies) but do so apart from love. This tells us that true love originates from the heart.

When we love, we will be patient and kind with others. We'll not envy their success because it will be our passion to see them win. We'll never boast of ourselves and will refrain from all haughtiness and pride. We'll not demand our own way. We will not be irritable because of our impatient attitudes. We'll keep no record of when we've been wronged but will choose to forgive and release any debts. We'll never smile upon injustice; our passion will be for mercy and truth. We'll never give up on people or lose faith, and we will always believe the best. We'll always see others as innocent unless proven guilty, and even then we will remain hopeful for repentance and restoration. We will be full of hope and endure any hardship for the benefit of the kingdom or another's well-being. Bottom line: we will live for the godly edification of others, which is only found in their conformity to Christ and the fulfillment of His will for their lives.

A Leader Who Influenced Many

A few years back, I attended the funeral of a very close friend. His name was Jack Wallace. He founded Detroit World Outreach, in Detroit, Michigan, a multiracial church that grew to four thousand members in just ten years. Jack was traveling to Zimbabwe to preach at a crusade when he collapsed with a heart attack just after getting off the plane.

Thousands of people attended Jack's funeral: leaders of ministries from all over the United States, community leaders, and vice presidents of major corporations along with what society calls blue-collar workers, street people, and moms on food stamps. This was the demographic of his church. Many who didn't know Jesus as Lord attended the funeral as well, people including hotel and restaurant personnel along with others in the community whom he greatly impacted in his personal encounters.

The attendance of the citizens from outside Jack's church didn't surprise me. Jack and I spent considerable time together outside his church, and I was so blessed by how he behaved toward everyone he met. He treated each individual as valuable and precious. He tipped the waitresses and valets handsomely. I sometimes hedged a bit, thinking his behavior might be a tad excessive, but this stupid mindset was corrected one day when Jack told me how valuable and precious all these people were to God. Jack didn't just make you feel as if you were the most important person when you were with him. When you were with Jack, you really were the most important person to him.

The funeral service was four and a half hours long. Many of the leaders who were close to him were asked to get up and share for a few minutes. After hearing from four or five of us about our closeness to Jack and what he meant to us, one very well-known leader finally got up and said, "I thought I was his best friend!" Everyone laughed.

We all knew that Jack viewed us and treated each of us as his closest friend. Not only did this great leader impact nations through his crusades and television broadcasts, but he also impacted all those he came in contact with on an individual basis. It didn't matter if you were the CEO of a major corporation or someone on welfare. Jack knew how to communicate with you and love you as a human being. Not only was Jack faithful to his calling and gifts, but he also caused his minas to multiply in every area of life.

A Janitor Who Has Influenced Multitudes

Some of the individuals who've had the most profound impact on my life are people you will never see behind pulpits. One of them was a financial worker at Rockwell International. His name is Mike, and I came to know him only two years after I became a Christian. He was seated close to me at work, and we used to talk about the things of God during breaks and at lunchtime. Later, we connected for hours in each other's homes and at church. It was Mike's integrity and practical wisdom from the Scriptures that impacted me the most. I was also affected by the way he honored, loved, and respected his wife, children, and any individual who came across his path.

I eventually left Rockwell and went into ministry. A short while later, Mike also left the company and started his own accounting firm, which is still in existence today. His business became very successful. He's helped over twelve thousand clients with their tax returns and bookkeeping, and five thousand of those clients come to him on a regular basis. They've been with him for years because of his honesty and integrity.

I asked Mike recently how many of his clients he had ministered the Word of God to. He said, "John, a conservative estimate would be 90 percent." That would be over ten thousand people.

I was floored. I then asked how many he had led to salvation. His reply was, "Hundreds." He said, "Just last week I led a Cuban man to the Lord and prayed with him to be healed of cancer."

Mike has also helped many ministries set up their bookkeeping. Our ministry, when we were in our infant stage, was one of them. Mike saw the call on my life and for years did my tax returns at no charge. Mike's life has impacted people in so many ways.

I remember in our long conversations Mike talking about the janitor who influenced his life more than anyone else had. I called him recently to again ask about this man. Mike began to weep on the phone.

He said, "John, six of my nine aunts and uncles ended up in an insane asylum. My own mother ended up in one as well. Both of my grandfathers were shot by other men. My family was very messed up, and I was headed for this destiny.

"However, due to financial stress, my mother sent me to another family for them to care for me. I lived with them for seven years. The man of the house was a janitor of a local paper mill. His name was Charlie. His integrity, commitment to Jesus, and love for people broke the curse off my life. Every week he took me to church and taught me the ways of God. His influence on my life helped form who I am today. My daughter once wrote a paper and entitled it 'The Greatest Man I Never Knew.' It was about Charlie."

You'll most likely never hear about Charlie anywhere on earth outside this book. However, his influence has extended to the thousands Mike has ministered to. Also, his influence touched me through Mike. So the millions I've had the privilege to minister to have all been reached indirectly through Charlie as well. Do you see how one janitor multiplied his minas and will one day be rewarded greatly?

Influence to Legacy

This reminds me of a true account that one of my employees read to me recently. It is about an atheist named Max Jukes and a godly man named Jonathan Edwards. Here's the story:

> Max Jukes, the atheist, lived a godless life. He married an ungodly girl, and from the union there were 310 who died as paupers, 150 were criminals, 7 were murderers, 100 were drunkards, and more than half of the women were prostitutes. His 540 descendants cost the State one and a quarter million dollars.
>
> But, praise the Lord it works both ways! There is a record of a great American man of God, Jonathan Edwards. He lived at the same time as Max Jukes, but he married a godly girl. An investigation was made of 1,394 known descendants of Jonathan Edwards of which 13 became college presidents, 65 college professors, 3 United States senators, 30 judges, 100 lawyers, 60 physicians, 75 army and navy officers, 100 preachers and missionaries, 60 authors of prominence, one a vice-president of the United States, 80 became public officials in other capacities, 295 college graduates, among whom were governors of states and ministers to foreign countries. His descendants did not cost the state a single penny.[1]

That is yet another case of multiplying minas. These men—Charlie, Mike, and Jonathan Edwards—have affected so great a number of lives. Their influence led to great legacies. Yet it wasn't their public ministry that impacted these multitudes we speak of. It was their personal lives.

This is the privilege God gives every one of us. How you respond to a police officer, the way you speak of your pastor, how you treat your children, the manner in which you conduct your financial affairs, the words you use to speak to individuals, and the list continues—these all affect the lives of others around you. Will you be a builder or a stumbling block?

> Yes, each of us will have to give a personal account to God. So don't
> condemn each other anymore. Decide instead to live in such a way
> that you will not put an obstacle in another Christian's path. . . . Let
> us aim for harmony in the church and try to build each other up.
> (Romans 14:12–13, 19 NLT)

Paul speaks this in direct relationship to the Judgment Seat of God. Every influence we've had on individuals will come into clear examination there. It is most important we keep this before us at all times. It will motivate us to win rather than to look out for ourselves.

Rebecca Ruter Springer lived in the nineteenth century and was given an extended visit of heaven before her final departure to her reward. Upon returning, she wrote her classic book entitled *Intra Muros*. In it she quotes a relative who spent much time with her in heaven. She reported that this relative, her husband's brother, was close to the Master. His words to her were:

> "If only we could realize while we are yet mortals, that day by day we
> are building for eternity, how different our lives in many ways would
> be! Every gentle word, every generous thought, every unselfish deed,
> will become a pillar of eternal beauty in the life to come."[2]

Leading Others to Jesus

The greatest influence we can have on an individual is to lead that person to Christ. When you understand eternal judgments, you will be motivated to tell those you know the plan of salvation. We read, "He who is wise captures human lives [for God, as a fisher of men—he gathers and receives them for *eternity*]" (Proverbs 11:30 AMP).

As a young believer, I used to feel the pressure of preaching the gospel to every individual I came in contact with. However, I later learned to look to the Holy Spirit for guidance in when and what to speak. I realized that even Jesus stated He only did what He saw His Father doing. When we walk with God, there is a flow, not a compulsion that leads to frustration and turns people away.

However, the urge to lead others to eternal life will be ever present until we are taken home. The love of God fuels this desire. To lead someone to Christ causes all the angels, as well as God Himself, to rejoice with unspeakable joy. It carries a certain reward. Jesus says, "The harvesters are paid good wages, and the fruit they harvest is people brought to eternal life" (John 4:36 NLT).

I had the privilege of leading my wife to the Lord on our first date. Shortly after coming to Jesus, I made a commitment to not date another girl until God brought my wife to me. I figured God brought Eve to Adam; He could do the same for me.

I had dated many girls before becoming a Christian. After my conversion, I dated a few Christian girls and found it was interfering with my walk with God. There were rips and tears in our souls when we broke the relationships. It didn't take long to discover it wasn't healthy for me. So I made a commitment to pray before going out with another girl.

At the time, my wife was a party girl. Another guy on campus said she was the wildest girl on campus. I don't know if that was entirely true, but it was close to accurate. When my relationship with Lisa started, I hadn't been out with a girl for a year and a half because every time I'd ask, the Lord would tell me not to go. However, I felt compelled by the Holy Spirit to ask Lisa to an upcoming Bible study picnic. She accepted.

After the picnic, Lisa and I walked on the campus and I shared the gospel with her from midnight till 1:30 in the morning. She interrupted me and requested to get saved immediately. Shortly afterward, both of us knew it was God's will for us to marry. I can honestly say I got the better end of the deal. I wouldn't be the man I am today had it not been for her.

Lisa has touched millions of lives. She is a prolific author and an advocate for injustice, and she speaks at conferences all over the world. What if I hadn't taken the chance to reach out to her? What if my fear of her making fun of me had kept me from telling her about Jesus? I believe God would have sent someone else. I would have missed out on God's best choice for my wife and would not have a part in all the people she has eternally ministered to. Thank God for His gifts!

Remember, a seed will multiply, but a seed looks insignificant. Don't ever take the leading of the Holy Spirit for granted, and most especially, don't ignore Him. The most "insignificant" things God has led me to do have turned out to be the most significant multiplication factors in my life. God wants you to multiply. And God also wants to reward you for your multiplication.

A Final Exhortation

So much is at stake. We can't take our entrusted time here on earth lightly. People's eternal destinies are dependent upon our obedience to the plan of God. It's His will that all be saved and conformed into the image of Jesus. He doesn't want any left behind.

An entire generation was lost in the wilderness after coming out of Egypt. They had one of the greatest leaders of all time, but still they failed. We can have magnificent leaders, but it is up to all of us as a generation to fulfill the plan of the Master Builder. He has decreed, "This gospel of the kingdom will be preached in all the world as a witness to all the nations, and then the end will come" (Matthew 24:14). Let's not miss our assignment! It's time, the season is upon us, and He's at the door! If we don't fulfill our destiny, then God will have to raise up another generation like He did with Joshua's to complete His house, for He has already decreed that His house will be full.

We do our part to fulfill God's plan by multiplying what He's entrusted to us. Don't be discouraged. Don't see your part as insignificant. Don't lose your passion. Don't lose sight of the heavenly vision made clear in the New Testament, which has been outlined in this book. Not only are others in your generation counting on you—some are in desperate need for you to reveal Jesus to them, and others are in need of your extending His encouragement and strength. Your eternal destiny also awaits you. You can succeed by utterly depending on His grace. He is faithful!

I appeal to you as a fellow citizen of the kingdom. Fulfill your calling and make your election sure. Run your race fully to the end. You'll look back ten million years from this moment and rejoice that you did. You cannot be too committed to the will of God. So run your race to win!

As final words of encouragement, I leave you with one of Paul's earnest prayers for all the saints:

> May the Lord make your love for one another and for all people grow
> more and more and become as great as our love for you. In this way
> he will strengthen you, and you will be perfect and holy in the pres-
> ence of our God and Father when our Lord Jesus comes with all who
> belong to him. (1 Thessalonians 3:12–13 TEV)

Scripture contains many verses regarding eternal rewards,
far more than can be printed in this book. For a list of passages
revealing the major areas of eternal judgment and reward,
visit DrivenByEternity.com/EternalRewards.

DISCUSSION QUESTIONS

SECTION 6: CHAPTERS 13–14

1. Are there aspects of your life (or even something central to it) that seem unimportant or unimpressive to you? Think about these things from heaven's perspective. Why might your faithfulness in those seemingly insignificant areas be significant to God?

2. For most of us, the drive to compete or compare is instinctive. What changes about our approach to the kingdom of God when we aren't focused on how we measure up against anyone else?

3. Is your life rich with multiplication? How can you better steward your time, prayer, talents, and resources?

4. At the very beginning of our journey, we discussed 1 John 4:17, which says that we can be confident before the Judgment Seat of Christ. Knowing what you do now, can you explain why that is?

5. How can you, right now, be intentional to build a life of eternal influence?

APPENDIX
HOW TO RECEIVE SALVATION

*If you confess with your mouth that Jesus is Lord and believe in
your heart that God raised him from the dead, you will be saved.
For it is by believing in your heart that you are made right with
God, and it is by confessing with your mouth that you are saved.*

—Romans 10:9–10 NLT

God wants to see you positioned for eternal success. He's passionate
about you and the plan He has for your life. But there's only one way
to start the journey to your destiny: by receiving salvation through God's
Son, Jesus Christ.

Through the death and resurrection of Jesus, God has made the way
for you to enter His kingdom as a beloved son or daughter. The sacrifice
of Jesus on the cross made eternal and abundant life freely available to
you. Salvation is God's gift to you; you cannot do anything to earn or
deserve it.

To receive this precious gift, first acknowledge your sin of living independently of your Creator (for this is the root of all the sins you have
committed). This repentance is a vital part of receiving salvation. Peter
made this clear on the day that five thousand were saved in the book of
Acts: "Repent therefore and be converted, that your sins may be blotted
out" (Acts 3:19). Scripture declares that each of us is born a slave to sin.
This slavery is rooted in the sin of Adam, who began the pattern of will-
ful disobedience. Repentance is a choice to walk away from obedience
to yourself and Satan, the father of lies, and to turn in obedience to your
new Master, Jesus Christ—the One who gave His life for you.

You must give Jesus lordship over your life. To make Jesus "Lord" means you give Him ownership of your life (spirit, soul, and body)—everything you are and have. His authority over your life becomes absolute. The moment you do this, God delivers you from darkness and transfers you to the light and glory of His kingdom. You simply go from death to life—you become His child!

If you want to receive salvation through Jesus, pray these words:

God in Heaven, I acknowledge that I am a sinner and have fallen short of Your righteous standard. I deserve to be judged for eternity for my sin. Thank You for not leaving me in this state, for I believe You sent Jesus Christ, Your only begotten Son, who was born of the virgin Mary, to die for me and carry my judgment on the cross. I believe He was raised again on the third day and is now seated at Your right hand as my Lord and Savior. So on this day, I repent of my independence from You and give my life entirely to the lordship of Jesus.

Jesus, I confess you as my Lord and Savior. Come into my life through Your Spirit and change me into a child of God. I renounce the things of darkness which I once held onto, and from this day forward I will no longer live for myself. By Your grace, I will live for You who gave Yourself for me that I may live forever.

Thank You, Lord. My life is now completely in Your hands, and according to Your Word, I shall never be ashamed.

Welcome to the family of God! I encourage you to share your exciting news with another believer. It's also important that you join a Bible-believing local church and connect with others who can encourage you in your new faith. Feel free to contact our ministry (visit Messenger International.org) for help finding a church in your area.

You have just embarked on the most remarkable journey. May you grow in revelation, grace, and friendship with God every day!

Notes

Chapter 1

1. *Webster's Encyclopedic Unabridged Dictionary of the English Language* (New York: Gramercy, 1993), s.v. "eternity."
2. *The American Heritage Dictionary of the English Language,* Fourth Edition (New York: Houghton Mifflin, 2000), s.v. "eternity." Eternity: *the state or quality of being eternal;* eternal: *existing outside of time;* hence: *the state of existing outside of time.*
3. Merrill F. Unger, *The New Unger's Bible Dictionary,* ed. R. K. Harrison (Chicago: Moody, 1988), BibleSoft PCStudyBible Version 4.
4. Robert Young, *Young's Literal Translation of the Holy Bible* (Grand Rapids, MI: Baker, 1986).

Chapter 3

1. Revelation 2:23 AMP
2. Luke 16:2
3. Hebrews 4:13 AMP
4. John 8:24
5. Acts 4:12 AMP
6. James 2:10 TLB
7. Ephesians 2:8–9 NLT (the name *God* was changed to *Jalyn* to fit the story)
8. Ecclesiastes 9:5–6 NLT
9. Proverbs 24:20 NLT
10. Proverbs 13:13
11. Matthew 22:13–14
12. Revelation 22:14–15
13. Titus 1:16 NLT (the name *God* was changed to *Jalyn* to fit the story)
14. Luke 6:46 TEV
15. Matthew 7:21–23 TLB (the word *heaven* was changed to *Affabel* to fit the story)
16. James 2:14, 17–20 NLT (the name *God* was changed to *Jalyn* to fit the story).
17. Ezekiel 18:25, 27–28 TLB

18. Psalm 50:16–21 TLB
19. Matthew 22:13
20. Proverbs 30:12
21. Matthew 24:12–13 TEV
22. 2 Peter 2:20–21 TEV (the name *Jesus Christ* was changed to *Jalyn* to fit the story)
23. Ezekiel 18:24–27 NLT
24. Matthew 24:13
25. Revelation 3:5 NASB
26. Proverbs 21:16 NIV
27. Matthew 22:13–14 (the pronoun *him* was changed to *her* to fit the story)
28. Hebrews 10:26–27, 30–31 NLT (the name *God* was changed to *Jalyn* to fit the story)
29. James 3:1 NLT (the word *church* was changed to *school* and the name *God* was changed to *Jalyn* to fit the story)
30. Mark 9:42
31. Luke 12:45–48 NLT
32. Jude 13 TEV
33. Matthew 22:13–14
34. Revelation 16:5–7 TEV

Chapter 4
1. *The American Heritage Dictionary,* Third Edition (New York: Houghton Mifflin, 1992), s.v. "elementary."

Chapter 5
1. Movie Reviews: *The Matrix.* http://www.pluggedinonline.com /movies/movies/a0000128.cfm. Accessed September 5, 2005.
2. Alexander Roberts and James Donaldson, eds., *The AnteNicene Fathers.* "Polycarp: Letter to the Philippians," 10 vols. (Grand Rapids, MI: Wm. Eerdmans Publishing Company, 1985), ch. 1.
3. Alexander Roberts and James Donaldson, eds., *The AnteNicene Fathers.* "Polycarp: Letter to the Philippians," 10 vols. (Grand Rapids, MI: Wm. Eerdmans Publishing Company, 1985), ch. 2.
4. Alexander Roberts and James Donaldson, eds., *The AnteNicene Fathers.* "Clement of Rome Letter to the Corinthians," 10 vols. (Grand Rapids, MI: Wm. Eerdmans Publishing Company, 1985), ch. 32.

5. Alexander Roberts and James Donaldson, eds., *The AnteNicene Fathers.* "Clement of Rome Letter to the Corinthians," 10 vols. (Grand Rapids, MI: Wm. Eerdmans Publishing Company, 1985), ch. 34.

6. David W. Bercot, ed., *A Dictionary of Early Christian Beliefs* (Hendrickson Publishers, Inc., 1998), 586.

7. Ibid.

8. Josh McDowell, *Evidence That Demands a Verdict* (San Bernardino, CA: Here's Life Publishers, 1972), 50–52.

Chapter 6

1. Kenneth E. Hagin, *I Believe in Visions* (Tulsa, OK: Faith Library Publications, 1984), 68–71 (second edition; tenth printing).

2. From the UBS Handbook Series. © 1961–1997 by United Bible Societies.

3. David W. Bercot, ed. *A Dictionary of Early Christian Beliefs* (Hendrickson Publishers, Inc., 1998).

4. Ibid.

5. Ibid.

6. Ibid.

7. Ibid.

8. *The American Heritage Dictionary of the English Language*, Fourth Edition. Houghton Mifflin Co., 2004 (software edition).

Chapter 8

1. Luke 14:12–14

2. Mark 12:43–44 TEV

3. Colossians 1:28 (the name *Christ* was changed to *Jalyn* to fit the story)

4. Ezekiel 13:10–11 NIV

5. 1 Corinthians 3:12–15 NLT

6. 1 Thessalonians 2:19–20 NLT

7. Matthew 12:36–37 TEV

8. Proverbs 12:14 TEV

9. Jeremiah 11:20

10. Jeremiah 17:10 NLT (the name *the Lord* was changed to *Jalyn* to fit the story)

11. This conversation was adapted from Matthew 25:34–40 TEV

12. 2 Corinthians 9:10

13. 2 Corinthians 9:9 AMP
14. Luke 14:11 AMP
15. Luke 19:17 NLT
16. Revelation 2:26–27 NIV
17. Matthew 25:21

Chapter 9

1. Names in this story have been changed to respect privacy.

Chapter 10

1. James Strong, *Strong's Exhaustive Concordance of the Bible* (Peabody, MA: Hendrickson Publishers, 1988).
2. *Biblesoft New Exhaustive Strong's Concordance*, (Seattle, WA: Biblesoft, Inc., ver. 4, 1994).

Chapter 12

1. This section was adapted from content that first appeared in my book *Relentless: The Power You Need to Never Give Up* (Colorado Springs, CO: Waterbrook Press, 2011), 217–219.

Chapter 13

1. *Webster's Encyclopedic Unabridged Dictionary of the English Language* (New York: Gramercy, 1993), s.v. "envy."
2. *The American Heritage Dictionary of the English Language*, Fourth Edition. Houghton Mifflin Co., 2004 (software edition).

Chapter 14

1. Leonard Ravenhill, *Sodom Had No Bible* (Minneapolis, MN: Bethany House, 1971), 155.
2. Rebecca Ruter Springer, *My Dream of Heaven: A Nineteenth Century Spiritual Classic: Originally Known As Intra Muros* (Cincinnati, OH: Harrison House), 21.

DRIVEN BY ETERNITY

DRIVEN BY ETERNITY

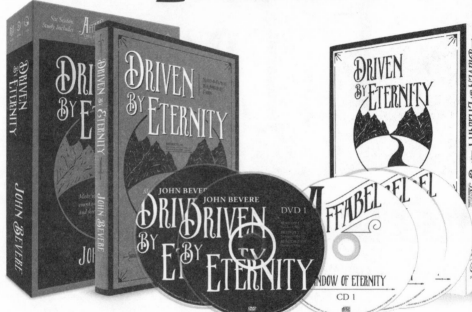

Study Includes:

6 video sessions on 2 DVDs (30 minutes each)
Driven by Eternity book
Affabel: Window of Eternity audio drama on 3 CDs

Order Today

Online: MessengerInternational.org | Call: 1-800-648-1477

MESSENGER STREAMING

Stream life-transforming videos
by John and Lisa Bevere.

Visit MessengerStreaming.com to learn more.

senger International exists to
individuals, families, churches,
nations realize and experience
transforming power of God's
d. This realization will result
ves empowered, communi-
transformed, and a dynamic
onse to the injustices
juing our world.

CLOUD LIBRARY

Cloud Library is an online platform that allows pastors and leaders around the world to access free digital resources in their own languages. We use this platform to share resources with believers in restricted or hard-to-reach areas worldwide.

Learn more at CloudLibrary.org

BOOKS BY JOHN

A Heart Ablaze*
The Bait of Satan*
Breaking Intimidation*
Drawing Near*
Driven by Eternity*
Enemy Access Denied
Extraordinary*
The Fear of the Lord*
Good or God?*
The Holy Spirit: An Introduction*

Honor's Reward*
How to Respond When You Feel Mistreated
Relentless*
Rescued
The Story of Marriage*
Thus Saith the Lord?
Under Cover*
Victory in the Wilderness
The Voice of One Crying

*Available in curriculum format

Messenger International was founded by John and Lisa Bevere in 1990. In over two decades of ministry, Messenger International's God-entrusted messages have transformed millions of lives worldwide. Today, our mission to teach, reach, and rescue encompasses a wide variety of efforts to disciple the nations.

Call: **1-800-648-1477**

Email: **Mail@MessengerInternational.org**

Visit us online at: **MessengerInternational.org**

Connect with John Bevere:

JohnBevere.com